AFRICA AND THE WORLD TRADE ORGANIZATION

Mshomba provides a systematic study of Africa as it relates to the World Trade Organization (WTO). He examines the WTO's enforcement mechanism, its broadened mandate as illustrated by the Agreement on Trade-Related Aspects of Intellectual Property Rights, agriculture in the Doha Round, issues relating to transparency in government procurement, and the endeavor to streamline assistance to developing countries through an "Aid for Trade" initiative. The author integrates theory and practice, with a clear presentation of important economic concepts and a rigorous analysis of key issues and proposals. He presents African countries as having an important role to play in the WTO, especially as they actively engage in bargaining through various coalitions. Mshomba acknowledges that WTO negotiations will always be complex and at times contentious due to wide economic and political differences between countries. He views the differences, however, as creating opportunities for a mutually beneficial exchange of goods, services, and ideas.

Richard E. Mshomba is Professor of Economics at La Salle University in Philadelphia. Born and raised in Tanzania, he received a Ph.D. in economics from the University of Illinois at Urbana-Champaign. His areas of research are development economics and international economics, with a focus on African countries. Mshomba is the author of *Africa in the Global Economy* (2000), a *Choice* Outstanding Academic Book. He is a frequent guest analyst on Voice of America on economic issues pertaining to Africa. He has also been a guest analyst on National Public Radio, Irish Public Radio (Radio Telefís Éireann), Radio Netherlands, and a number of other radio stations. He is a frequent contributor of op-ed pieces to *The Arusha Times* in Tanzania.

Mshomba was awarded the Pew Faculty Fellowship in International Affairs, John F. Kennedy School of Government, Harvard University, 1993–1994. He received the 2005 Lindback Award for Distinguished Teaching at La Salle University. Mshomba travels regularly to the village where he grew up in Tanzania, where he and his wife are engaged in educational and development initiatives.

# AFRICA AND THE WORLD TRADE
# ORGANIZATION

### RICHARD E. MSHOMBA
*La Salle University*

**CAMBRIDGE**
UNIVERSITY PRESS

*To the De La Salle Christian Brothers,*
*for their dedication to education throughout the world.*

# CONTENTS

# Contents

# TABLES AND FIGURES

FIGURES

# ACKNOWLEDGMENTS

*How shall I make a return to the Lord for all the good he has done for me?*
*(Psalm 116: 12)*

This book is literally the culmination of a lifetime of learning and the support of family, teachers, friends, priests and other religious workers, colleagues, schools, and universities. I was born and raised in the village of Sinon in Arusha, Tanzania. My constant prayer when I was in primary school was that I would be selected to attend secondary school. In the 1960s in Tanzania, only 5 percent of those who finished primary school could go to secondary school. The idea that one day I would be a university professor was beyond my wildest dreams. Yet the foundation of my professional career is the education I received in those early years and the love and guidance of my parents. My mother and father were subsistence farmers; the memory of their strong work ethic, wisdom, and generosity continues to inspire me.

I thank Ambrose and Flora Itika, Assumpta Ndimbo, and Daniel and Supera Njoolay for their unwavering support over the years. My profound gratitude goes to the wonderful Holy Ghost Fathers and especially to my hero, the late Bishop Dennis Durning. I would also like to thank Richard Geruson, my first economics professor, who advised me to major in economics and who has been a generous mentor to me. He has remained a close friend. My profound gratitude also goes to my immediate and extended families – the Mshombas of Arusha, Tanzania; the Durnings of Glenside,

Pennsylvania; and the O'Hallorans of Cary, Illinois, whose prayers and encouragement I can always count on. I am also thankful for the support of Bishop Herbert Bevard and my fellow parishioners at St. Athanasius Catholic Church in Philadelphia.

I am grateful to my colleagues in the Economics Department at La Salle University for their support as well. They share with me materials they come across that might be useful to my research. My special thanks go to David George, who took time away from his own research to read and discuss my manuscript and to offer insightful comments. It would not have been possible to complete this book in a reasonable amount of time without a generous research leave and sabbatical leave (two consecutive semesters) from La Salle University, for which I am very grateful. I also commend and thank La Salle's librarians for their expertise and efficiency. The reference and inter-library loan librarians are simply the best.

In conducting research for this book, I spent a few weeks in Geneva consulting with ambassadors, commercial attachés, and WTO officials. I am very thankful for their time and information. My special thanks go to Marwa Kisiri, Patrick Low, and Claudia Uribe for their insights and also for assisting me in making appointments with other officials.

I would like to thank my students for their interest in my work. In particular, I am grateful to Peter Ajak and Christine Quinn, who read the manuscript and checked to be sure the bibliography was consistent with what is in the text. Christine also prepared the diagrams in Chapter 4. I would also like to thank Thomas Herrle, Christopher McNabb, and Gregory Robinson for the many conversations I have had with them on Africa and economic issues.

I benefited tremendously from a review by Voxi Amavilah, who provided extensive and extremely helpful comments on each chapter. Amavilah is one of those rare individuals who assists you with your research and then thanks you for asking them for their help. I also benefited from my discussions and correspondence with

## Acknowledgments

Michael D. Kerlin. In addition, I extend my sincere gratitude to two anonymous reviewers for their very useful comments. Their suggestions helped me with this manuscript and gave me ideas for my future research. I would also like to extend my heartfelt gratitude to my dear friend and colleague, Harvey Glickman, for his mentoring and valuable insights.

It is an understatement to say that I could not have completed this book without the support of my wife, Elaine. She assumed a larger share of our responsibilities to allow me more time for research. She also edited and discussed the entire manuscript with me. Trained as a lawyer, she is keen on detail, organization, and clarity, which she helped provide with her painstaking editing. I am also grateful to our sons – Alphonce, Dennis, and Charles – for their encouragement, curiosity, bike rides, playfulness, and humor. They were also helpful in other ways, ranging from verifying data to asking questions like, "if you can write a book that has so many words, why can't you write a children's book?"

It goes without saying that individuals who have helped me with this book may not necessarily agree with my analyses and conclusions. I also take responsibility for any errors or omissions.

– Richard E. Mshomba

# ABBREVIATIONS

| | |
|---|---|
| ACP | African, Caribbean, and Pacific Countries |
| ACWL | Advisory Center on WTO Law |
| ADB | African Development Bank |
| ADF | African Development Fund |
| AERC | African Economic Research Consortium |
| AGOA | African Growth and Opportunity Act |
| AMDS | AIDS Medicines and Diagnostics Service |
| AMS | Aggregate Measure of Support |
| AU | African Union |
| CAC | Codex Alimentarius Commission |
| CFC | Common Fund for Commodities |
| CPAR | Country Procurement Assessment Reports |
| CPI | Corruption Perception Index |
| CRS | Catholic Relief Services |
| DAC | Development Assistance Committee |
| DAC-OECD | Development Assistance Committee of the Organization for Economic Cooperation and Development |
| DDA | Doha Development Agenda |
| DFID | Department for International Development (United Kingdom) |
| DSB | Dispute Settlement Body |
| DSU | Dispute Settlement Understanding |
| EBA | Everything But Arms |
| EC | European Community |

| | |
|---|---|
| ECA | Economic Commission for Africa |
| ECU | European Currency Unit |
| EPAs | Economic Partnership Agreements |
| EU | European Union |
| FAO | Food and Agricultural Organization |
| FDI | Foreign Direct Investment |
| GATS | General Agreement on Trade in Services |
| GATT | General Agreement on Tariffs and Trade |
| GDP | Gross Domestic Product |
| GPA | Agreement on Government Procurement |
| GSP | Generalized System of Preferences |
| HDI | Human Development Index |
| HIPC | Heavily Indebted Poor Countries |
| IBRD | International Bank of Reconstruction and Development |
| ICAC | International Cotton Advisory Committee |
| ICJ | International Court of Justice |
| ICTSD | International Center for Trade and Sustainable Development |
| IDA | International Development Association |
| IF | Integrated Framework for Trade-Related Technical Assistance for Least-Developed Countries |
| ILO | International Labor Organization |
| IMF | International Monetary Fund |
| ITC | International Trade Center |
| ITO | International Trade Organization |
| JITAP | Joint Integrated Technical Assistance Program |
| LDC | Least-Developed Countries |
| MDGs | Millennium Development Goals |
| MFN | Most Favored Nation |
| NEPAD | New Partnership for Africa's Development |
| NIH | National Institutes of Health (U.S.) |
| OAU | Organization of African Unity |
| ODA | Official Development Assistance |

| | |
|---|---|
| OECD | Organization for Economic Co-operation and Development |
| PACT | Program for Building African Capacity for Trade |
| PDI | Previously Disadvantaged Individuals |
| PEPFAR | President's Emergency Plan for AIDS Relief (U.S.) |
| PhRMA | Pharmaceutical Research and Manufacturers of America |
| PPP | Purchasing Power Parity |
| PRSPs | Poverty Reduction Strategy Papers |
| SADC | Southern African Development Community |
| SDR | Special Drawing Rights |
| SEATINI | Southern and Eastern African Trade Information and Negotiations Institute |
| SITC | Standard International Trade Classification |
| SONAPRA | Societé Nationale pour la Promotion Agricole (Benin's state-owned National Agricultural Promotion Company) |
| SWAp | Sector-Wide Approach |
| TBT | Technical Barriers to Trade |
| TGP | Transparency in Government Procurement |
| TRIPS | Trade-Related Aspects of Intellectual Property Rights |
| UNAIDS | Joint United Nations Program on HIV/AIDS |
| UNCITRAL | United Nations Commission on International Trade Law |
| UNCTAD | United Nations Conference on Trade and Development |
| UNDP | United Nations Development Program |
| UNIDO | United Nations Industrial Development Organization |
| USAID | U.S. Agency for International Development |
| USDA | U.S. Department of Agriculture |
| WHO | World Health Organization |
| WIPO | World Intellectual Property Organization |
| WTO | World Trade Organization |

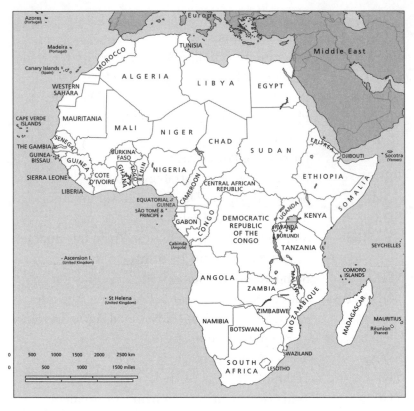

Map of Africa
*Source:* Network Startup Resource Center (http://www.nsrc.org/
AFRICA/africa.gif). Reprinted by permission.

# 1 INTRODUCTION

THE OBJECTIVE OF THIS STUDY IS TO EXAMINE THE WORLD
Trade Organization (WTO) – its enforcement mechanism;
its broadened mandate, illustrated by the Agreement on Trade-
Related Aspects of Intellectual Property Rights (TRIPS); agriculture in the Doha Round of the WTO; the WTO's pursuit of
additional agreements; and its endeavor to streamline assistance
to developing countries through an "Aid for Trade" scheme – all in
the context of Africa.

Before the WTO was established in 1995, few people knew there
was an international organization that set trade rules. However, the
WTO was preceded by and is a product of the General Agreement
on Tariffs and Trade (GATT), in operation since 1948. The WTO
has gained exposure and notoriety primarily from demonstrations
against it at the WTO Ministerial meetings. These demonstrations
are usually well orchestrated and manage to draw much media
attention, often eclipsing the agenda items of the Ministerial meetings. Many trade economists who are usually quite comfortable
with their theories have been put on the defensive as a result of the
growing negative publicity that the WTO and globalization have
received. Among them is the renowned Jagdish Bhagwati, who has
published a book solely defending globalization (Bhagwati, 2004).

However, criticism of the WTO is not necessarily a campaign
against trade and globalization. The criticism is often targeted at
the expanding mandate of the WTO, in terms of enforcement,

its broadening coverage, and the glaring asymmetry (in terms of the capacity to negotiate) between developing and developed countries.

Nonetheless, before discussing the WTO, it is important to offer a few words about trade. There are opportunity costs for producing anything and, therefore, societies are constantly working out how best to use their scarce resources. Trade is one of the most important mechanisms through which countries can allocate their resources efficiently in a way that allows them to consume more than what they can produce domestically. For example, the United States is the largest consumer of coffee in the world, consuming about 20 percent of the world's supply. However, the United States does not produce any coffee, even though it has the technology to produce it. Because it does not have a comparative advantage in the production of coffee, the United States finds it is cheaper to import coffee from miles away – from Brazil, Colombia, East Africa, and even Vietnam – than to produce it itself. The resources that would have been used to produce coffee in greenhouses are instead used to produce other goods and services. While the hypothetical example of producing coffee in the United States may be dismissed as absurd, it is not entirely different from the reality of the United States subsidizing domestic producers of sugar at a cost two to three times the price of importing it under free market conditions – a clearly inefficient allocation of resources.

Trade, by its very nature, causes a reallocation of resources. Notwithstanding what trade theory postulates, resources are never perfectly mobile between industries or geographical locations. No matter how beneficial trade might be to the society as a whole, and perhaps even to everyone in the society in the long run, it always creates short-run losses for some. Therefore, it should not be surprising that in every country, there will always be people who will be against the trade of at least some goods or services.

Goods and services are produced in various countries as well as under different labor, health, intellectual property, and environmental laws and regulations. Although these differences contribute additional opportunities for trade, they are also sources of opposition to trade.

Moreover, international trade involves countries that are large and small, high-skilled and low-skilled, rich and poor, democratic and authoritarian, land-locked and coastal, and so on. This diversity creates different approaches to trade, different impacts of trade, and different sensitivities to trade, adding yet another layer of complexity and potential for disagreement about trade rules.

In addition, poor countries are often described by activist groups as unable to compete and, thus, as exploited – still another reason for voices against trade. The idea that poor countries cannot compete, however, is often the result of confusion between absolute advantage and comparative advantage. Consider the simple illustration below.

Even if a country does not have an absolute advantage in producing anything, it will still have a comparative advantage in producing some products. A country has an absolute advantage in producing a product if it can produce it at a lower absolute cost than its trading partners. Suppose on average a farmer in Senegal can produce 5 tons of cotton or 4 tons of peanuts, and on average a farmer in the United States can produce 10 tons of cotton or 15 tons of peanuts. In this hypothetical example, the United States has an absolute advantage in producing both products. Senegal, however, has a comparative advantage in the production of cotton.

Comparative advantage refers to lower opportunity cost than that of competitors. Producers in one country have a comparative advantage if their opportunity cost in producing the product is lower, for whatever reason, than that of producers in another country. In the example above, the opportunity cost of producing a ton of cotton in Senegal is 0.8 tons of peanuts, whereas the opportunity cost of producing a ton of cotton in the United States. is 1.5 tons of peanuts. If Senegal and the United States traded according to their comparative advantage, that is, Senegal exported cotton to the United States while the United States exported peanuts to Senegal, both countries would benefit. When producing goods or services according to their comparative advantage, both countries use their resources more efficiently. In other words, specialization on the basis of comparative advantage increases productivity and, therefore, the gains from trade.

By steering countries toward an efficient use of resources, an infusion of new technologies, and greater competition, trade is an important tool for economic growth. Of course, economic growth is not automatic, considering that other factors, such as macro-economic instability, civil war, or health pandemics, can drag the economy down. Even when trade leads to economic growth, it does not necessarily translate into real economic development, that is, improvement in people's standard of living in terms of access to basic needs and social services. Trade is sometimes even blamed for a lack of development in some countries, as if trade were to have been a "magic bullet." The reality is that trade must be complemented by other policies, including effective education and health policies, for economic growth to bring about development.

Given the benefits of trade and, at the same time, the potential for arbitrary trade barriers, an international organization like the WTO can play a critical role in promoting fair and predictable trade rules and advocating for developing countries. Nonetheless, the WTO will always be a controversial organization and an easy target, no matter how constructive it might be, due to the diversity and multitude of trade issues and self-interests represented by various countries and groups.

In addition, the debate over the WTO is often distorted by exaggeration and, sometimes, by pure noise and empty diplomatic gestures. It has become increasingly difficult to distinguish genuine trade issues from propaganda and purely ideological stances. This book attempts to uncover and analyze some of the real issues pertinent to African countries.

African countries have an ambivalent relationship with the WTO, of which they are a part. They understand the benefits of trade and the need for international agreements that guide and enforce trade rules. They appreciate the economies of scale of negotiating these agreements at the multilateral level. In addition, they are keenly aware of the financial and technical assistance and preferential treatment they receive as a result of the WTO initiatives.

Despite these benefits, however, some elements of the WTO make African countries guarded or even resentful. Pressure, political maneuvering, and, at times, paternalism on the part of developed countries toward African countries seem to be salient features of the WTO. When the WTO was established, many African countries signed agreements without fully understanding them or their long-term potential impact. Of course, those agreements were softened by exceptions, extensions, and assistance for developing countries. Another source of skepticism has been the (perceived) small size of assistance and the unpredictable disbursement of the promised assistance. African countries are also concerned that the WTO coverage is increasingly having a more direct and broader impact on trade policies in Africa, thus reducing their domestic policy space.

## A SHORT HISTORY OF GATT AND THE WTO[1]

At the end of the Second World War, nations made efforts to establish international institutions that would address political and economic issues in the world. The United Nations was founded in 1945 to promote peace and international cooperation. The International Bank for Reconstruction and Development (the World Bank) and the International Monetary Fund (IMF) were also established in 1945 to provide long-term and short-term loans, respectively.

---

[1] The discussion for this section is drawn from Mshomba (2000).

GATT was established in 1947 (and became operational in 1948) with the mission to liberalize world trade.

GATT was formed from parts of the International Trade Organization (ITO), a proposed specialized agency of the United Nations. It was established with minimal institutional arrangements to expedite its approval because it was supposed to be temporary. Its functions were ultimately to be assumed by the ITO. However, the ITO never came into existence because the U.S. Congress refused to ratify it, claiming it would undermine its national sovereignty in trade policy. Opposition in the United States was so strong that President Truman did not even bother to send the proposal to the Congress.

Twenty-three countries signed the original treaty establishing GATT in 1947.[2] In addition, participation in GATT was extended to colonies of GATT members, under Article XXVI:5 of GATT. GATT contracting countries applied this provision to all their colonies in Africa, with one exception. France did not apply this provision to sponsor Morocco to participate in GATT (Tomz et al., 2005). Thus, by extension, nearly all African countries were part of GATT from its very inception.[3] To the extent that colonialism was fundamentally an exploitative political and economic system, the extension of GATT's rights and obligations to the colonies was also seen as a means for exploitation. This history has contributed to the suspicion and skepticism with which African countries came to accept GATT and its successor, the WTO.

---

[2] Governments that signed to establish or join GATT were officially known as contracting countries (parties). Signatories of the WTO are known as WTO members. The twenty-three founding countries of GATT were Australia, Belgium, Brazil, Burma, Canada, Ceylon, Chile, China, Cuba, Czechoslovakia, France, India, Lebanon, Luxembourg, Netherlands, New Zealand, Norway, Pakistan, South Africa, Southern Rhodesia, Syria, United Kingdom and the United States. http://www.wto.org/english/thewto_e/minist_e/min96_e/chrono.htm

[3] South Africa and Southern Rhodesia (Zimbabwe) were among the original contracting countries of GATT. However, these countries were under minority White rule that was notoriously repressive of Africans.

A colony to which GATT benefits and obligations were applied had three options when it achieved independence: (a) join GATT immediately as a full contracting party; (b) establish *de facto* participation status while deciding about its future domestic trade policy; or (c) simply end its participation in GATT. As of December 31, 1993, there were 114 fully contracting parties plus 19 *de facto* participants in GATT (U.S. International Trade Commission, 1994: 41).

While GATT was technically only a provisional treaty throughout its 48 years of existence, over time it actually amounted to an increasing number of complex agreements, administered and enforced by its operating body. These agreements were designed to reduce barriers to trade. There were eight rounds of multilateral trade negotiations under GATT, including the Uruguay Round (1986–1993), from which the WTO was born. The first seven rounds of negotiations were held as follows: (1) in Geneva in 1947; (2) in Annecy, France, in 1949; (3) in Torquay, England, in 1950–1951; and (4) through (7) in Geneva, in 1955–1956, 1961–1962 (the Dillon Round), 1964–1967 (the Kennedy Round), and 1973–1979 (the Tokyo Round), respectively (Raj, 1990). Each round of negotiations sought and accomplished, to varying degrees, a reduction of trade barriers among members.

It is estimated that the first six rounds of negotiations reduced average tariffs in developed countries from about 40 percent to about 8 percent (Laird and Yeats, 1990). The seventh round, the Tokyo Round, was relatively farther reaching in scope. In addition to reducing tariffs, it also reduced non-tariff barriers. These included government procurement requirements, restrictive licensing procedures, and health and safety standards which created unnecessary obstacles to international trade. This achievement was important because as average tariff rates in industrial nations decreased, the propensity to use non-tariff barriers increased. Under the Tokyo Round, industrial countries also reduced their tariffs by a weighted average of 36 percent over a period of 8 years, bringing their average tariff to about 5 percent.

Like the rounds preceding it, however, the Tokyo Round of negotiations failed to integrate textiles and apparel and agriculture into GATT. Inclusion of these areas was not to come until the last round of multilateral trade negotiations under GATT, the Uruguay Round. The Uruguay Round was launched in 1986 and concluded on December 15, 1993. A new international organization, the WTO, was established through the Uruguay Round to replace GATT.

The WTO went into effect on January 1, 1995. The WTO facilitates the implementation, administration, and operation of agreements. It also brings all rules and agreements reached under GATT into a single body of operation. Under the WTO, member countries subscribe to all of its rules and agreements. This is an important departure from the old system under GATT, whereby members could pick and choose the agreements to which they wanted to subscribe. "Whereas, in the past, countries could take an *à la carte* approach to the agreements, membership of the WTO implied membership of all its multilateral agreements" (Raby, 1994: 13). Actually, four plurilateral agreements remained when the WTO came into existence – the Agreement on Government Procurement, the Agreement on Trade in Civil Aircraft, the International Dairy Agreement, and the International Bovine Meat Agreement. The last two were terminated in 1997, because matters relating to those areas could be dealt with by the Agreements on Agriculture and on Sanitary and Phytosanitary.[4] Nonetheless, countries were under pressure to sign all other agreements. This pressure was felt more acutely by developing countries because the WTO agreements included

---

[4] Unlike a multilateral agreement which is binding on the entire membership of GATT/WTO, a plurilateral agreement is binding only on those countries that have decided to be signatories of the agreement.

intellectual property and trade in services, areas in which developed countries have comparative advantage. Another significant change under the WTO was that the dispute settlement procedures were streamlined and unified. The procedures restrain nations from taking unilateral actions in addressing disputes, as discussed in Chapter 2.

A basic principle of the WTO and its predecessor, GATT, is non-differentiated treatment, commonly called the *most favored nation* (MFN) principle. The MFN principle means a member country must treat all other members equally in respect to trade policy. If a member country lowers the tariff rate on a commodity entering from one member country, for example, it must likewise lower the tariff rate on that commodity from all other member countries. Exceptions to the MFN rule are made for preferential tariff treatment for developing and least-developed countries, and for free trade areas and other levels of economic integration.

AFRICAN COUNTRIES' MEMBERSHIP IN THE WTO AND
VARIOUS COALITIONS

As of December 2007, the WTO had 152 members, including 42 African countries. In addition, there were 31 observer governments, including nine African countries. Only two African countries – Eritrea and Somalia – had neither membership nor observer status. *De facto* participation is not an option under the WTO.

African countries in the WTO have formed a coalition called the African Group. Many of them also belong to several other coalitions, including the African, Caribbean, and Pacific Countries (ACP) Group, the Least-Developed Countries (LDC) Group, the G77, and the G33 (the latter two are discussed below), as shown in Tables 1.1 and 1.2. The African Group, the ACP Group, and the LDC Group also coordinate under an umbrella group called the G90.

TABLE 1.1 African Countries' Membership in the WTO, ACP Group, LDC Group, and G33: December 2007

| Country | WTO Member (x) Observer (o) | ACP | LDC | G33 |
|---|---|---|---|---|
| Algeria | o | | | |
| Angola | x | x | x | |
| Benin | x | x | x | x |
| Botswana | x | x | | x |
| Burkina Faso | x | x | x | |
| Burundi | x | x | x | |
| Cameroon | x | x | | |
| Cape Verde | x | x | x | |
| Central African Republic | x | x | x | |
| Chad | x | x | x | |
| Comoros | o | x | x | |
| Congo, Dem. Rep. of | x | x | x | x |
| Congo, Rep. of | x | x | | |
| Côte d'Ivoire | x | x | | x |
| Djibouti | x | x | x | |
| Egypt | x | | | |
| Equatorial Guinea | o | x | x | |
| Eritrea | | x | x | |
| Ethiopia | o | x | x | |
| Gabon | x | x | | |
| Gambia | x | x | x | |
| Ghana | x | x | | |
| Guinea | x | x | x | |
| Guinea-Bissau | x | x | x | |
| Kenya | x | x | | x |
| Lesotho | x | x | x | |
| Liberia | o | x | x | |
| Libya | o | | | |
| Madagascar | x | x | x | x |
| Malawi | x | x | x | |
| Mali | x | x | x | |

TABLE 1.1 *(continued)*

| Country | WTO Member (x) Observer (o) | ACP | LDC | G33 |
|---|---|---|---|---|
| Mauritania | x | x | x | |
| Mauritius | x | x | | x |
| Morocco | x | | | |
| Mozambique | x | x | x | x |
| Namibia | x | x | | |
| Niger | x | x | x | |
| Nigeria | x | x | | x |
| Rwanda | x | x | x | |
| Sao Tomé and Principe | o | x | x | |
| Senegal | x | x | x | x |
| Seychelles | o | x | | |
| Sierra Leone | x | x | x | |
| Somalia | | x | x | |
| South Africa | x | x | | |
| Sudan | o | x | x | |
| Swaziland | x | x | | |
| Tanzania | x | x | x | x |
| Togo | x | x | x | |
| Tunisia | x | | | |
| Uganda | x | x | x | x |
| Zambia | x | x | x | x |
| Zimbabwe[1] | x | x | | x |

[1] The economy of Zimbabwe deteriorated precipitously in the 2000s to the extent that in June of 2006, the United Nations Committee for Development Policy recommended that Zimbabwe be downgraded to the status of a least-developed country. However, the government of Zimbabwe refused to give its consent to be downgraded (Deen, 2006).

Sources:
*WTO members, http://www.wto.org/English/thewto_e/whatis_e/tif_e/org6_e.htm.*
*ACP states, http://www.acpsec.org/en/acp_states.htm.*
*Least-Developed Countries list, http://www.un.org/special-rep/ohrlls/ldc/list.htm.*
*G33 members, http://www.wto.org/english/tratop_e/agric_e/negs_bkgrnd04_groups_e.htm#key.*

TABLE 1.2  Percentage of African Countries in Various Groups: December 2007

| Group | Total Membership | | | Group Members that are also WTO Members | | |
|---|---|---|---|---|---|---|
| | Total | African Countries | Percentage of African Countries | Total | African Countries | Percentage of African Countries |
| WTO | 152 | 42 | 28 | 152 | 42 | 28 |
| ACP | 79 | 48 | 61 | 57 | 39 | 68 |
| Least-Developed Countries | 50 | 34 | 68 | 33 | 26 | 79 |
| G77 | 133 | 53 | 40 | 102 | 42 | 41 |
| G33 | 42 | 14 | 33 | 42 | 14 | 33 |

*Sources:*

WTO members, *http://www.wto.org/English/thewto_e/whatis_e/tif_e/org6_e.htm.*

ACP states, *http://www.acpsec.org/en/acp_states.htm.*

Least-Developed Countries list, *http://www.un.org/special-rep/ohrlls/ldc/list.htm.*

G77 members, *http://www.g77.org/doc/members.html.*

G33 members, *http://www.wto.org/english/tratop_e/agric_e/negs_bkgrnd04_groups_e.htm#key.*

In terms of numbers, African countries enjoy significant representation in the WTO through various coalitions, as shown in Table 1.2. As of December 2007, African countries represented 28 percent of the WTO membership. Fifty countries were classified by the United Nations as least developed, of which 33 were WTO members. Of the 33 least-developed WTO member countries, 26 were African. All African countries except five in North Africa (Algeria, Egypt, Libya, Morocco, and Tunisia) are members of the ACP Group. The G77 is a coalition of developing countries founded in 1964 to promote their interests in multilateral negotiations at various forums. The membership of the G77 grew from 77 countries when it was founded to 133 countries in 2007. All 53 African countries are members of the G77. The G33 is a coalition of a subset of developing countries in the WTO that has focused on negotiations on agriculture, particularly on special products and a special safeguard mechanism.

The practice of belonging to these and other coalitions is explained by history, geography, common broad economic interests, and the efficiency of sharing information and scarce resources. More importantly, it is necessitated by the desire to have some leverage in the WTO negotiations. Leverage for African countries usually comes from their sheer number and the merits of their arguments, not from economic strength. Exports and imports of most African countries are miniscule proportions of world trade. For example, in 2004, Sub-Saharan African countries in aggregate contributed only 1.6 percent of world exports, half of it originating from Nigeria and South Africa. Excluding Nigeria and South Africa, exports of Sub-Saharan Africa in 2004 were slightly less than those of Poland (World Bank, 2005: 298–299).

The negative side of belonging to this multiplicity of coalitions is that it spreads thin the scant diplomatic and technical resources that African countries possess. In fact, proposals from these coalition groups are usually the product of a few core countries in a group, with the core countries determined by technical capacity, the personalities and experience of diplomats and commercial attachés, and what is at stake.

While African countries have been able to build coalitions among themselves and with other countries, these coalitions are often tenuous due to the diversity of African countries and their diverse economic interests. Some of the diversity regarding agricultural subsidies is discussed in Chapter 4. Table 1.3 reveals a very wide range of economic diversity among countries in terms of economic indicators. The Human Development Index (HDI) is calculated based on life expectancy at birth, the average number of years of schooling, and gross domestic product (GDP) per capita in purchasing power parity (PPP).[5] While most African countries are ranked in the lowest range of the HDI, seven African countries have an HDI of over 0.7.[6] Table 1.3 also lists the aid-dependency ratios (aid as a percent of gross national income), which show how heavily dependent some African countries are on foreign aid.

On average, the ratio of the GDP per capita of the five "poorest" African countries to that of the five "richest" African countries is about 1 to 22. These economic disparities manifest themselves in many other ways, such as in greatly differing manufacturing capacities and shares of exports within regional blocs. Economic integration in some regional blocs has been delayed due to these

---

[5]  The HDI for 2004 ranked 177 countries. Norway was ranked number one with the highest HDI of 0.965. Most African countries were ranked lowest. Except for East Timor (142nd), Yemen (150th), and Haiti (154th), the 140th to 177th positions were taken by African countries.

[6]  This is only an illustration of the disparity and must be understood with caution. The HDI (and even more so, the GDP per capita) in its aggregate form does not capture other aspects of development and certainly does not capture development inequalities within countries. For example, the United Nations Development Program (UNDP), the organization that calculates and publishes the HDI, reports that, "Kenya has an HDI that ranges from 0.75 in Nairobi (almost on par with Turkey) to 0.29 in Turkana, a pastoral area in the north of the country. If Turkana were a country, it would be off the current HDI by a considerable margin, reflecting the region's recurrent droughts, poor access to health and water infrastructure and high malnutrition rates" (UNDP, 2006: 271).

TABLE 1.3 Development Indicators and Aid-Dependency Ratios

| Country | HDI | GDP per Capita Dollars (PPP* ) | GDP Average Annual Growth Rate | Aid-Dependency Ratios (AID/ GNI** ) |
|---|---|---|---|---|
| | 2004 | 2004 | 2000–2004 | 2004 |
| Seychelles | 0.842 | 16,652 | 1.1 | n.a. |
| Mauritius | 0.800 | 12,027 | 1.0 | 0.6 |
| Libya | 0.798 | 7,570 | 2.0 | 0.1 |
| Tunisia | 0.760 | 7,768 | 4.3 | 1.2 |
| Algeria | 0.728 | 6,603 | 4.8 | 0.4 |
| Cape Verde | 0.722 | 5,727 | 2.5 | n.a. |
| Egypt | 0.702 | 4,211 | 3.5 | 1.9 |
| Equatorial Guinea | 0.653 | 20,510 | 2.5 | n.a. |
| South Africa | 0.653 | 11,192 | 3.2 | 0.3 |
| Morocco | 0.640 | 4,309 | 4.5 | 1.4 |
| Gabon | 0.633 | 6,623 | 2.2 | 0.6 |
| Namibia | 0.626 | 7,418 | 3.2 | 3.1 |
| Sao Tomé and Principe | 0.607 | 1,231 | 2.0 | n.a. |
| Botswana | 0.570 | 9,945 | 0.8 | 0.5 |
| Comoros | 0.556 | 1,943 | 2.4 | n.a. |
| Ghana | 0.532 | 2,240 | 4.8 | 15.4 |
| Congo, Rep. of | 0.520 | 978 | 3.4 | 3.5 |
| Sudan (Northern) | 0.516 | 1,949 | 6.0 | 4.5 |
| Madagascar | 0.509 | 857 | 0.9 | 28.8 |
| Cameroon | 0.506 | 2,174 | 4.6 | 5.4 |
| Uganda | 0.502 | 1,478 | 5.8 | 17.3 |
| Swaziland | 0.500 | 5,638 | 1.7 | 4.9 |
| Togo | 0.495 | 1,536 | 2.6 | 3.0 |
| Lesotho | 0.494 | 2,619 | n.a. | 6.3 |
| Djibouti | 0.494 | 1,993 | 1.8 | n.a. |

*(continued)*

TABLE 1.3 *(continued)*

| Country | HDI | GDP per Capita Dollars (PPP*) | GDP Average Annual Growth Rate | Aid-Dependency Ratios (AID/ GNI**) |
|---|---|---|---|---|
| | 2004 | 2004 | 2000–2004 | 2004 |
| Zimbabwe[1] | 0.491 | 2,065 | −7.0 | 4.0 |
| Kenya | 0.491 | 1,140 | 1.5 | 4.0 |
| Mauritania | 0.486 | 1,940 | 5.3 | 11.1 |
| Gambia | 0.479 | 1,991 | 2.5 | 16.0 |
| Senegal | 0.460 | 1,713 | 4.6 | 13.9 |
| Eritrea | 0.454 | 977 | 3.3 | 28.5 |
| Rwanda | 0.450 | 1,263 | 5.1 | 25.8 |
| Nigeria | 0.448 | 1,154 | 4.9 | 1.0 |
| Guinea | 0.445 | 2,180 | 2.9 | 7.3 |
| Angola | 0.439 | 2,180 | 8.1 | 6.6 |
| Tanzania | 0.430 | 674 | 6.8 | 16.2 |
| Benin | 0.428 | 1,091 | 4.5 | 9.3 |
| Côte d'Ivoire | 0.421 | 1,551 | −1.5 | 1.0 |
| Zambia | 0.407 | 943 | 4.4 | 21.2 |
| Malawi | 0.400 | 646 | 1.8 | 25.9 |
| Congo, Dem. Rep. of | 0.391 | 705 | 3.5 | 28.6 |
| Mozambique | 0.390 | 1,237 | 8.5 | 21.4 |
| Burundi | 0.384 | 677 | 2.7 | 54.6 |
| Ethiopia | 0.371 | 756 | 3.7 | 23.0 |
| Chad | 0.368 | 2,090 | 14.3 | 11.8 |
| Central African Republic | 0.353 | 1,094 | −1.4 | 7.9 |
| Guinea-Bissau | 0.349 | 722 | 2.9 | 28.3 |
| Burkina Faso | 0.342 | 1,169 | 5.2 | 12.7 |
| Mali | 0.338 | 998 | 6.3 | 12.2 |
| Sierra Leone | 0.335 | 561 | 15.8 | 34.3 |
| Niger | 0.311 | 779 | 4.1 | 17.5 |

TABLE 1.3 *(continued)*

| Country | HDI | GDP per Capita Dollars (PPP*) | GDP Average Annual Growth Rate | Aid-Dependency Ratios (AID/ GNI**) |
|---|---|---|---|---|
| | 2004 | 2004 | 2000–2004 | 2004 |
| World | 0.741 | 8,833 | 2.5 | 0.2 |
| Low-income countries | 0.556 | 2,297 | 5.4 | 2.8 |
| Sub-Saharan Africa | 0.472 | 1,946 | 3.9 | 5.3 |
| South Asia | 0.599 | 3,072 | 5.8 | 0.8 |

[1] Zimbabwe's economy suffered a catastrophic decline in the 2000s. By the end of 2007, it had the lowest GDP per capita (PPP) in Africa – less than $200 – and the end of this trend was nowhere in sight.

* Purchasing power parity (PPP) takes into account countries' different relative costs of living and inflation rates.

** GNI, gross national income; n.a., not available.

*Source: UNDP (2006) for HDI and GDP per capita; World Bank (2005) for GDP growth rates; and World Bank (2006) for aid-dependency ratios.*

disparities, which often cause friction, jealousy, and contempt among African countries. In addition, some countries are engaged in cross-border conflicts.

Nonetheless, it is apparent that when faced with a common challenge, African countries can put their differences aside and speak in unison as the African Group. Their common historical background of colonialism enables them to forge a united position on a number of issues. Moreover, they also share some unifying economic similarities (attributed, in part, to colonialism). For example, they all tend to be highly trade oriented, as shown in Table 1.4 by the high merchandise trade ratios, that is, the sum of exports and imports as a percent of GDP. They all depend heavily on the countries of the Organization for Economic Cooperation and

Development (OECD) as markets for their exports and imports.[7] About 70 percent of African countries' exports are destined for OECD countries. It is clear from Table 1.4 that agriculture is the most important economic sector in generating export revenue for many African countries. Therefore, it should not come as a surprise that agriculture has featured prominently in the Doha Round, and that trade policies of the OECD countries are of the utmost importance to African countries.

Many factors complicate negotiations for African countries in the WTO. One is the friction between developed countries themselves. The recurring impasse on agricultural policies is due in no small measure to disagreements between the United States and the European Union. It is not unusual for African and other developing countries to be standing on the sidelines waiting for the major powers to reach a compromise before they can join in the negotiations. Another factor is the diversity of African countries' interests, as alluded to above. While, in general, African countries place a high premium on the unity of the African Group, their interests vary and are sometimes in conflict with each other. Therefore, efforts of an African country toward a given outcome can vary from that of being an advocate at the forefront to indifference and even sabotage through bilateral agreements.

Yet another complicating factor in negotiations is that African countries are lumped together with other developing countries. Developed countries may want to give additional preferential treatment to African countries, but that may not always be possible without giving the same treatment to other developing countries. For example, the apprehension of developed countries regarding

---

[7]    As of 2008, the OECD had 30 members: Australia, Austria, Belgium, Canada, Czech Republic, Denmark, Finland, France, Germany, Greece, Hungary, Iceland, Ireland, Italy, Japan, Korea (South), Luxemburg, Mexico, Netherlands, New Zealand, Norway, Poland, Portugal, Slovak Republic, Spain, Sweden, Switzerland, Turkey, United Kingdom, and United States.

TABLE 1.4 Merchandise Trade Ratios and the Structure
of Merchandise Exports: 2004

| Country/ Countries | Merchandise Trade Ratio* | Food and Agricultural Raw Materials | Fuels, Ores, and Minerals | Manufactures |
|---|---|---|---|---|
| | | Structure of Exports – Percentages of Total** | | |
| Algeria | 60 | 0 | 97 | 2 |
| Angola | 104 | 0*** | 93*** | 6*** |
| Benin | 38 | 90 | 0 | 9 |
| Botswana | 76 | n.a. | n.a. | n.a. |
| Burkina Faso | 33 | 88 | 4 | 8 |
| Burundi | 34 | 93 | 2 | 5 |
| Cameroon | 33 | 43 | 52 | 5 |
| Central African Republic | 21 | 27 | 36 | 37 |
| Chad | 70 | n.a. | n.a. | n.a. |
| Congo, Dem. Rep. of | 50 | n.a. | n.a. | n.a. |
| Congo, Rep. of | 129 | n.a. | n.a. | n.a. |
| Côte d'Ivoire | 66 | 65 | 13 | 20 |
| Egypt | 26 | 17 | 47 | 31 |
| Eritrea | 74 | n.a. | n.a. | n.a. |
| Ethiopia | 47 | 88 | 1 | 11 |
| Gabon | 66 | 11 | 82 | 7 |
| Gambia | 54 | 70 | 3 | 27 |
| Ghana | 78 | 82 | 4 | 14 |
| Guinea | 36 | 3 | 72 | 25 |
| Guinea-Bissau | 60 | n.a. | n.a. | n.a. |
| Kenya | 45 | 52 | 27 | 21 |
| Lesotho | 162 | n.a. | n.a. | n.a. |
| Liberia | 231 | n.a. | n.a. | n.a. |
| Libya | 91 | 1*** | 95*** | 4*** |

*(continued)*

TABLE 1.4 *(continued)*

| Country/ Countries | Merchandise Trade Ratio* | Structure of Exports – Percentages of Total** | | |
| --- | --- | --- | --- | --- |
| | | Food and Agricultural Raw Materials | Fuels, Ores, and Minerals | Manufactures |
| Madagascar | 51 | 67 | 9 | 22 |
| Malawi | 66 | 83 | 0 | 16 |
| Mali | 50 | 98*** | 0*** | 2*** |
| Mauritania | 53 | n.a. | n.a. | n.a. |
| Mauritius | 79 | 27 | 0 | 71 |
| Morocco | 55 | 21 | 10 | 69 |
| Mozambique | 57 | 25 | 71 | 3 |
| Namibia | 75 | 49 | 8 | 41 |
| Niger | 30 | 34 | 57 | 8 |
| Nigeria | 48 | 0 | 98 | 2 |
| Rwanda | 21 | 59 | 30 | 10 |
| Senegal | 55 | 38 | 23 | 39 |
| Sierra Leone | 40 | 93 | 0 | 7 |
| South Africa | 49 | 11 | 31 | 58 |
| Sudan | 37 | 16 | 81 | 2 |
| Swaziland | 163 | 23 | 1 | 76 |
| Tanzania | 35 | 66 | 14 | 20 |
| Togo | 88 | 40 | 13 | 47 |
| Tunisia | 80 | 12 | 11 | 78 |
| Uganda | 31 | 79 | 5 | 15 |
| Zambia | 69 | 26 | 64 | 10 |
| Zimbabwe | 87 | 47 | 25 | 28 |
| World | 45 | 9 | 11 | 77 |
| Low-income countries | 38 | 18 | 31 | 50 |
| Sub-Saharan Africa | 55 | 19 | 49 | 31 |
| South Asia | 28 | 12 | 11 | 76 |

* (Exports + imports)/GDP *100. ** May add up to less or more than 100 due to rounding. *** The data are for 1990. n.a., not available.
*Source: World Bank (2006).*

the utilization of compulsory licensing to acquire generic drugs was rooted in the potential abuse by and competition from countries like Brazil, China, and India, and not so much in losing African countries as a market for patented drugs. (Compulsory licensing is discussed in Chapter 3.)

Perhaps the most important complicating factor is that African countries receive preferential treatment and substantial financial aid from their historical nemeses – developed countries. Negotiations in the WTO are not isolated from other interactions with developed countries. Many African countries are dependent on aid from OECD countries, as shown in Table 1.3. In 2004, the ratio of aid per capita (i.e., aid from OECD countries) to gross national income per capita was more than 10 percent in more than 20 countries. Only a naïve diplomat would approach WTO negotiations single-mindedly, without considering the country's aid dependency. Moreover, developed countries have direct and subtle ways of reminding African countries of the assistance and benefits they are receiving or have been promised. This dependency on aid compromises what little leverage African countries might have. Nonetheless, African countries are seeking even more assistance through the WTO's Aid for Trade initiative.

Promises and commitments for various forms of aid to developing countries sweeten all WTO agreements. The accompanying aid or technical assistance is usually to assist recipient countries in amending their legislation and enacting new laws to conform to the agreements. Dissatisfaction with the size and sometimes incoherent nature of assistance promised by WTO members is the reason behind the Aid for Trade program through which assistance to developing countries will be enhanced and better coordinated.

■ ■ ■

So many trade agreements and related issues fall under the realm of the WTO that any book on the WTO can cover only a small percentage of them. This book is no exception. What follows is an overview of the topics chosen for this book and its organization.

Chapter 2 examines the operation of the WTO's dispute settlement mechanism and explores factors that have limited African countries' utilization of the mechanism. It also analyzes some of the proposals submitted by the African Group regarding the Dispute Settlement Understanding (DSU). The DSU is the lead chapter because it clearly distinguishes the WTO from its predecessor, GATT, and fosters commitment to and enforcement of all other agreements. Discussion of this agreement also plainly reveals the wide differences that exist between African countries and developed countries. The chapter ends with a case study of the services of the Advisory Centre on WTO Law (ACWL).

Chapter 3 provides a theoretical and historical perspective on patents and examines the TRIPS Agreement in relation to public health care. This agreement reflects the broadening scope of the WTO, when compared to GATT. The TRIPS Agreement provides a uniform standard to protect intellectual property rights. The focus of the chapter is on the minimum standard to protect patents and on provisions meant to ensure that countries are not constrained by patents in dealing with public health care crises. The agreement is of the utmost relevance to African countries because of the inherent tension that exists between the protection of intellectual property rights (the priority of developed countries) and access to cheap medicines (the priority of African countries). In addition, the discussion on the TRIPS Agreement serves to show the progress African countries are making in terms of their capacity to negotiate.

Chapter 4 considers the agricultural sector, the most important economic sector in Africa, in the context of the Doha Round, launched in 2001. This chapter studies the potential impact on African countries of reducing agricultural subsidies in developed countries, taking into account special and preferential treatment extended to African countries. The Doha Round of negotiations has suffered a number of setbacks, due in no small part to disagreements on the extent to which there should be reforms of domestic policies and preferential treatment in agriculture. The chapter ends with a case that examines the effects of the confluence of domestic and external policies on the cotton industry in Benin.

Chapter 5 examines the pursuit of an agreement on transparency in government procurement and discusses why African countries resist such expanded coverage of the WTO. Given that governments buy many goods and services, government procurement policies can be significant in fostering infant industries, especially in developing countries. Yet such policies can also serve as important trade barriers. A plurilateral Agreement on Government Procurement already exists. Developed countries would like to see a multilateral agreement, at least on *transparency* in government procurement. African countries are concerned, however, that such an agreement would hinder them in developing certain industries. If history is a guide, there will be new agreements in the future, and this is likely to be one of them. The issue of government procurement also raises important questions regarding government corruption in Africa, a topic that is becoming increasingly taboo in diplomatic circles. An official with the WTO Secretariat told the author that political correctness has effectively forbidden the use of the "c" word ("c" for corruption) in formal WTO negotiations, when describing conditions in developing countries.

Chapter 6 discusses the Aid for Trade program, an endeavor by the WTO to improve and streamline assistance to developing countries. A recurring theme when one speaks with African trade officials is that African countries need assistance to increase their capacity to take advantage of the WTO agreements and the preferential treatment accorded to them. They wonder, for example, how useful the Generalized System of Preferences (GSP), the

African Growth and Opportunity Act (AGOA), or Everything But Arms (EBA) will be if they cannot increase their capacity to produce and export more. An objective of the Aid for Trade program is to reduce supply-side constraints in developing countries. This is an important initiative for Africa, given its potential to increase the export capacity of African countries and improve relations between African countries and developed countries in the WTO.

Chapter 7 is the conclusion.

# 2 DISPUTE SETTLEMENT
UNDERSTANDING

THE DISPUTE SETTLEMENT UNDERSTANDING (DSU), Annex 2 of the WTO Agreement, represents a major, if not *the* major, difference between the WTO and its predecessor, GATT. It provides a coherent and predictable timetable and system of consultation and enforcement of WTO obligations intended to reduce trade barriers and price-distorting policies and to maintain minimum uniform standards.

Initially, under GATT, dispute settlements were processed primarily through diplomatic channels, but over time, they became more adjudicatory (Hudec, 1990 and 1993; Jackson, 1998; Zimmermann, 2005). However, this mechanism was significantly limited because each and every stage of the dispute settlement process – that is, referral of a dispute to a panel procedure, adoption of the panel report, and authorization of the countermeasures – required a positive consensus (WTO, 2003). This meant that the process could be delayed or blocked by a respondent or a losing party. Still, as Jackson (1998) points out, by the mid-1980s it was diplomatically very difficult for a respondent to block a request for a panel procedure. Even the blockage of panel reports was more rare than one would have expected. In a theoretical model by Chang (2002), the low propensity of blocking panel rulings is explained by diplomatic costs and the low degree of legal controversy.

However, as the degree of legal controversy increased following agreements on non-tariff barriers of the Tokyo Round (1973–1979), the incidence of blockage of panel rulings also increased. Each contracting party still had veto power to delay or block the dispute process or a panel report.

Another important shortcoming of the dispute settlement system under GATT was that the system was not integrated; the dispute settlement mechanism was not unified. Consequently, just as member countries could take an *à la carte* approach to selecting agreements on which to sign off, they could strategically use a similar approach in selecting a dispute settlement mechanism that would suit them best. In addition, the Tokyo Round created the possibility of one complaint being processed simultaneously through more than one mechanism, thus creating the potential for additional disputes over which mechanism to use. The Tokyo Round of negotiations produced plurilateral agreements, referred to as the "Tokyo Round Codes," which contained code-specific dispute settlement procedures (WTO, 2003, Chapter 2). Plurilateral agreements are those to which not all GATT/WTO members subscribe; rather, only subsets of the member countries subscribe to them.

Establishing strict enforcement of agreements in international organizations is often an impossible task because of fear of undermining national sovereignty. Such fear is the main reason that the International Trade Organization (ITO), conceived of in 1947, was never ratified. Instead, GATT, which was a more loosely structured and less restrictive body, was adopted as a provisional treaty. GATT operated in a provisional status for almost five decades, from 1948 to 1994.

Thus, it is no small accomplishment that the DSU was adopted. It reinforced the panel procedure and, at the same time, safeguarded the process by establishing an appellate procedure, as will be discussed in the section below. The WTO removed the inherent veto power, initially enjoyed by all contracting parties, to block the process or a panel report. In fact, it completely reversed the consensus procedure. A panel report or an Appellate Body ruling is automatically adopted unless there is a consensus against the ruling. Such a consensus is virtually impossible, considering the interests of the winning party. The DSU has also integrated the dispute settlement system, thus removing an *à la carte* approach to dispute settlement and eliminating the possibility of launching multiple disputes regarding the same case under various agreements.

### THE DISPUTE SETTLEMENT PROCEDURE

The dispute settlement procedure can consist of as many as five stages, with a timetable as follows: the *consultation* stage, up to 2 months; the *panel* stage, 6 to 11 months; the *appellate* stage, 2 to 4 months; the *compliance* stage, up to 15 months; and the *compensation and suspension of concessions* stage, indeterminate. The procedure can end at any stage.

At the first stage, the *consultation* stage, a complainant submits a written request for consultations with a member that: (a) is detected to have breached an obligation and (b) whose infringement causes an adverse effect. "In cases where there is an infringement of the obligations assumed under a covered agreement, the action is considered *prima facie* to constitute a case of nullification or impairment" (Article 3.8 of DSU). There is a presumption that failure to observe an agreement makes void or reduces benefits accruing to the complainant under that agreement. Therefore, the defending country has the burden to rebut the charge and is required to reply and enter into consultations within 10 days and 30 days, respectively, after receiving the request for consultations. If the defending country fails to meet either deadline, or if consultations fail to produce a settlement within 60 days after the receipt of the request for consultations, the complainant may request a panel.

The *panel* stage involves establishing a panel and terms of reference, determining a timetable for the panel process including submission of written reports by parties to the dispute, assessing the facts of the case, and submitting a report. The panel is composed of three panelists, though a panel can be composed of five panelists if there is mutual agreement between the parties to the dispute. Deliberations of the panel are confidential. The panel is expected to submit its final report within 6 months (and no more than 9 months) after composing the panel and establishing the terms of reference. The panel report (ruling) is to be adopted within 60 days after its circulation, unless one of the parties in the dispute has given notification of an appeal.

The *appellate* stage is clearly a refinement of the dispute settlement mechanism that prevailed under GATT. This stage involves the work of the Appellate Body, whose proceedings are also confidential. The appellate review is "limited to issues of the law covered in the panel report and legal interpretations developed by the panel" (Article 17.6 of DSU). The Appellate Body has 60 days (and no more than 90 days) from the date of notification of an appeal to the time it circulates its report. The report is subsequently adopted within 30 days unless there is a consensus against the ruling, something that is almost impossible to achieve.

The *compliance* stage involves implementation of the ruling and recommendations of the panel report, if there is no appeal, or of the Appellate Body. Compliance is expected to be swift and completed within 15 months. The Dispute Settlement Body (DSB) maintains surveillance of the implementation of the recommendations and rulings.

*Compensation and suspension of concessions* is the final stage in the legal framework of the DSU. While this stage is necessary in order to put some teeth into the mechanism, in an ideal situation, it would not be necessary. Its main purpose is to induce compliance and, therefore, to the extent that it is effective, this stage, just as those preceding it, is expected and meant to be temporary. If a defending country fails to comply with the recommendations and rulings, it may negotiate compensation with the complainant. If such negotiations do not produce mutually acceptable compensation or yield compliance, the DSB can authorize the complainant to suspend concessions or other obligations to the country that was found in breach of the rules. In plain language, the complainant can be authorized to retaliate, for example, by placing trade barriers on goods from the country determined to be in infringement. In principle, retaliation should be in the same sector in which the defending country has been found in violation.

Of course, not all cases are treated the same. The dispute settlement mechanism has additional arrangements for handling disputes that involve multiple complainants, third parties,[1] perishable goods and other cases deemed urgent, and developing countries. The discussion that follows focuses on provisions for developing countries.

In line with other WTO agreements, the DSU seeks to acknowledge cases involving developing countries as "handle with care" cases. Favorable differential treatment for developing countries is invoked in seven of the twenty-seven articles of the DSU, including Article 24, devoted to special procedures for the least-developed countries.[2] These provisions call for special attention to problems and interests of developing countries and for legal assistance to those countries. If a complaint is against a developing country, that developing country is to be given ample time to prepare and present its argument. In the panel stage, if a dispute involves a developing country and a developed country, the former can request to have at least one panelist from a developing country. The panel is

---

[1] A third party is any member with substantial interest in the dispute before a panel, who has notified the Dispute Settlement Board of its interest (Article 10.2 of DSU). A third party cannot appeal a panel report.

[2] Articles 3.12, 4.10, 8.10, 12.10, 12.11, 21.2, 21.7, 21.8, 24, and 27.2.

also expected to report explicitly on the extent to which allowable provisions for differential and favorable treatment for developing countries have been utilized. In the compliance stage, if the complainant is a developing country, "the DSB shall take into account not only the trade coverage of measures complained of, but also their impact on the economy of developing country Member concerned" (Article 21.8 of DSU). Article 24 of the DSU calls for additional consideration for least-developed countries. For example, members are asked to exercise restraint in bringing cases that ask for compensation from or seek retaliation against least-developed countries.

A provision in Article 22 of the DSU on suspension of concessions and other obligations (retaliation) is of special relevance to developing countries, although it is not limited to them. The complainant may seek to cross-retaliate, that is, to retaliate in sectors not covered by the violated agreement, if it determines that it is not practical or effective to retaliate in the same sector in which the defending country has been found in violation.

It is important to point out that, unlike institutions such as the World Bank or the International Monetary Organization (IMF), the WTO does not have a precise classification of countries in terms of their development.[3] Each member country declares its own development status. However, a country that categorizes itself as a "developing country" does not receive preferential treatment automatically. It can be challenged on its decision to take advantage of more favorable treatment for developing countries. As for least-developed countries, the WTO adopts the designation by the United Nations, which in 2007 had fifty countries in that classification, thirty-three of which were members of the WTO. Of these

---

[3] According to the World Bank website, in 2008 the World Bank classified countries according to the 2007 gross national income per capita, calculated using the Atlas method (as opposed to the purchasing power parity method). The groups were: low income, $935 or less; lower middle income, $936–$3,705; upper middle income, $3,706–$11,455; and high income, $11,456 or more.

TABLE 2.1 Number of Cases Brought to the WTO: 1995–2005

| Year | Case Numbers | Total |
|------|-------------|-------|
| 2005 | DS325-DS335 | 11 |
| 2004 | DS305-DS324 | 20 |
| 2003 | DS277-DS304 | 28 |
| 2002 | DS243-DS276 | 34 |
| 2001 | DS216-DS242 | 27 |
| 2000 | DS186-DS215 | 30 |
| 1999 | DS155-DS185 | 31 |
| 1998 | DS111-DS154 | 44 |
| 1997 | DS65-DS110 | 46 |
| 1996 | DS23-DS64 | 42 |
| 1995 | DS1-DS22 | 22 |

Source: *http://www.wto.org/english/tratop_e/dispu_e/dispu_status_e.htm.*

least-developed WTO members, twenty-six were African countries (see Table 1.1 in Chapter 1).

DISPUTES

A full comparison of the current utilization of the DSU with the
utilization of the dispute settlement mechanism under GATT is
beyond the scope of this study. Not only was the mechanism under
GATT less unified and less rigorous, GATT had fewer members
and covered fewer agreements. It is sufficient to note that in the
nearly fifty-year tenure of GATT, only about 300 disputes were
brought for consultation. Hudec (1990 and 1993) provides a syn-
opsis of the GATT disputes for the 1948–1974 and 1948–1989 periods, respectively.

According to the WTO website, in the first eleven years of the
WTO (i.e., January 1, 1995 to December 31, 2005), there were 335
requests for consultation (see also WTO, 2005). The annual number of cases has ranged from a low of eleven in 2005 to a high of
forty-six in 1997, with fluctuations as shown in Table 2.1.

Tables 2.2 through 2.5 include only "old" cases, that is, those filed before January 1, 2005.[4] Table 2.2 shows the distribution of the 324 complaints into two broad categories of countries, those filed by high-income countries and those filed by developing countries.[5] Ideally, developing countries would be disaggregated to separate least-developed countries from other developing countries. However, thus far, only one least-developed country – Bangladesh – has directly participated in the DSU. In February 2004, Bangladesh brought a complaint against India on anti-dumping measures on imports of batteries. In 2006, Bangladesh and India informed the DSB that they had reached a mutually agreeable solution.

The first number in each cell of Table 2.2 is the absolute number of cases in the relevant category. In parentheses is the number of cases as a percentage (rounded) relative to the total number of cases. Seven disputes were brought by multiple complainants.[6] Six of them are tallied in Table 2.2 under "high-income and developing countries"; the seventh was recorded with the "bilateral" cases because all complainants were developing countries.[7]

Quantifying DSU cases by country groups, whether based on economic development or geographical location, is not a precise exercise. As noted above, some disputes are filed by multiple complainants from different regions and different economic groups. In addition, some disputes are brought jointly by high-income countries and developing countries. There is no consensus about whether to treat a consultation requested by multiple complainants as one or more than one consultation. For example,

---

4   This is done to prevent characterizing relatively new cases as being inactive because a panel has not yet been established, or as lacking a mutually acceptable solution.

5   High-income countries that have participated either as complainants or respondents are Australia, Belgium, Canada, Denmark, European Communities, France, Greece, Hong Kong, Ireland, Japan, Netherlands, New Zealand, Norway, Portugal, Singapore, South Korea, Sweden, Switzerland, United Kingdom, and the United States.

6   DS234, DS217, DS158, DS58, DS35, DS27, and DS16.

7   DS58, a case on imports of shrimp brought by India, Malaysia, and Pakistan against the United States.

TABLE 2.2  Requests for Consultations: January 1,
1995–December 31, 2004

| | Complainants | | | |
| | | | High-Income | |
| Respondents | High-Income Countries | Developing Countries | and Developing Countries* | Total |
|---|---|---|---|---|
| High-Income Countries | 142 (44%) | 56 (17%) | 5 (2%) | 203 (63%) |
| Developing Countries | 64 (20%) | 56 (17%) | 1 (–) | 121 (37%) |
| TOTAL | 206 (64%) | 112 (35%) | 6 (2%) | 324 (100%) |

*These are cases brought by multiple complainants that include at least one
developing country and one developed country.*
*Source: WTO (2005).*

Holmes et al. (2003) and Brewer and Young (1999) count the
number of complaints by the number of complainants, rather
than by the number of cases. Zimmerman (2005) counts the
number of disputes by the number of cases, an approach that
is used in this study as well. Counting multilateral cases by the
number of complainants would have increased the number of
requests for consultation by twenty-eight, changing the total
from 324 to 352.[8] Moreover, although the United States generally brings its disputes against the "European Communities"
(EC) as a group, it also has disputes against individual members
of the EC.[9]

---

[8]  For a discussion of issues regarding quantification of cases, see Brewer and Young
(1999).
[9]  The WTO materials refer to the European Union (EU) as such or as the European
Communities (EC). The EC is a member of the WTO, as is each of its twenty-seven
member states.

Of the 324 cases brought in the first ten years of the WTO, high-income countries were involved in 83 percent and developing countries were involved in 56 percent. The sum of 139 conveys that 39 percent of cases involved both high-income and developing countries. Almost 70 percent of the disputes brought by developed countries were against other developed countries, while disputes filed by developing countries were equally distributed between the two groups. The United States and the EC were involved in almost two-thirds of the cases brought in the first ten years of the WTO, or in about 80 percent of all disputes in which high-income countries were involved. Most of the high-income complaints against developing countries were directed at four relatively large economies – Argentina, Brazil, India, and Mexico. (China, which acceded to the WTO in 2001, will most likely join this short list in a few years.) This should not be surprising. Exports from the United States and EC to many individual developing countries are too small a percent of total exports for a violation by the importing country to reduce in any significant way benefits accruing to the United States or EC.

In their study, Holmes et al. (2003) conclude that trade share is a robust predictor of a country's participation in dispute settlement. It is likely that the single most important explanation for the higher share of disputes to which high-income countries are a party is the large trade shares with each other. However, there are other logical explanations. High-income countries may be constrained in filing disputes by their consideration of problems developing countries face, a self-discipline encouraged by the WTO. High-income countries might also be concerned about the potential for stirring up negative publicity if they brought cases against small developing countries. Moreover, high-income countries have other, and presumably more subtle, ways of leveraging a reduction in trade barriers in developing countries without resorting to the DSU. Another explanation could simply be that developing countries – especially the least-developed – receive many exceptions, making it hard to find them in violation of agreements. Of course, these explanations do not necessarily explain why least-developed countries have not been active complainants; some possible explanations are provided later in this chapter.

As described above, the DSU has a comprehensive process for handling disputes, including the privilege of either party to appeal a panel's report. However, the hope is always for the involved parties to genuinely try to resolve their disputes at the consultation stage. While the threshold in determining the success rate of consultations is rather subjective, 56 percent of the 324 disputes did not move to the panel stage. Table 2.3 shows the number of cases in which there was no panel established or settlement reported. Although it is still possible for complainants in these cases to request the establishment of panels in the future, only "old" cases (covering the period from January 1, 1995 to December 31, 2004) were included in the data. Table 2.4 shows the number of cases in

TABLE 2.3  No Panel Established and No Notification
of Settlement: January 1, 1995–December 31, 2004*

| | | Complainants | | | |
|---|---|---|---|---|---|
| R e s p o n d e n t s | | High-Income Countries | Developing Countries | High-Income and Developing Countries | Total |
| | High-Income Countries | 33 (23%) | 18 (32%) | 2 (40%) | 53 (26%) |
| | Developing Countries | 23 (36%) | 31 (55%) | 0 (0%) | 54 (45%) |
| | TOTAL | 56 (27%) | 49 (44%) | 2 (33%) | 107 (33%) |

* The first number in each cell is the absolute number of relevant cases. The second number (in parentheses) is the percentage, the base being the corresponding number in Table 2.2.
Source: WTO (2005) and http://www.wto.org/english/tratop_e/dispu_e/dispu_status_e.htm.

TABLE 2.4  Mutually Agreed-Upon Solutions or Inactive:
January 1, 1995–December 31, 2004*

| | | Complainants | | | |
|---|---|---|---|---|---|
| **R** | | | | High-Income | |
| **e** | | High-Income | Developing | and Developing | |
| **s** | | Countries | Countries | Countries | Total |
| **p** | | | | | |
| **o** | High-Income | 34 | 9 | 0 | 43 |
| **n** | Countries | (24%) | (16%) | (0%) | (21%) |
| **d** | Developing | 18 | 14 | 1 | 33 |
| **e** | Countries | (28%) | (25%) | (100%) | (27%) |
| **n** | | | | | |
| **t** | | 52 | 23 | 1 | 76 |
| **s** | TOTAL | (25%) | (21%) | (17%) | (23%) |

* The first number in each cell is the absolute number of relevant cases. The second number
(in parentheses) is the percentage, the base being the corresponding number in Table 2.2.
*Source: WTO (2005) and http://www.wto.org/english/tratop_e/dispu_e/dispu_
status_e.htm.*

TABLE 2.5  Sums of Numbers in Tables 2.3 and 2.4 in
Corresponding Cells: January 1, 1995–December 31, 2004*

| | | Complainants | | | |
|---|---|---|---|---|---|
| **R** | | High- | | High-Income | |
| **e** | | Income | Developing | and Developing | |
| **s** | | Countries | Countries | Countries | Total |
| **p** | | | | | |
| **o** | High-Income | 67 | 27 | 2 | 96 |
| **n** | Countries | (47%) | (48%) | (40%) | (47%) |
| **d** | Developing | 41 | 45 | 1 | 87 |
| **e** | Countries | (64%) | (80%) | (100%) | (72%) |
| **n** | | | | | |
| **t** | | 108 | 72 | 3 | 183 |
| **s** | TOTAL | (52%) | (64%) | (50%) | (56%) |

*The first number in each cell is the absolute number of relevant cases. The second number
(in parentheses) is the percentage, the base being the corresponding number in Table 2.2.
*Source: WTO (2005) and http://www.wto.org/english/tratop_e/dispu_e/dispu_
status_e.htm.*

which the parties reached a mutual agreement at the consultation stage, including a few that have been declared inactive. Table 2.5 adds up the numbers appearing in Tables 2.3 and 2.4.

The first number in each cell in Tables 2.3, 2.4, and 2.5 is the absolute number of relevant cases. The second number in each cell (in parentheses) is the percentage, the base being the corresponding number in Table 2.2. For example, in Table 2.4, in the top left cell, 34 is the number of cases brought by high-income countries against other high-income countries where mutual agreement was achieved; 24% (34 out of 142) is the percentage of such cases in which mutual agreement was achieved.

There is a higher tendency for cases that involve developing countries to end up with no panel established and no settlement notification than cases that involve only high-income countries. The tendency for "inaction" in cases involving only developing countries is 55 percent, compared to 23 percent of cases involving only high-income countries, as shown in Table 2.3. Overall, of all cases brought against and brought by developing countries, 72 percent and 64 percent, respectively, did not go beyond the consultation stage (Table 2.5). For high-income countries, the corresponding numbers for cases brought against and brought by high-income countries are 47 percent and 52 percent, respectively. Thus, cases involving developing countries have had a better chance of being dormant. This conclusion is not altered by various ways of counting cases with multiple complaints.

### AFRICAN COUNTRIES AND THE DSU

The discussion of African countries is intertwined with that of least-developed countries. As of December 2007, there were 152 members of the WTO, including forty-two African countries. Among the African countries, twenty-six (62 percent of them) are designated as least-developed countries. The "dominance" of African countries is even larger in the LDC Group (thirty-three countries) in the WTO. Almost 80 percent of the least-developed countries in the WTO are African countries.

Of the 335 disputes brought for consultation during the first eleven years of the existence of the WTO (January 1995 to December 2005), only six involved African countries – Egypt and South Africa – as primary parties (WTO, 2005). In all of those cases, Egypt and South Africa were countries against which complaints were bought. In chronological order, these cases were:

February 2005:   A case brought by Pakistan against Egypt involving anti-dumping duties on matches (DS327).[10] China, the EC, Japan, and the United States reserved their third party rights. The DSB established a panel in June 2005. Pakistan and Egypt reached a mutual understanding in March 2006.

January 2004:   A case brought by the United States against Egypt on measures affecting imports of textile and apparel (DS305). The United States and Egypt reached a mutual understanding in May 2005.

April 2003:   A case brought by Turkey against South Africa involving anti-dumping duties on imports of blankets (DS288). There has been no panel established and no settlement reported.

November 2000:   A case brought by Turkey against Egypt involving anti-dumping duties on imports of steel reinforcing bars (DS211). The dispute reached the panel stage and Egypt agreed to implement the recommendations and rulings of the DSB.

September 2000:   A case brought by Thailand against Egypt on the prohibition of imports of canned tuna (DS205). There has been no panel established and no settlement reported.

---

[10]   Dispute settlement (DS) cases are numbered in chronological order. One can always read the updates of a case by going to http://www.wto.org/english/tratop_e/dispu_e/dispu_status_e.htm and clicking on the case number.

April 1999:     A case brought by India against South Africa involving anti-dumping duties on imports of ampicillin and amoxicillin (DS168). There has been no panel established and no settlement reported.

As of December 2006, no African country has been involved as a principal complainant in any case under the WTO.[11] However, fifteen African countries have been involved as third parties in eight cases.[12] The single most famous case among these is the banana trade dispute between the United States and the EU (DS27). The cotton subsidies dispute between Brazil and the United States (DS267) has also received ample publicity, as will be discussed below.

---

[11] Under GATT, the WTO's predecessor, one finds only 2 cases where an African country was the principal complainant. In 1966, only two years after winning its independence, Malawi dared the United States into consultations regarding U.S. subsidies on tobacco (Hudec, 1990). While the agricultural sector was not under the jurisdiction of GATT, Malawi used Article XXXVII of GATT to challenge the U.S. subsidies, which allegedly allowed the United States to seize a larger export market. Article XXXVII:3 (c) required developed countries to:

have special regard to the interests of less-developed contracting parties when considering the application of other measures permitted under this Agreement to meet particular problems and explore all possibilities of constructive remedies before applying such measures where they would affect essential interests of those contracting parties.

The U.S. responded that the subsidies were not new and that they were simply being used to maintain an already established market share.

In 1984, South Africa challenged Canada because of a tax amendment by the Province of Ontario which, discriminately, exempted Maple Leaf Gold coins from a 7 percent tax that had been in existence. No other gold coins were exempted from the tax (Mosoti, 2006). Canada argued that the measure in question was not taken by Canada, but by a provincial government, which was not a contracting party of GATT. South Africa countered that "the federal government of Canada had not taken the measures, reasonably at its disposal and within its power, to ensure observance of its GATT obligations" (GATT, 1985: paragraph 9). The panel found that the discriminatory tax structure applied by Ontario was inconsistent with Canada's obligations to GATT. Although the panel's report was not adopted, the recommendation was for Canada to compensate South Africa for the competitive advantage it lost until the measure by Ontario was withdrawn. (For a full panel report, see GATT, 1985.)

[12] The cases are DS267, DS265, DS246, DS141, DS135, DS132, DS58, and DS27 (WTO, 2005). The countries are Benin, Cameroon, Chad, Côte d'Ivoire (2 cases), Egypt, Ghana, Kenya, Madagascar, Malawi, Mauritius (4 cases), Nigeria, Senegal (2 cases), Swaziland, Tanzania, and Zimbabwe.

First, the banana case, which some called the "banana war," attracted significant attention because of its rather fascinating intricacies, including the EC's complicated preferential system for imports of bananas from African, Caribbean, and Pacific (ACP) states; a conflict among developing countries that depend on banana exports; the corporate lobbying power involved in initiating the case[13]; and the United States' participation as the lead (and aggressive) plaintiff, even though not directly affected by the EC banana policy.[14] The following brief description captures the essence of the dispute.

In 1995, the United States, joined by Guatemala, Honduras, and Mexico (and Ecuador in 1996 immediately following its accession to the WTO), filed complaints alleging that the EC's banana regime for importation, sales, and distribution was inconsistent with WTO provisions (DS16 and DS27). Furthermore, by discriminating against U.S. firms that distributed bananas from Central and Latin America, the regime, allegedly, had an adverse effect on U.S. economic interests and, of course, on the economies of the co-complainants. As recipients of EC preferential treatment, four African countries – Cameroon, Ghana, Côte d'Ivoire, and Senegal – reserved their rights in the case as third parties and were trying to preserve the preferential treatment to which they had grown accustomed, dating back to even before the first Lomé Convention, signed in 1975.[15]

The WTO panel found the EC's banana trade regime to be inconsistent with its obligations. Subsequent appeals, stalling tactics by

---

[13] It has been alleged that the launching of the investigation and the filing of the formal complaint by the U.S. Trade Representative was a direct result of the relentless lobbying and generous financial donations by Chiquita (originally, the United Fruit Company) to the major political parties – Democratic and Republican – in the United States (Herbert, 1996; Raspberry, 1999).

[14] For an excellent discussion of the EC–U.S. banana trade dispute, see Read (2001).

[15] The first Lomé Convention formalized all preferential treatments of imports from the ACP countries. However, special provisions, such as the Banana Protocol, to safeguard imports from ACP countries were included in the Treaty of Rome that established the European Economic Community in 1957.

the EC, a unilateral (pre-emptive) declaration of punitive sanctions by the United States, and a complaint by the EC about the U.S. pre-emptive announcement, just added to the drama of the case. Left outside the main sphere of action during the negotiations between the EC and the United States were the developing countries on either side of the case, and neither side was satisfied with the deal struck by the two trading powers.

In 1999 the DSB permitted sanctions by Ecuador and the United States against the EC in this case. Mindful of its small size, Ecuador proposed cross-retaliation, that is, retaliation in a different sector. Specifically, Ecuador proposed denying intellectual property rights to European owners. As pointed out by Basso and Beas (2005: 19), this type of retaliation may:

lead to "socially acceptable" (or desirable) consequences. Instead of transferring the burden of the litigation onto society, which would happen if tariffs were doubled for imports from the non-implementing party, the burden is transformed into a social benefit, for example through increasing access to medicines, cultural goods, and entertainment products or just information.

This was the first case in which cross-retaliation through a suspension of TRIPS was requested, much to the chagrin of the arbitration panelists. The response of the arbitrators was essentially a warning to Ecuador about the complicated legal nature of their proposed path. They pointed out the complexities in determining the nationalities of intellectual property right holders. In addition, they reminded Ecuador that it was obligated to pre-TRIPS, World Intellectual Property Organization (WIPO) conventions: the *Paris Convention* for the protection of industrial property, the *Berne Convention* for the protection of literary and artistic works, and the *Rome Convention* for the protection of performers, producers of phonographs, and broadcasting organizations (WTO, 2000: 29–35).

While Ecuador was not able to retaliate, its creative proposal and, much more importantly, the United States' punitive trade sanctions imposed on EC products caused a change of heart by the EC. In 2001, the EC agreed to amend the banana regime to satisfy the United States and started to remove unlawful safeguards that favored imports of bananas from ACP countries. Nonetheless, the complainants contended that the EC's reform of the banana regime fell short.

In November 2006, Ecuador requested consultations with the EC, contending that the latter had not implemented the measures ordered by the Appellate Body (ICTSD, 2006 and 2006a). Later in February 2007, it requested the establishment of a panel and, shortly afterward, Cameroon, Colombia, Côte d'Ivoire, Dominica, the Dominican Republic, Ghana, Jamaica, Japan, St. Kitts and Nevis, St. Lucia, St. Vincent and the Grenadines, and the United States reserved their third-party rights. Subsequently, the United States requested the establishment of a panel, likewise claiming that the EC failed to bring its import regime of bananas into compliance with the WTO obligations. Belize, Brazil, Cameroon, Colombia, Côte d'Ivoire, the Dominican Republic, Ecuador, Jamaica, Japan, Mexico, Nicaragua, Panama, and Suriname reserved their third-party rights. It appears that the banana case will continue to be a source of disagreement between the United States and Central and Latin American countries on one side, and the EC and ACP countries on the other side. However, a successful establishment of Economic Partnership Agreements (EPAs) between the EC and ACP countries would reduce (if not remove) the validity of the banana case and similar cases against the EC.[16]

---

[16] The outcome of the banana case seemed to confirm that the non-reciprocal preferences provided by the EC to ACP countries were not covered by the Enabling Clause adopted in 1979 under GATT. The Enabling Clause allows developed countries to discriminate against other developed countries in favor of developing countries as it is applied to the Generalized System of Preferences program. The controversy with the EC preferences for ACP countries is that they discriminate against other developing countries – those that are not ACP countries. The Cotonou Agreement signed in 2000 was not covered by the Enabling Clause because it retained non-reciprocity of EC trade preferences for ACP countries. However, in 2001, the Doha Ministerial Council gave a temporary waiver to the non-reciprocal preferences provided by the EC to ACP countries. The Cotonou Agreement was to evolve into Economic Partnership Agreements (EPAs), that

The other dispute that has received considerable attention from the African Group in the WTO is the one brought by Brazil in 2002 against cotton subsidies in the United States (DS267).[17] Brazil was joined by Argentina, Australia, Benin, Canada, Chad, China, Chinese Taipei, the EC, India, New Zealand, Pakistan, Paraguay, and Venezuela as third parties. Although the participation by Benin and Chad in the dispute was only peripheral, their dire condition as least-developed countries, highly dependent on cotton exports, lead to an outcry against cotton subsidies. This was amplified by the "cotton initiative" launched jointly by Benin, Burkina Faso, Chad, and Mali a few months before the WTO ministerial meeting in Cancun, Mexico (WTO, 2003d). (See the case on Benin and its cotton industry at the end of Chapter 4.)

In 2004, a DSU panel ruled that certain U.S. subsidies to cotton farmers were inconsistent with the U.S. obligations under the Agreement on Agriculture. Though the United States appealed, the Appellate Body concurred with most of the panel's findings. While this was a major victory for Brazil and African countries, the United States usually takes its time in making corrections in such politically sensitive sectors. Following Ecuador's example,

---

is, reciprocal agreements between the EC and ACP countries, by 2008 (ICTSD, 2001). By January 1, 2008, twenty ACP countries, including eighteen African countries, had signed interim economic partnership agreements with the EC on trade in goods only; all fifteen Caribbean countries had signed full economic partnership agreements with the EC (Zwane, 2008), as shown below. Negotiations were to continue until all seventy-nine ACP countries had reached full economic partnership agreements with the EC.
*Interim agreements on trade in goods*:
*Africa:* Angola, Botswana, Burundi, Comoros, Côte d'Ivoire, Ghana, Kenya, Lesotho, Madagascar, Mauritius, Mozambique, Namibia, Rwanda, Seychelles, Swaziland, Tanzania, Uganda, and Zimbabwe.
*Pacific Region:* Papua New Guinea and Fiji.
*Full economic partnership agreements*:
*Caribbean Region:* Antigua and Barbuda, Bahamas, Barbados, Belize, Dominica, the Dominican Republic, Grenada, Guyana, Haiti, Jamaica, Saint Lucia, Saint Vincent and the Grenadines, Saint Christopher and Nevis, Suriname, and Trinidad and Tobago.

[17] Brazil requested consultations with the United States in 2002 and consequently requested establishment of a panel in 2003.

Brazil entertained the possibility of using cross-retaliation against U.S. services and intellectual property. However, a strong warning from the United States subdued Brazil's enthusiasm. Brazil ended up reaching a bilateral deal with the United States (ICTSD, 2005), with the understanding that the United States would comply with the cotton ruling by the Appellate Body. Given the discussion below about preferential treatment to developing countries, it is important to understand the threat issued by the United States.

No sooner had Brazil filed notice of its intention with the WTO this month [October 2005] than it got a heavy-handed admonition from B. Zoellick, the deputy secretary of state and former U.S. Trade Representative. He told reporters in Brasilia that it will take time for Congress to fix as complicated a problem as the cotton subsidies and that retaliation would only aggravate U.S. lawmakers. Then he brandished a threat to eliminate Brazil's right to export goods such as plywood, auto parts and metals duty-free under a special program for developing countries. "Keep in mind, Brazil sells about $2.5 billion under a special-preference program to the United States," Zoellick said according to a transcript of his remarks. "I think it is dangerous for people to go down these paths because one retaliates, and all of a sudden you might find out that something else happens" (Blustein, 2005).

As it happened, this stern warning did not restrain Brazil altogether. Alleging that the United States had not adopted the corrective measures called for by the Appellate Panel, in August 2006 Brazil requested a compliance panel to examine U.S. implementation of the recommendations and rulings (WTO, 2006). Contesting Brazil's contention and claiming that they had complied with the rulings, the United States tried to block the establishment of a compliance panel. Nonetheless, a compliance panel was formed, which later determined that the United States failed to bring its cotton subsidy programs into compliance (ICTSD, 2007a). It is likely that contentions over the cotton case between Brazil and the United States will continue for an extended period and will push the DSU mechanism to its limits.

Some could argue that the increased use of the dispute settlement process weakens the political process for settling disputes. However, there is no reason to assume that the two processes are mutually exclusive. In fact, the two processes can reinforce each other to the extent that they serve as reasonable alternatives or complementary processes. The political (diplomatic) process of settling a dispute has a better chance of succeeding when parties know that the legal process can be pursued, should it be necessary. Strategically, countries will always pursue the process that has a higher probability of success, other things being equal. Note that less than 50 percent of all disputes go beyond the *consultation* stage. In addition, it is fair to assume that there are unrecorded disputes that are resolved amicably through the political process that do not even get to the *consultation* stage. Regarding the cotton case, African countries relied on the political process and the authority of the Ministerial Conference, while at the same time utilizing the dispute settlement body in their role as third parties.

As it turned out, the strategy used by Benin, Burkina Faso, Chad, and Mali paid off. By relying on diplomacy and pursuing their case primarily through the WTO General Council, rather than through the DSU (except for Benin and Chad, as third parties), they managed to make a stronger case from a development point of view, rather than from a legal point of view. This path also made the United States and other developed countries less defensive and more willing to assist. In August 2004, the WTO General Council reached a decision in favor of development assistance for the cotton sector in Africa, particularly in West African countries (WTO, 2004). For example, Canada, Denmark, the EC, Germany, Japan, the Netherlands, the United States, and a number of multilateral agencies have responded with resources and creative ways to support the cotton industry in West Africa.[18]

---

[18] These agencies include the African Development Bank (ADB), the Development Assistance Committee of the Organization for Economic Cooperation and Development

Assistance has included rehabilitation of feeder roads, the building of irrigation infrastructure, the introduction of more productive cotton varieties, improving extension services, and improving cotton grading and classing. According to the U.S. Agency for International Development (USAID), "cotton classing is a major constraint to international marketing of cotton from [West Africa]. Estimates are that improved classing of cotton could potentially add as much as US$ 0.07 to US$ 0.10 per pound to the sale of cotton in world markets" (WTO, 2004a: 17). That would be approximately a 12 to 15 percent increase in price.

A cursory glance at the African countries' utilization of the DSU to this point might lead one to question the relevance of this chapter. The number of disputes brought by or against African countries might be seen as suggesting the agreement is irrelevant to African countries. Certainly neither the African Group (forty-two countries) nor the Least-Developed Country Group (thirty-three countries) in the WTO dismiss the agreement. They view it in the context of the implementation of all other agreements. However, they are not satisfied with what they see, contending that the dispute settlement system is biased against low-income developing countries – that is, against most African countries. They view the lack of active participation by African countries in disputes as being due to some inherent structural difficulties within the system. Operating under that premise, these two groups have been actively working in concert to craft proposals for amending the agreement to make it user-friendly for poor countries.

MAJOR PROBLEMS WITH THE DSU

African countries see four major problems with the DSU: the system is complicated and too expensive; developing countries are

(DAC-OECD), the Food and Agricultural Organization (FAO), the International Monetary Fund (IMF), the International Trade Center (ITC), the United Nations Industrial Development Organization (UNIDO), and the World Bank.

not adequately represented; the system does not clearly embrace a development agenda; and the compensatory and enforcement dimensions of the system are biased against African countries (WTO 2002a, 2002c, 2003b).

1. *The system is complicated and too expensive.* The operative word here is "expensive." The complicated nature of the system, as characterized by African countries, is taken to be intrinsic. The complexity of the system makes it too expensive for African countries to utilize effectively. Thus, most prominent for African countries in their proposals is a plea for financial assistance and arrangements that would reduce their costs to use the system. Specifically, the African Group and the LDC Group make two recommendations. They recommend a permanent standing fund (with funds presumably raised mostly from high-income countries) to help them develop the capacity to use the dispute settlement system. In addition, they recommend due consideration for the possibility of consultations involving least-developed countries to be conducted in the capitals of least-developed countries.

Recognizing developing countries' handicap in utilizing the dispute settlement system, the WTO in 2001 established an Advisory Center on WTO Law (ACWL) to provide services to those countries, free of charge or at lower rates than those available in the market. For example, the hourly rate for dispute settlement proceedings for least-developed countries is barely 10 percent of the market price. Services include legal advice, training of government officials in WTO law, and support in WTO dispute settlement proceedings. (See the case study about the ACWL at the end of this chapter.) Mosoti (2006) explains that the dispute settlement mechanism is a public good in the sense that, through litigation, there is improved clarity of WTO rules. The establishment of the ACWL is an acknowledgment that it is in the interest of all WTO members that developing countries are empowered to use the dispute settlement system.

As noted above, another recommendation is for the WTO to consider the possibility of holding consultations in the capitals of least-developed countries for dispute cases in which least-developed countries are involved (WTO, 2002c). The idea is to avoid the high cost of hosting officials from African capitals in Geneva. For a dispute settlement case, various government officials would likely be needed to offer informational support to the WTO representative(s). Most African countries have only one or two officials in Geneva handling WTO matters.

Although the suggestion to hold consultations in the capitals of least-developed countries seems reasonable, it is not at all clear that it would be ideal. Government officials sent to a particular venue for a particular purpose tend to be more prepared and more readily available for the task at hand than they would be in their home capitals. A least-developed country having consultations in its capital would also reduce its ability to exchange ideas on a case with other officials from least-developed countries in Geneva or experts at the ACWL or the United Nations Conference on Trade and Development (UNCTAD). One must also consider potential additional costs for other parties in the case.

There would even be additional direct costs to the hosting least-developed countries. WTO disputes require specific legal expertise that is typically not available in least-developed countries and, therefore, it would need to be imported. Foreign legal experts would charge extra for travel and hotel expenses and also for the inconvenience of being away from other cases and clients. These are additional costs that would most likely not be covered by the ACWL.

Another caveat about having consultations in the capitals of least-developed countries is that government officials (to whom consultations are brought closer) may sabotage the initiative. Traveling to Geneva is a unique opportunity and financially quite rewarding for those from a least-developed country. In fact, traveling to Geneva plus the *per diem* may be just the incentive needed to boost the morale of these mostly overworked and underpaid officials and technocrats.

As an example, at the conclusion of the Uruguay Round of GATT, a representative of an African country invited the WTO secretariat to his country to give a workshop on the new agreements to officials at the ministry of trade and industry. However, some individuals at the ministry sabotaged the effort because they wanted instead to be brought to Geneva. Considering the cost difference, that would have meant training only two people instead of training many more at the ministry's headquarters. The compromise was to have the workshop in a different city in the country, away from the capital, to give participants at least some modest *per diem*.

When asked which dispute cases they might have brought against their trading partners had the cost of proceedings not been prohibitively high, some African officials point to the lack of technical capacity to even ascertain truly disputable cases. This problem does not have an instant solution. However, the ACWL is making an important contribution with its legal advice for least-developed countries and developing countries, as discussed in the case study at the end of this chapter.

In addition, African countries should try to emulate the public–private network model of the EC. In order to utilize the WTO dispute settlement system effectively, the EC developed a close working relationship with trade associations, corporations, and their lawyers (Shaffer, 2006). With information supplied by the private sector, the EC has been able to create a detailed database listing foreign trade barriers, which is continuously updated. African countries do not have anywhere near the resources needed to develop such a database, but the first step is simply nurturing a relationship that encourages collaboration between the government and the private sector, and having an attitude that promotes trade. Shaffer (2006) explains how before the establishment of the WTO, European trade policy was defensive in posture, focusing on defending domestic producers from foreign goods. However, in 1996, the EC announced a new "Market Access Strategy" aimed at opening foreign markets to European goods. This led the EC to be more engaged in using the dispute settlement system as a complainant to advance its public and private interests (Shaffer, 2006). Again, it is not realistic to expect African countries to be able to do what the EC (and the United States and other developed countries) can. However, participation as a complainant in the WTO legal system by any country requires an outward-looking strategy.

2. *Developing countries are not adequately represented.* Diplomatic and technical representation of developing countries in the WTO in general is very limited. Many developing countries, especially least-developed countries, usually have just one or two trade generalists in Geneva, whereas developed countries can afford specialists in specific areas of negotiations. According to the African Group and the LDC Group, there is also unbalanced and inadequate representation of developing countries in the dispute settlement system. The African Group has proposed a geographical balancing of representation in the dispute proceedings. It argues that such a balance will reflect "the various backgrounds and inherent concerns of the entire WTO membership" (WTO, 2002a: 6).

Currently, for disputes between a developing country and a developed country, Article 8.10 of DSU entitles the developing country to at least one panelist from a developing country, "if the developing country so requests." (Panels are usually composed of three panelists.) It is interesting that Article 8.10 is needed to ensure that developing countries are not completely left out; one would have assumed that the sheer number of developing countries in the WTO and the requirement that a panel should consist of members with "sufficiently diverse background and a wide spectrum of experience" (Article 8.2 of the DSU) would guarantee at least one representative from a developing country in each panel.

Nonetheless, some developing countries do not find Article 8.10 of the DSU sufficient to achieve the geographical balance that they consider important. This is made clear by a proposal from the LDC

Group. The Group wants Article 8.10 of the DSU to be modified to entitle the developing country to two panelists from developing countries, the first one to be automatically granted, and the second if the developing country so requests. The Group also proposes even more tailored representation to safeguard their interests in disputes between a least-developed country and a developing country.

When a dispute is between a least-developed country and a developing or developed country, the panel shall include at least one panelist from a least-developed country Member and if the least-developed country Member so requests, there shall be a second panelist from a least-developed country (WTO, 2002c: 2).

Perhaps experience has shown African countries that the economic level of a panelist's own country influences his or her interpretation of rules and agreements. Whether this is an objective conclusion or not, there is a presumption of existing, or potential for the existence of, systematic bias against developing countries if they are not adequately represented in the panels.

It is practically impossible to decipher panel reports and Appellate Body reviews in terms of potential biases against developing countries or any other group of countries. First and foremost, each dispute is unique. Second, in the end it is often not clear which side is the winner. This is evidenced, for example, when both the complainant and the defending country appeal to the Appellate Body following the panel's report. In the complaint (DS285) brought by Antigua and Barbuda against U.S. restrictions on the cross-border supply of gambling and betting services, both sides appealed certain findings of the panel (WTO, 2005: 58–60). Third, even in a case with a relatively clear winner, typically the country would not have won on every claim that it brought or that was brought against it. One of a few exceptions is a case (DS243) where the panel reported that India failed in all its claims to establish inconsistency (violation) in U.S. rules of origin for textiles and apparel products (WTO, 2005: 80). Fourth, some complaints are brought jointly by developing and developed countries. A good example is the infamous banana case (DS16 and DS27) that was brought jointly by Ecuador, Guatemala, Honduras, Mexico, and the United States against the EC (WTO, 2005: 148).

A fifth reason for difficulty in identifying bias against developing countries is that, even in cases where the primary parties are a developing country on one side and a developed country on the other, third party countries may diversify the complainant's side and/or respondent's side. For example, in Peru's case against the EC's trade description of sardines (DS231), Canada, Chile, Colombia, Ecuador, Venezuela, and the United States reserved their rights as third parties (WTO, 2005: 85). In the case brought by the United States against Mexico's anti-dumping measures on imports of high-fructose corn syrup (DS132), Jamaica and Mauritius reserved third-party rights (WTO, 2005: 132). In a case brought by India against conditions for the EC tariff preferences (DS246), Bolivia, Brazil, Colombia, Costa Rica, Cuba, Ecuador, El Salvador, Guatemala, Honduras, Mauritius, Nicaragua, Pakistan, Panama, Paraguay, Peru, Sri Lanka, Venezuela, and the United States reserved third-party rights (WTO, 2005: 77).

As of June 2005, panel and Appellate Body reviews had been completed for approximately thirty disputes in which the primary parties were a developing country on one side and a developed country on the other. The cases were distributed equally between developing and developed countries. That is, there were fifteen cases brought by developed countries against developing countries and fifteen brought by developing countries against developed countries. For almost all those cases, the complainant won a few claims. Taking the view that the complainant is considered a winner if vindicated in at least one of its complaints, there is no revealed bias against developing countries.

A failure to deduce any bias does not necessarily mean it does not exist; moreover, people can be biased unintentionally. The bias can simply be a benign susceptibility to outside pressure or an unconscious outcome of one's upbringing and the world to which he or she was exposed. The proposals by the African Group and the LDC Group to ensure representation of developing countries have merit to the extent that: (a) there are gray areas in interpreting rules and agreements, even for trade and law experts; and (b) panelists' experience with their own countries tend to influence their interpretation of the rules in those gray areas.

Of course, the most important criterion must remain the integrity and professional qualification of the individual being considered for a panel. Mosoti (2006: 443) cautions that

insisting on developing-country nationals might actually exclude some other WTO experts who are perhaps better suited to bring development concerns to the fore of the dispute settlement system, by virtue of their training, breadth of experience, and moral authority.

Moreover, the kind of experiential and geographical balancing of panels sought by African countries may never be satisfied. There will continue to be a propensity to narrowly reclassify regions or groups. For example, the LDC Group already finds being grouped with developing countries is too general, as their proposal suggests. Geographical balancing is even more problematic. In a dispute involving an African country, would it be sufficient that some panelists are from developing countries, or must they come from Africa? In a dispute involving a country in southern Africa, would it be sufficient that some panelists are from Africa, or must they come from southern Africa?

3. *The system does not clearly embrace a development agenda.* Proposals by the African Group and the LDC Group, whether regarding panel composition or procedures for appellate review, seem to be underscored by one fundamental assertion: the DSU mechanism is not sensitive to development interests of developing countries. The LDC Group claims that the mechanism is too legalistic, "often to the detriment of the evolution of a development-friendly jurisprudence" (WTO, 2002c: 2). Therefore, its proposal is geared at

aligning the DSU mechanism with development objectives. In the same spirit, the African Group wants the success of the DSU to be determined not only by the speed of proceedings and the number of disputes finalized, but it "should be equally determined on the basis of the extent to which findings and recommendations fully reflect and promote the development objectives" (WTO, 2002a: 7).

"Development" is a term with a very high premium in political economy discussions. It is even more powerful when the development argument is made by African countries. Why, one might ask, would anyone or any system stand in the way of development for these impoverished countries? Moreover, unlike the first two decades of their independence when, according to Ake (1996: 9), the development argument was merely "a means for reproducing political hegemony," a few African countries are, these days, genuinely undertaking development initiatives.

Development—that is, sustainable increase in the standard of living of the population – must be the guiding principle for all economic policies. However, no matter how compelling the development argument might be, it has its limitations when it comes to the DSU system. The most appropriate stage for the development argument is at the negotiation of agreements. Once an agreement has been reached, a member country should not wave the development card as an excuse for failing or refusing to meet its obligations.

It can be argued that most African countries as well as other developing countries signed the WTO agreements at the conclusion of the Uruguay Round of GATT without a clear understanding of the long-term impact of these agreements. This was due in part to the complexity of the agreements and the limited technical and diplomatic representation by African countries, compounded by the fact that various agreements were negotiated simultaneously.[19]

---

[19] Whereas developed countries had specialists for each area of negotiation, African countries were largely represented by generalists, and some African countries had no representatives at all. Competent as those few African representatives may have been, they were too few in number and their resources too limited to grasp all the intricacies of

Nonetheless, correcting for any revealed biases against development must be done by renegotiating agreements and amending them accordingly. For example, TRIPS has been renegotiated and revised to address special challenges faced by the least-developed countries. While the DSU system can and will signal the need for such revisions and the need for technical assistance, it must enforce the rules, not set the rules, if the system is to work effectively.

The development argument has another more general weakness. It subtly assumes that freer markets are averse to development. In their proposals, African countries and least-developed countries seem to project the idea that any rulings against them would reflect insensitivity to the development agenda. In aggregate, WTO agreements push countries toward more openness and toward allowing market forces to determine the allocation of goods and resources. African countries have often pointed to market imperfections as a reason for government controls and intervention, and no one would deny that market imperfections are prevalent in developing countries and that the government has an important role to play. However, it is important to note that claims of market imperfections are sometimes simply weak excuses to introduce and maintain rent-generating activities. Moreover, some of the policies that many African countries implemented in the name of development, in fact created market imperfections and weakened the economies of those countries.

Consider, for example, the price and production controls in various sectors (goods, services, finance, and agriculture) that were the norm in many African countries from the 1960s to the mid-1980s as a means to deal with monopolistic tendencies. The price and production controls created shortages, as well as wasteful government monopolies whose remnants are still features of some African economies. Agricultural reforms that would have increased

economics, history, law, science, strategy, and politics involved (Blackhurst and Lyakurwa, 2005; Ohiorhenuam, 2005; Mshomba, 2000).

producer prices were resisted by those connected with the marketing boards (which, at the time, included the whole apparatus of the single ruling party in most countries) in the name of development. The result was a decline in production of agricultural exports and an increase in cross-border smuggling (May, 1985; Mshomba, 1993).

Another example of an ineffective policy implemented in the name of development was reflected by the almost impenetrable trade barriers of the pre-structural adjustment era. African countries justified those barriers by making the infant industry argument. Yet the public suffered the typical costs of protection – shortages and high prices – without gaining advantage in industrial production. It took, in part, external pressure for some countries to move toward development-friendly policies, such as reducing export taxes on subsistence farmers and reducing trade barriers that were a severe burden on consumers. Of course, many of the sheltered factories collapsed as soon as there was any glimpse of outside competition.

Some viewed the collapse of such factories as evidence that the World Bank, the IMF, and, later, the WTO did not understand development and had a bias against developing countries. However, is a country really made worse off by allowing goods from other countries (including other poor African countries) to compete with domestic goods produced by a perpetually subsidized, and inefficiently run, government facility? An argument does not qualify as pro-development in nature just because it comes from a representative from a developing country. In addition, an argument is not anti-development just because there is a group in a developing country that would lose in the short run.

The development argument in the WTO is typically framed as if disputes are and would only be between developing and developed countries.[20] Even if that were the case, what would prevent

---

[20] Note that the development argument is also a recurring excuse for failing to meet mutually agreed timetables for regional economic integration in Africa. For details, see Chapter 6 in Mshomba (2000).

developed countries from also using the development argument in their favor? Countries vary tremendously in terms of their development, but because there is no limit to development, any country can potentially use the argument. If one is to automatically assume that the argument is invariably stronger when it comes from a developing country, what is to be made of a dispute between two developing countries or two least-developed countries? Developing countries in the Americas have gotten comfortable bringing cases against each other; six such cases were brought from 1995 to 1999 and twenty-three such cases were brought from 2000 to 2004 (WTO, 2005).

Again, consider the banana case discussed earlier, with developing countries on either side of the case (though some just as third parties). Should the argument categorically favor the poorer country in the dispute? The point here is not that development goals should not matter, but that the development argument is weak. In fact, the argument poses potential danger to *development* when applied automatically to the dispute settlement system.

4. *The compensatory and enforcement dimensions of the system are biased against African countries.* This is the area in which African countries have their most compelling argument against the current DSU system. The final stage in the legal framework of the DSU is compensation and suspension of concessions. However, as will be discussed below, compensation is rare, and retaliation, especially by smaller countries, causes additional economic loss to the complainant and is ineffective. In addition, retaliation causes less of an impact on the respondent than the trade loss caused by the respondent. Thus, if an African country was a complainant and reached this stage in the dispute settlement process, the compensatory and enforcement provisions do not give the African country enough leverage to attain satisfaction or to make the violating country change its policies.

For illustration, let $A$ be an African country and $B$ be the United States. Suppose country $A$ submits a complaint that certain trade measures imposed by country $B$ breached the latter's obligation and consequently caused adverse effects in country *A*. The case proceeds through consecutive stages and finally the Appellate Body upholds the panel's conclusion that the measures at issue are inconsistent with country *B*'s obligations. Country *B* is then expected to inform the DSB of its intention to implement the recommendations of the DSB and to complete the implementation within fifteen months of the adoption of the Appellate Body report.

Consider a situation where country *B* does not change its measures extensively or quickly enough to satisfy the complainant, country *A*. If the DSB sides with the complainant, country *A* will be entitled either to compensation from country *B* or the right to retaliate with its own trade barriers against country *B*.

Compensation means country *B* must reduce mutually agreed upon trade barriers on some other products. However, note that compensation is voluntary and, thus, extremely rare. Moreover, compensation by country *B* would be bound by the *most favored nation* principle; that is, a member country must treat all other members equally with respect to trade policy. Therefore, if country *B* were to reduce trade barriers on some products from country *A*, it must do so on those products from other member countries as well, that is, on a *most favored nation* basis – another reason why compensation is rare. In addition, suppose the unlawful trade policy of country *B* was against country *A*'s most dominant export commodity, as cotton is for a number of West African countries. In that case, reducing trade barriers for other products, that is, minor exports from country *A*, would be meaningless for country *A*. Given that country *A* would not find this remedy satisfactory, country *B* would be even less inclined to use it as a way to provide compensation.[21]

If, as can be expected, compensation fails to resolve the dispute, the DSB can authorize country *A* to suspend concessions or other obligations to country *B*. That is, country *A* can retaliate

---

[21] For more about why compensation is rarely preferred, see Anderson (2002).

by placing trade barriers on goods from country *B*. The level of retaliation by country *A* is to be equivalent to the level of nullification and impairment (i.e., the trade loss) caused by country *B*. In principle, to the extent possible, retaliation should be in the same sector in which the defending country has been found in violation. However, African countries have hardly any intra-industry trade with their major trading partners to make retaliation a viable choice.[22] In addition, for African countries, retaliation causes (a) additional economic loss (a net welfare loss) to the complainant and is ineffective; and (b) less of an impact on the respondent than the trade loss caused by the respondent.

### Retaliation Causes Additional Economic Loss and is Ineffective

Whatever the trade barrier might be that caused the dispute in the first place, it causes a net loss to the complainant due to a reduced volume of exports (from the complainant) and potentially reduced unit prices of the exports (due to the decreased demand for the products). This represents a deterioration in the terms of trade.[23] The ripple effect of reduced export revenues for developing countries is usually far reaching because they need foreign currency to pay for imports and repay foreign loans. Asking these countries to retaliate by imposing their own trade barriers is literally asking them to dig themselves into a deeper hole of overall economic loss. Trade barriers distort domestic prices, which in turn distort domestic production and consumption. This causes a production

---

[22] Intra-industry trade involves international trade in which a country both exports and imports products in the same industry. For example, when the United States both exports and imports cars, it is referred to as intra-industry trade. African countries mainly export primary products and import manufactured products. There is little intra-industry trade in Africa compared to developed countries.

[23] The price of a country's export goods relative to the price of its import goods is known as the country's terms of trade. Deterioration in the terms of trade is a fall in the price of exports relative to the price of imports.

distortion loss and a consumption distortion loss, on top of redistributing income from millions of domestic consumers to a few domestic producers. When one considers the overall economic impact, trade barriers – inefficient policies – in one country do not justify trade barriers in another. Of course, the WTO is painfully aware of this reality and hopes that retaliation or the threat of retaliation, when necessary, will lead to the lowering of trade barriers by respondents. In other words, they expect retaliation to be rare and temporary.

Furthermore, for retaliation to induce change, it must have some noticeable economic impact on the respondent's economy. The economies of African countries are too small for their trade barriers to induce policy change in the United States or the EC, for example. According to the *Direction of Trade Statistics* (published by the IMF), from 2000 to 2004, the United States and the EC exports of goods to Africa were, respectively, about 1 percent and 2 percent of their total exports of goods. Individual African countries would inflict no real damage to the United States or the EU export potential, even if those African countries were to impose prohibitive tariffs across the board. In addition, given that they are price takers, African countries cannot improve their terms of trade by imposing trade barriers.

On the flip side, if the United States, the EC, or any other large trading partner were to retaliate against a trade barrier placed by an African country, it would inflict considerable damage on the latter, thus effectively forcing the African country to remove the barrier. About 20 and 45 percent of Africa's exports are destined for the United States and the EC, respectively. Whether it concerns imports or exports, the United States and the EC are much more important to Africa, than Africa is to the United States or the EC. This phenomenon suggests that the retaliation remedy is asymmetrical and inherently unfair.

Large economies must not be encouraged to take unfair advantage of their size. However, to the extent that the asymmetry reduces the propensity for African countries to increase trade barriers for fear of retaliation, it can be a blessing in disguise for Africans, considering the benefits of trade. Of course, African countries would benefit even more from trade if their *trading partners* reduced trade barriers.

If, indeed, retaliation by small African countries inflicts no real damage on large economies, the same can be said about trade barriers *initiated* by those African countries. Being a minor player would suggest not only that exerting effective pressure on major players is not possible, but also that major players may not be sufficiently harmed by these policies for them (the major players) to exert pressure for the removal of those policies. Even at the establishment of the WTO, the marginalization of small African countries was apparent. Their commitments were seen, to some extent, as a token. Least-developed countries, most of which are in Africa, were asked to "just give us a number" at which they wanted to bind their tariffs (Mshomba, 2000: 115). Therefore, trade barriers initiated by small African countries that violate WTO agreements would most likely go unchallenged in the dispute settlement mechanism by large economies.

Ironically, the greater disadvantage for small African countries is not so much that their retaliation would be ineffective, but that their trade barriers may simply be ignored. Those trade barriers could potentially be maintained, hurting African economies for quite some time. In other words, there may not be enough outside pressure to reduce trade barriers, a reduction that would have an overall positive impact, especially to African consumers.

This is not how African representatives approach the situation. Their concern is the apparent inherent inability of their countries to effectively retaliate against trade barriers imposed by large economies. African countries have, therefore, proposed collective retaliation (WTO, 2002a: 3).

There should be a provision stating that: in the resort to the suspension of concessions, all WTO Members shall be authorised to collectively suspend concessions to a developed Member that adopts measures in breach of WTO obligations against a developing Member, notwithstanding the requirement that suspension of concessions is to be based on the equivalent level of nullification and impairment of benefits.

It is difficult to believe that African countries are serious about this proposal, considering its potential for escalating trade barriers and the negative repercussions of such trade embargos. However, the proposal highlights the frustration felt by developing countries. Moreover, the concept of collectivity is not altogether foreign to the WTO, where collective bargaining in the form of coalitions, by region or economic classification, is common and sometimes effective.

### Retaliation Causes Less of an Impact on the Respondent Than the Trade Loss Caused by the Respondent

The WTO requires that retaliation by the complainant against the respondent's exports be proportional to the trade loss on a one-to-one basis. The total value of prohibited imports by the complainant should be equivalent to the value of the complainant's reduced exports to the respondent that resulted from the respondent's breach of WTO obligations. Naturally, if the WTO is going to endorse retaliation, it must also set limits. Whatever the limits are, equivalence, on the basis of overall economic loss, cannot be achieved. This is especially the case for a small complainant whose retaliation can only add to its own economic loss without necessarily inducing a policy reversal by the respondent.

Anderson (2002) suggests authorizing retaliation by the complainant that is some multiple of the damage caused by the respondent. Although this may indeed help large complainants influence compliance faster, it would simply multiply the economic loss experienced by small complainants if they were to be gullible enough to adopt the full extent of permissible retaliatory trade barriers.

Even if retaliation were effective, the term "equivalence" loses its meaning almost completely, considering that retaliation is usually authorized when the breach of the WTO obligations has already persisted for at least three years. Retaliation is not authorized with the view to correct for the reduction of exports that has already happened. It is supposed to match the concurrent damage and be halted as soon as the respondent complies, even though, in theory, "the DSB shall take into account not only the trade coverage of measures complained of, but also their impact on the economy of developing country Members concerned" (Article 21.8 of the DSU).

The current DSU system also lacks the capacity to correct for long-term or irreversible damage to the complainant caused by the respondent's breach of WTO obligations. This may include a permanent displacement of workers, the loss of skills, a reduced ability to attract direct investment, and shifts in demand to substitute goods (not necessarily produced by the complainant). For example, the price support program for sugar in the United States and the EC caused rapid growth in the demand for high-fructose corn syrup. In 1973 high-fructose corn syrup accounted for less than 2 percent of United States caloric sweetener consumption. By 1987, it accounted for 36 percent (Gardner, 1990: 47). This increase was partly due to the price floor for sugar in the United States. Even if the price support system were eliminated, the world demand for sugar would still not increase to the level it would have, if there had not been any sugar subsidies. The same can be said about the potential impact of the price support program for cotton in shifting demand from natural fibers to synthetic fibers in the United States. Note that while export subsidies by the United States lower the world price of cotton, they cause the domestic price of cotton in the United States to increase.

To illustrate the potentially irreversible loss of skills that can occur through a respondent's breach of WTO obligations, consider that the skills of crop husbandry in Africa are passed from one generation to another through actual participation in farming. If a family is displaced from cotton production, it means that parents will not be able to pass their knowledge of growing and caring for cotton to their children. In turn, that means that even when cotton subsidies in OECD countries are finally removed and/or the price of cotton bounces back, there will be fewer people who know how to cultivate cotton.

In 2002, Mexico presented a proposal asserting that, "the fundamental problem of the WTO dispute settlement system lies in the period of time during which a WTO-inconsistent measure can be in place without the slightest consequence"(WTO, 2002d: 1). Mexico proposed an acceleration of proceedings to obtain authorization for retaliation and retroactive application of the DSB rulings. Similar proposals were made by the African Group (WTO, 2002a) and the LDC Group (WTO, 2002c). To emphasize the serious injury caused to developing countries by illegal measures restricting their exports, the African Group proposed retroactive remedies even for measures that were withdrawn before the commencement or finalization of dispute proceedings. In addition, Mexico proposed authorizing the complaining party to take preventive measures against alleged WTO-inconsistent measures while dispute proceedings were pending. This authority was to be granted when the complainant considered that the respondent's breach of obligation would cause or threatened to cause damage that would be difficult to repair.

Aware that retaliation by small developing countries may simply add to more domestic injury, Mexico and African countries have made additional recommendations. Mexico proposed that if acceptable compensation could not be negotiated, the complainant should be given the option to trade the right to retaliate to another member (WTO, 2002d: 6). A preliminary study of Mexico's proposal for using auction theory lends cautionary support to the efficacy of the proposal from an economic point of view (Bagwell et al., 2004). However, it warns that introducing auctioning countermeasures into the DSU system may not necessarily be a good idea, considering potential political ramifications that might arise. Proposals by the African Group and the LDC Group call for compensation to be mandatory and not only in the form of further market access, but also monetary compensation.[24]

None of these proposals would have a direct impact on the export industry hurt by the WTO-inconsistent measures. One would imagine that the preventive measures proposed by Mexico could take the form of a complainant subsidizing the industry. However, developing countries have severe budget constraints. This is where the merit of monetary compensation lies, because those funds could be used to support the afflicted export sector. Ironically, the chance of receiving financial support for the affected export sector seems better when a charge is pursued through the WTO General Council rather than through the DSU. At least the approach taken by West African countries regarding their cotton sector, as discussed above, suggests this phenomenon.

African countries are so vulnerable that threats of trade barriers alone, by a large trading partner such as the United States or the EU, can be sufficient to destroy their export industries. In 1994, a few months before the WTO came into effect, the United States threatened Kenya with import quotas on shirts and pillowcases. These threats alone dissuaded potential investors from investing in Kenya and caused producers of apparel in Kenya to look for new host countries even before the quotas were actually set or became effective. Likewise, the threats prompted U.S. importers to look for other sources. The current DSU system is not structured to address any damages caused by threats of trade barriers, even though they can be just as damaging as actual trade barriers. It would be very difficult to calculate a mutually acceptable estimate

---

[24] Proposals by developing countries calling for monetary compensation and collective retaliation were also floated during the GATT period, dating as far back as 1965 (Hudec, 2002).

of damages caused by threats, but it is worth a serious discussion in the WTO.

Although other actions are not considered trade barriers in a technical sense, they can be applied with partiality. Consider travel warnings posted on the U.S. State Department's website. It is not clear, for example, why Kenya was on the U.S. travel warning list in 2006, while Egypt has continued to escape the list even after bloody terrorist attacks at Egyptian tourist spots. Given the impact that these travel warnings have on trade, tourism, and foreign direct investment, the WTO should at least be apprised of the factors used to include a member country on the warning list.

### OTHER CONSIDERATIONS REGARDING THE LOW LEVEL OF AFRICAN PARTICIPATION IN THE DSU

Other important considerations regarding the low level of participation by African countries in the dispute settlement process include (1) the role of individual firms; (2) the role of the media, NGOs, and domestic consumers; (3) non-WTO avenues for negotiating trade disputes; (4) the role of preferential treatment and financial assistance for African countries; and (5) the lack of credible disputes between African countries and developed countries.

### *The Role of Individual Firms*

The discussion above may lead one to conclude that disputable trade barriers by a small African country have no significant impact on large developed countries and, therefore, are left completely unchallenged. However, even casual observation of the real world would refute such a conclusion. Large developed countries are known both to have trade barriers on goods from small developing countries and to complain about trade barriers by seemingly small countries with minuscule market size.

To appreciate the forces behind trade barriers and, more importantly here, the forces behind submission of complaints to the DSB, it is imperative to consider the interests of individual firms. Although WTO membership consists of national governments, international trade is, in practice, not conducted by national governments but rather by companies, companies that are concerned with their profit margins. While trade barriers by an African country may not have any noticeable impact on the overall U.S. economy, for example, it may have an impact on a U.S. company's short-run profits.

There is a firm or firms (typically multi-national corporations) behind every dispute. The driving force and the propensity to lobby for action are determined by an individual firm's losses or anticipated losses. The question of whether the disputed trade barrier has an impact on the overall terms of trade is irrelevant to an exporting firm. In addition, even when the market of the country with disputable trade barriers is small relative to the exporting firm's total sales, the firm might still lobby vigorously for their removal if that market is projected to grow. Moreover, if one small country's trade barriers were neglected, who is to say that other small countries would not follow suit and impose similar trade barriers? Pursuing a country with disputable trade barriers is not only meant to force that country to open its market, but also to deter other countries from putting into place similar barriers.

The Market Access Strategy developed by the EU in 1996 enables firms to notify the EU's Trade Directorate General (TDG) directly of trade barriers, or to notify the TDG indirectly through respective trade associations or a member state official. The EU estimates that over 90 percent of the identified trade barriers are reported by individual firms or their trade associations (Shaffer, 2006).

Section 301 of the U.S. Trade Act of 1974 enables individual firms to petition the U.S. Trade Representative (as Chiquita did in the banana case) for an investigation of alleged violations of the trade rules of a foreign country. In addition, the Office of the U.S. Trade Representative can initiate an investigation itself. The fact that individual enterprises, whether in the United States or in a developing country, are behind initiations of dispute settlements, should not come as a surprise as they have first-hand information about disputed trade barriers. Moreover, trade rules and rule changes are not always publicly reported, and only those enterprises directly affected manage to identify and account for their occurrence. For this reason, when criticism is leveled against corporations for their influence in initiating cases, that criticism should not go unchallenged. If there is an alleged violation of an agreement, it should matter little who initiates the investigation. What is important is for the relevant panel and the Appellate Body to consider the facts regarding the alleged violations and interpret agreements objectively and with impartiality. If WTO agreements are reached with the full intention that they guide trade activities between nations, then those who report violations should not be criticized simply because they are motivated by self-interest.

Of course, this is not to say that all WTO agreements take into account fully the salient development challenges that African and other developing countries face. The TRIPS Agreement is a good example of an agreement that fell short in appreciating the needs and capacity of African countries, as discussed in Chapter 3. This is where the question arises as to the degree of corporations' self-interest, or rather their influence, and the fairness of some agreements on which disputes are based. Corporations can have significant influence in the framing of trade issues and the outcome of negotiations, as well as in the initiation of dispute cases. For this reason, some critics even go so far as to argue that corporations are culpable of having "hijacked" the WTO.

While this argument cannot simply be dismissed out of hand, for there is some truth to it, accepting it at face value would also be misguided. Like other participants in world trade, such as French farmers, cotton growers in the United States and Africa, or consumers anywhere, corporations deserve a voice in international trade rules through their governments.

A major controversy that has emerged regarding the participation of corporations and NGOs in dispute settlement procedures has to do with whether panels and the Appellate Body may accept and consider *amicus curiae* briefs (WTO, 2003: Chapter 9).[25] By definition, *amicus curiae* briefs are submissions by entities that are neither a party nor a third party to the dispute. These briefs typically come from NGOs and industry associations with the intent to influence outcomes of disputes.[26]

Article 13 of the DSU gives panels "the right to seek information and technical advice from any individual or body which it deems appropriate." In addition, the Appellate Body's report on a case brought in 1996 by India, Malaysia, Pakistan, and Thailand concerning the U.S. import prohibition of certain shrimp and shrimp products, stated that Article 12 of the DSU allows panels to consider or reject unsolicited *amicus curiae* briefs (WTO, 1998: paragraphs 102–110). The controversy over unsolicited briefs only intensified when the United States filed a proposal on transparency, recommending opening dispute arguments and proceedings to the public and setting guidelines for handling *amicus curiae* submissions (WTO, 2002). Many countries were opposed to the U.S. proposal, particularly to the suggestion that unsolicited briefs by non-parties be allowed. The position of the African Group is that any unsolicited information should be submitted to the parties and not directly to the panels. The African Group and many other developing countries are concerned that allowing direct submissions by non-parties (NGOs and business associations) to the panels or Appellate Body would weaken the inter-governmental nature of the WTO (WTO, 2002a, 2002b, 2003b). The African Group has a compelling argument

---

[25] Amicus curiae means "friend of the court."
[26] For a study that examines the strategies used by NGOs to submit *amicus curiae* briefs, see Butler (2006).

that must be seriously considered. Nonetheless, corporations and NGOs should be able to inform their governments without being automatically labeled as insensitive, greedy, or commandeers of the WTO.

Individual national governments are in the WTO to represent their constituencies, including corporations, distributors, consumers, investors, farmers, and NGOs. There is also no reason to assume that if an agreement is good for corporations, it must be bad for the rest of the participants. Trade, as is well known, is not a zero-sum game.

Part of the criticism regarding the power of corporations stems from those who are frustrated by some suspicious domestic lobbying tactics in many countries. Apparently Chiquita, for example, resorted to making large sums of "soft contributions" to political parties to push the U.S. Trade Representative to move on the banana case. However, it would be naïve to expect that the WTO could or should monitor and control an individual country's domestic mechanisms for initiating an investigation.

Even if it could be argued convincingly that corporations have and tend to use significant power to trample the interests of developing countries, it would seem that the DSU mechanism serves as a neutralizing force, rather than accomplice, in the face of such abusive power. The fact that a corporation can convince its government to initiate a case against a trading partner does not mean that the complainant will necessarily win the case. Without the DSU body and its legitimacy, corporations, if politically powerful, would simply push their governments into unmitigated protectionist actions, justified in the name of domestic interests and/or retaliation.

Thanks in part to corporations that lobby their governments to file cases, active engagement of the DSU body in deliberating and ruling on cases has become a beacon that signals a need for technical assistance for developing countries and re-examination of WTO agreements. It has also made possible scrutiny of domestic trade laws that may be incompatible with the articles of the DSU, despite disagreement about the panel rulings of such cases.

In 1998, the EC filed a complaint (DS152) with respect to Sections 301–310 of the U.S. Trade Act of 1974, contending that particular trade law was inconsistent with the articles of the DSU because it enabled the United States to act unilaterally in determining and imposing punitive sanctions (WTO, 2005: 124). One year later, a DSU panel found in favor of the United States, concluding that the U.S. Trade Act of 1974 was not inconsistent with the articles of the DSU. Surprisingly, the panel ruling was not based on the legal interpretation of the U.S. trade law, but rather on the declaration by the U.S. administration that it will not actually use the law or act unilaterally.

The panel noted that its findings were based in full or in part on US undertakings articulated in the Statement of Administrative Action approved by the US Congress at the time it implemented the Uruguay Round agreements and confirmed in the statements by the US to the panel (WTO, 2005: 124).

A weakness in this line of reasoning is apparent. It is similar to a ruling that it is not inconsistent with the law for a country to possess illegal deadly weapons, as long as there is a declaration by that country that it will not fire the weapons.[27] While the panel ruling for this case (and undoubtedly others) leaves a lot to be desired, the dispute settlement process has, nevertheless, bound the U.S. government more firmly to its political declaration not to impose punitive sanctions unilaterally. In other words, one must not only look at what the DSU system has failed to achieve, but also at what it has been able to accomplish.

## The Role of the Media, NGOs, and Domestic Consumers

The presumably ineffective retaliation by a small developing country against a large developed country, even when the small country

---

[27] For an extended critical evaluation of the panel ruling on the U.S. sanctions law and its inconsistency with other DSU panel decisions, see Raghavan (2000).

has won a case, is one explanation given by African countries regarding why they have not been active participants in the DSU system. However, when a small country wins a case against a large country, the media, NGOs such as Oxfam and Third World Network, and domestic consumers in the large country can galvanize the public to pressure the government to retract its unlawful trade policies.

The Brazil-U.S. cotton subsidies case certainly benefited from publicity garnered mainly by allegations that the U.S. cotton subsidies had detrimental effects on desperately poor African countries dependent on cotton exports. In fact, these allegations and the solidarity of the African Group with other developing countries on other contentious issues were part of the reason why the WTO Ministerial meeting in 2003 in Cancun, Mexico, did not succeed. Pressure on the United States to remove cotton subsidies gained even more momentum when Brazil won the case.

Even the banana case benefited from the media and pressure by NGOs, although it did not need as much advocacy as the cotton case because it had large and influential countries on both sides. In the banana case, although Ecuador was authorized to impose sanctions against the EC, it refrained from retaliating. Ecuador was concerned that retaliation would only hurt its economy without necessarily pressing the EC into compliance.[28] When Ecuador proposed cross-retaliation through intellectual property rights, it quickly learned how complicated and dangerous that could be. Notwithstanding this reality, winning the case gave Ecuador and other Latin American countries more ammunition with which to criticize the EC's banana regime through the media.

It is also important to emphasize that trade barriers, whether lawful or unlawful according to the WTO agreements, hurt domestic consumers and firms that use targeted products as inputs. For

---

[28] A reviewer pointed out that, while a retaliating country may be harmed by its action in the short run, such an action could be justified to the extent that it lessens the probability of the trading partner increasing barriers in the future.

example, agricultural export subsidies in the United States and the EC hurt food processors and producers of soft drinks in those countries, not to mention the taxpayers. Restrictions of imports of steel in the United States hurt the automobile and construction industries, and so forth. Thus, some firms in the country to which a complaint is directed are potential allies of the countries filing the complaint. These potential allies can be important in supplying information that may help the complainants win the case, while also providing for overall political pressure for removal of the trade barriers.

Finally, it should be added that the contention that large countries will use their economic power to ignore WTO rulings is often an exaggeration. Large countries, like other countries, strive for good diplomatic relations with other WTO members. When large countries lose cases, even to developing countries, they do not automatically resort to bully-like defiance; rather, they resort to appeals and compliance, even if marginally and strategically. African countries should not be afraid of bringing cases against large countries if they have legitimate issues. A win by a small complainant against a large country would most likely produce a change in trade policy, even if the small complainant were not able to retaliate. Thus, although it seems compelling to argue that African countries have little reason to be active in the dispute settlement mechanism because the enforcement system is biased against them, the argument is actually not as strong as one might think.

## Non-WTO Avenues for Addressing Trade Disputes

There are other, more important explanations why African countries have not been active in the dispute settlement mechanism. Besides the fact that the system is complicated and expensive, as already discussed, an additional explanation is that there are non-WTO avenues for addressing trade disputes. International trade disputes have existed for centuries and have been "resolved" in a variety of ways, ranging from diplomacy to wars. For example, in the mid-nineteenth century, Great Britain and other Western countries responded to a Chinese prohibition of opium by attacking Chinese coastal cities with gunboats (Beeching, 1975). China was not only forced to open its ports to British opium and later to opium from other Western countries, but also lost Hong Kong to Great Britain.

Bilateral negotiations, especially between African countries and their trading partners, are still a dominant mode of operation. Even when African countries negotiate as a subgroup or as a whole continent with their trading partners, as they sometimes do through the New Partnership for Africa's Development (NEPAD), they do not necessarily work directly through the WTO. Thus, while the DSU system provides a unified and predictable process for addressing disputes, it is not the only avenue available, nor is it necessarily the avenue of first choice for settling or pre-empting disputes. The "cotton initiative" launched by West African countries was brought to the WTO General Council and relied on the political process.

### The Role of Preferential Treatment and Financial Assistance for African Countries

Should an African country bring a case against the EC or the United States, it would do so from a very weak position, with almost no leverage whatsoever. African and other developing countries receive a variety of preferential treatment from developed countries. For example, they are the beneficiaries of the Generalized System of Preferences (GSP) program, implemented under the auspices of GATT and its successor, the WTO. Under the GSP program, developed countries are allowed and encouraged to provide preferential reduction or removal of trade barriers on products from developing countries.[29] All African countries that are members of the WTO are eligible for U.S. and EU GSP benefits.

---

[29] For an extensive discussion of the GSP program and its benefits (or lack thereof) to African countries, see Chapter 3 in Mshomba (2000).

TABLE 2.6 African Countries' Key Preferential Access to the U.S. and EU Markets: January 31, 2006*

| Country (WTO Member) | ACP Beneficiary | AGOA** Eligible | EBA Eligible |
|---|---|---|---|
| Angola | X | X | X |
| Benin | X | XX | X |
| Botswana | X | XX | |
| Burkina Faso | X | X | X |
| Burundi | X | X | X |
| Cameroon | X | XX | |
| Cape Verde | X | XX | X |
| Central African Rep. | X | | X |
| Chad | X | X | X |
| Congo, Dem. Rep. of | X | X | X |
| Congo, Rep. of | X | X | |
| Côte d'Ivoire | X | | |
| Djibouti | X | X | X |
| Egypt | | | |
| Gabon | X | X | |
| Gambia | X | X | X |
| Ghana | X | XX | |
| Guinea | X | X | X |
| Guinea-Bissau | X | X | X |
| Kenya | X | XX | |
| Lesotho | X | XX | X |
| Madagascar | X | XX | X |
| Malawi | X | XX | X |
| Mali | X | XX | X |
| Mauritania | X | | X |
| Mauritius | X | XX | |
| Morocco | | | |
| Mozambique | X | XX | X |
| Namibia | X | XX | |
| Niger | X | XX | X |
| Nigeria | X | XX | |

(*continued*)

TABLE 2.6 *(continued)*

| Country (WTO Member) | ACP Beneficiary | AGOA** Eligible | EBA Eligible |
|---|---|---|---|
| Rwanda | X | XX | X |
| Senegal | X | XX | X |
| Sierra Leone | X | XX | X |
| South Africa | X | XX | |
| Swaziland | X | XX | |
| Tanzania | X | XX | X |
| Togo | X | | X |
| Tunisia | | | |
| Uganda | X | XX | X |
| Zambia | X | XX | X |
| Zimbabwe | X | | |

* All listed countries are eligible for the U.S. and EU GSP programs.
** X, countries eligible for the general AGOA benefits; XX, countries eligible for the general AGOA benefits and special apparel benefits.
*Sources:*
*WTO Members, http://www.wto.org/english/thewto_e/whatis_e/tif_e/org6_e.htm.*
*ACP Members, http://europa.eu.int/comm/development/body/country/country_en.cfm.*
*AGOA eligible, http://www.agoa.gov/eligibility/country_eligibility.html.*
*EBA eligible, http://europa.eu.int/comm/trade/issues/global/gsp/eba/ug.htm.*

The United States and the EU (and other developed countries such as Canada and Japan) provide additional preferential treatment to Africa, as shown in Tables 2.6 and 2.7. The U.S. African Growth and Opportunity Act (AGOA) that took effect in May 2000 further increases U.S. openness to African products in a preferential way. The EU has special trade arrangements with Mediterranean countries, including four African countries – Algeria, Egypt, Morocco, and Tunisia. The Cotonou Agreement, signed in 2000, retained EU trade preferences for ACP countries at least until 2007. In 2001, the EU expanded its already relatively open policy toward the least-developed countries with what they

TABLE 2.7  Tariffs under Preferential Schemes

| Preferential Agreement | Average Tariff Rate (All HS-6 Products) | Average Tariff Rate (Tariff Peak Products) |
|---|---|---|
| Canada | | |
| GSP | 4.3 | 28.2 |
| LDCs | 4.4 | 22.8 |
| MFN | 8.3 | 30.5 |
| European Union | | |
| GSP | 3.6 | 19.8 |
| ACP LDCs | 0.8 (0) | ~ 0 |
| Non-ACP LDCs | 0.9 | ~ 0 |
| MFN | 4.3 | 27.8 |
| Japan | | |
| GSP | 2.3 | 22.7 |
| LDCs | 1.7 | 19.0 |
| MFN | 4.3 | 27.8 |
| United States | | |
| GSP | 2.3 | 16 |
| AGOA LDCs | 0.0 | n.a. (~ 0) |
| Non-AGOA LDCs | 1.8 | 14.4 |
| MFN | 5.0 | 20.8 |

*HS, harmonized system. This is an international method of classifying products used for customs documents and for the application of tariffs; HS, "digit" refers to the level of classification of products: the smaller the digit, the less differentiated the products. Some countries differentiate products beyond the 6-digit level. However, the HS-6 level is commonly used to compare tariff rates because it is the highest level of differentiation that all countries use; LDC, least-developed countries; "Tariff peak products," products subject to tariff rates three times or more than the average tariff rate.*
*Source: Table 3 in Mattoo and Subramanian (2004) – Reprinted by permission.*

call the Everything But Arms (EBA) initiative (Yu and Jensen, 2005). The EBA removes quotas and tariffs on all products, except for weapons and ammunitions, coming from forty-nine least-developed countries, including thirty-four African countries. The sugar, banana, and rice markets are being liberalized gradually, to appease farmers in the EC and prevent an economic shock in some of the ACP countries that have become dependent on historical preferential quotas. (The economic disruption would have occurred because some LDCs are not ACP countries and, thus, previously did not receive preferential treatment under the Cotonou Agreement.) The liberalization process for these three products is scheduled to be completed in 2009.

Preferential arrangements are, in practice, non-binding commitments. The preference-giving country (region) usually sets the criteria for eligibility. These include safeguard measures that, essentially, caution preference-receiving countries not to be too successful in their export volumes or risk a suspension of preferences. Preferential treatment is, therefore, generally unpredictable and temporary in nature. A preference-giving country can suspend its program in whole or in part. It can add, remove, and/or re-designate a product or country at its own discretion.

This situation is not conducive to making African countries aggressive in the dispute settlement system. Even Brazil's knee-jerk reaction to retaliate against the United States after winning the cotton subsidies case was quickly calmed by the spell of preferential treatment. Much weaker than Brazil, African countries must try to strike a delicate political and cost-benefit balance in view of the benefit they receive from preferential access that can be suspended unilaterally. (Of course, although they benefit from preferential access, it can be detrimental in the long run, because it reduces incentives for diversification.) African countries are so dependent on preferential treatment (or at least the idea of it), that their concern is often the rapid decrease in the most favored nation (MFN) tariffs that erode the margin of preference.[30]

---

[30] The idea of the most favored nation principle in the WTO is to have each member country treat all other members equally with respect to trade barriers. Exceptions are made for preferential treatment that benefit developing countries and also for free trade areas. The margin of preference is the difference between the MFN tariff and the GSP or AGOA or EBA tariff, for example.

Lack of leverage due to preferential treatment is compounded by Africa's perpetual requests (sometimes demands) and need for financial assistance from developed countries. Consider one of the more recent initiatives by African leaders in 2001, NEPAD. Before NEPAD, there was the Lagos Plan of Action for the Economic Development of Africa (1980), Africa's Priority Program for Economic Recovery (1986), the African Alternative Framework to Structural Adjustment for Social-Economic Recovery and Transformation (1989), and the Abuja Treaty (1994). What may set NEPAD apart from previous continent-wide development initiatives is the way its language and economic orientation is explicitly in harmony with what is espoused by the World Bank, the IMF, and the WTO. With the NEPAD initiative, African leaders emphasize the role of the private sector, trade, regional cooperation, transparency, and even accountability (hopefully not only to donors but also, and more importantly, to their own people). However, similar to earlier initiatives, its implementation is remarkably reliant on foreign assistance.[31]

It is an understatement to say that Africa needs assistance. NEPAD's assumed role to bring the continent into a new age of peace, security, stability, economic growth, and prosperity is dependent on donors (often referred to as partners). Implementing NEPAD's ambitious programs requires $64 billion annually, most of which is requested from outside the continent (African Union: 2001: paragraph 144). Some critics of this seemingly unavoidable dependency, including President Yahya Jammeh of Gambia, have called NEPAD, figuratively, a kneepad, that is, something to kneel on while begging (Bafalikike, 2002).[32] Metaphors aside, African

---

[31] For an extensive evaluation of the chances of NEPAD to succeed in its proclaimed political and economic programs to promote stability and development, see Taylor (2005).

[32] "I am not criticising Nepad," Jammeh said, "but the way it was conceived to be dependent on begging. Nobody will ever develop your country for you. What we want is an African Development Trust Fund where we put our resources and give loans to African countries to develop. But if you want to develop Africa by begging, you must train so that you have strong knees and that is why they call it Kneepad. If you rely on Nepad,

countries appear to be perpetually knocking at the rich countries' doors for assistance. This level of dependence surely must make African countries hesitant to bring cases against their donors (partners) through the DSU system.

As for developed countries, they can use criteria for preferential access to their markets and conditions for financial assistance to propel African countries to "voluntarily" reduce barriers to trade and foreign investment, without necessarily resorting to the WTO dispute settlement mechanism. For example, the Cotonou Agreement between the EU and ACP countries signed in 2000 was reached with the understanding that the arrangement would evolve into Economic Partnership Agreements (EPAs) by the end of 2007. EPAs are premised as reciprocal obligations typical of a free trade agreement. Likewise, eligibility for AGOA requires that a country is:

making continual progress toward establishing the following: market-based economies; the rule of law and political pluralism; elimination of barriers to U.S. trade and investment; protection of intellectual property; efforts to combat corruption; policies to reduce poverty, increasing availability of health care and educational opportunities; protection of human rights and worker rights; and elimination of certain child labor practices. (http://www.agoa.gov/eligibility/country_eligibility.html)

Developed countries may also want to avoid formal complaints against African countries through the DSU system because such cases would likely attract a lot of negative publicity for the complainants (the bullies, as they would be referred to) from various groups. Moreover, developed countries have some more direct and less public ways of pressuring African countries to conform to their wishes. For example, the U.S. embassies in Africa usually distribute U.S. position papers to their host countries before WTO meetings, both as a courtesy and to forewarn them not to "rock the

buy more pads for your knees because you will die on your knees and you will never get anything" (Bafalikike, 2002: 18).

boat." An African country's head representative in the WTO negotiations tells how he once received a call from a U.S. trade official in Geneva alerting him that his position (the position of the African diplomat) on a particular issue was not compatible with that of his boss in the capital – the Minister of Trade. Apparently, the U.S. official had called the African Minister of Trade and charmed him with some promise of continued aid to his country and the two agreed they would straighten out the African official in Geneva, so he would be receptive to the U.S. position on the issue. The U.S. official was just being "kind" by letting his "colleague" in Geneva know.

## Lack of Credible Disputes Between African Countries and Developed Countries

As discussed previously, developed countries, which are African countries' major trading partners, have reduced or completely removed trade barriers in favor of African products. Therefore, their markets are open to African products far beyond the minimum requirements of the WTO agreements. As a result, complaints by African countries against developed countries can be expected to be negligible in number. This is partly why the cotton case has received so much attention.

Of course, this is not to suggest that developed countries have opened their markets as much as they should or could, especially considering non-tariff barriers on processed products and price distorting subsidies common in developed countries. However, from an obligatory point of view as determined by WTO agreements, African countries may have very little on which to bank complaints through the DSU system.

Disputes against African countries can also be expected to be minimal given the extensions and exceptions allowed for developing and least-developed countries. At the time the WTO was established, the commitment to reduce trade barriers by developing countries, especially by the least-developed countries, was in most cases merely symbolic. For example, these countries did not even bind some of their tariffs at all (as explained below) and where they did, they bound their tariffs above their applied tariffs. This practice made them fully compliant with most of the WTO commitments, from the very beginning of the implementation of the agreements.[33]

Table 2.8 shows binding coverage and bound and applied tariff rates for thirty-one African countries at the inception of the WTO. Binding coverage is the percentage of products subject to an agreed bound tariff rate. Bound tariff rates are tariff rate ceilings, that is, the maximum levels to which tariff rates can be raised. Applied tariff rates are the actual tariff rates on the imported goods. There is wide variation between countries in terms of the binding coverage, the average bound tariff rate, and the average applied tariff rate, so one must be extremely careful in making comparisons. Moreover, these are averages, so they do not show how protection is distributed among products. Nonetheless, the general observation can be made that in almost all cases, the bound tariff rates are considerably higher than the applied tariff rates, making compliance relatively easy.

The high tariff ceilings were allowed in part to lure the least-developed countries into this new international trade body and also to allow poor countries a wide range of flexibility in determining their development path. Moreover, unlike developed countries that have become accustomed to utilizing anti-dumping laws to safeguard their markets, African countries lack the experience and courage to apply such laws.[34] More importantly, African countries

---

[33] Developed countries employed similar tactics regarding the Agreement on Agriculture (Ingco, 1996; Tangermann, 1996).

[34] According to GATT Article VI, dumping occurs "if the export price of the product exported from one country to another is less than the comparable price, in the ordinary course of trade, for the like product when destined for consumption in the exporting country." Where domestic production is injured by dumped imports, a WTO member can apply anti-dumping duties to counteract dumping. However, the whole process of determining dumping and proving that dumping has caused injury to domestic

TABLE 2.8 Average and Bound Tariff Rates

| Country | Total Goods | | | | Industry | | | | Agriculture* | | |
|---|---|---|---|---|---|---|---|---|---|---|---|
| | Binding Coverage (Percent) | Average Bound Rate | Average Applied Rate | Wedge** (Percent) | Binding Coverage (Percent) | Average Bound Rate | Average Applied Rate | Wedge** (Percent) | Average Bound Rate | Average Applied Rate | Wedge** (Percent) |
| | (1) | (2) | (3) | (4) $\frac{(2-3)/3^*}{100}$ | (5) | (6) | (7) | (8) $\frac{(6-7)/7^*}{100}$ | (9) | (10) | (11) $\frac{(9-10)/10^*}{100}$ |
| Benin | 39.40 | 28.35 | 14.70 | 93 | 30.10 | 11.39 | 14.10 | -19 | 61.77 | 15.50 | 299 |
| Burkina Faso | 39.20 | 41.86 | 12.80 | 207 | 29.90 | 13.15 | 12.60 | 4 | 98.12 | 14.80 | 563 |
| Burundi | 21.80 | 68.34 | 7.40 | 824 | 9.90 | 26.83 | – | – | 95.36 | – | – |
| Cameroon | 13.30 | 79.87 | 18.30 | 336 | 0.10 | 50.00 | 17.30 | 189 | 80.00 | 23.69 | 238 |
| Central African Republic | 62.50 | 36.20 | 18.40 | 97 | 56.80 | 37.87 | 17.50 | 116 | 30.00 | 24.90 | 20 |
| Chad | 13.50 | 79.92 | 17.00 | 370 | 0.20 | 75.42 | 16.70 | 352 | 80.00 | 21.00 | 281 |
| Congo, Dem. Rep. of | 100.00 | 96.24 | 17.60 | 449 | 100.00 | 95.94 | – | – | 98.21 | – | – |

(continued)

[ 83 ]

TABLE 2.8 (continued)

| Country | Total Goods | | | | Industry | | | | Agriculture* | | |
|---|---|---|---|---|---|---|---|---|---|---|---|
| | Binding Coverage (Percent) | Average Bound Rate | Average Applied Rate | Wedge** (Percent) | Binding Coverage (Percent) | Average Bound Rate | Average Applied Rate | Wedge** (Percent) | Average Bound Rate | Average Applied Rate | Wedge** (Percent) |
| Congo, Rep. of | 16.00 | 27.47 | 18.60 | 48 | 3.10 | 15.21 | 17.20 | -12 | 30.00 | 24.00 | 25 |
| Côte d'Ivoire | 33.10 | 11.15 | 12.60 | -12 | 22.90 | 8.62 | 12.30 | -30 | 14.94 | 14.50 | 3 |
| Djibouti | 100.00 | 41.04 | 30.92 | 33 | 100.00 | 40.04 | 31.52 | 27 | 47.60 | 25.29 | 88 |
| Gambia | 13.60 | 100.94 | 13.60 | 642 | 0.50 | 56.36 | - | - | 102.42 | - | - |
| Ghana | 14.30 | 92.44 | 14.70 | 529 | 1.20 | 34.72 | 13.80 | 152 | 97.14 | 20.20 | 381 |
| Guinea | 38.90 | 20.12 | 6.24 | 222 | 29.50 | 10.00 | 6.22 | 61 | 39.70 | 6.45 | 516 |
| Guinea-Bissau | 97.70 | 48.65 | 14.00 | 248 | 97.30 | 50.00 | 13.30 | 276 | 40.00 | 17.00 | 135 |
| Kenya | 14.60 | 95.61 | 17.10 | 459 | 1.60 | 54.14 | 16.53 | 228 | 100.00 | 20.64 | 384 |
| Lesotho | 100.00 | 78.55 | 17.40 | 351 | 100.00 | 60.02 | - | - | 200.00 | - | - |
| Madagascar | 29.70 | 27.41 | 6.01 | 356 | 18.90 | 25.33 | 6.07 | 317 | 30.00 | 5.61 | 435 |
| Malawi | 26.10 | 82.74 | 13.57 | 510 | 14.90 | 43.32 | 13.24 | 227 | 121.27 | 18.55 | 554 |
| Mali | 40.60 | 28.82 | 11.24 | 156 | 31.60 | 14.15 | 10.40 | 36 | 59.17 | 16.06 | 268 |
| Mauritania | 39.30 | 19.64 | 10.60 | 85 | 30.00 | 10.48 | 10.00 | 5 | 37.67 | 13.80 | 173 |

| Country | | | | | | | | | | | |
|---|---|---|---|---|---|---|---|---|---|---|---|
| Mozambique | 13.60 | 97.50 | 13.80 | 606 | 0.40 | 6.60 | 12.50 | −47 | 100.00 | 18.10 | 458 |
| Niger | 96.80 | 44.29 | 14.50 | 205 | 96.20 | 38.13 | 14.40 | 165 | 83.09 | 15.10 | 450 |
| Rwanda | 100.00 | 89.28 | 10.00 | 792 | 100.00 | 91.54 | 9.20 | 895 | 74.38 | 13.20 | 463 |
| Senegal | 100.00 | 29.97 | 12.08 | 148 | 100.00 | 29.99 | 11.57 | 159 | 29.84 | 14.69 | 103 |
| Sierra Leone | 100.00 | 47.30 | 21.00 | 125 | 100.00 | 48.38 | – | – | 40.18 | – | – |
| Swaziland | 96.40 | 19.10 | 15.10 | 26 | 96.00 | 15.84 | – | – | 38.36 | – | – |
| Tanzania | 13.30 | 120.00 | 16.10 | 645 | 0.10 | 120.00 | 16.10 | 645 | 120.00 | 17.40 | 590 |
| Togo | 13.70 | 80.00 | 12.13 | 560 | 0.60 | 80.00 | 11.62 | 588 | 80.00 | 15.09 | 430 |
| Uganda | 15.70 | 73.27 | 8.79 | 734 | 2.90 | 50.39 | 8.39 | 501 | 77.69 | 12.54 | 520 |
| Zambia | 16.80 | 106.38 | 13.49 | 689 | 4.00 | 42.69 | 12.61 | 239 | 123.32 | 18.15 | 579 |
| Zimbabwe | 21.00 | 94.26 | 18.78 | 402 | 8.90 | 10.97 | 17.32 | −37 | 143.47 | 27.67 | 419 |

* For agriculture, binding coverage is 100 percent for all WTO members.

** The wedge shows the percentage by which the average bound rate exceeds the average applied rate, i.e., the percentage by which the applied rate could be increased to reach the bound rate.

Source: Table 2 in Mattoo and Subramanian (2004: 394–395). Reprinted by permission. Table 2 in Mattoo and Subramanian includes seventeen non-African countries and presents the differences between the bound rates and the applied rates in absolute terms.

were under pressure to sign off quickly on agreements that they did not fully understand and, therefore, they set high bound tariff rates as shields against the unknown.

For all practical purposes, most African countries are well insulated from complaints through the DSU system. They have a lot of room to flex their protection muscles before their policies can be found to be inconsistent with the WTO rules. Some countries can increase their overall average tariff by a multiple of six over the applied rate and still be in compliance with the

WTO agreements. Considering that these are simple averages and that not all products are subject to tariff ceilings, there is almost no limit on how high the tariff rates can be raised for selective products.

The WTO tariff obligations for most African countries are ineffective as a way to reduce trade barriers. It should, therefore, come as no surprise that developed countries utilize various preferential arrangements and financial assistance eligibilities to compel African countries to pursue trade-liberating policies beyond those WTO obligations. Even when preferential treatment or financial assistance might not result in reduced trade barriers in African countries, they restrain African countries from increasing protection, something these countries might otherwise do and still be within their WTO obligations. In the world of political economy, sometimes success is measured in terms of the ability to contain a trading partner's protection, rather than to advance its trade liberalization.

Of course, it is this ability of developed countries to influence trade policies in African countries through conditionality that is often under attack. Criticism of conditionality is easy and fashionable because of the nature of some of the conditions, the sovereignty

---

production requires institutional frameworks and technical expertise lacking in most African countries. South Africa seems to be an exception with its long history of anti-dumping legislation and readiness to initiate anti-dumping cases. Considering the number of cases filed worldwide from 1995 to 2003, South Africa is among the top five users of the anti-dumping apparatus (Feinberg and Reynolds, 2006 and Brink, 2005).

argument, and also the impression it gives of being more sensitive to the poor than those who are advocating freer markets. However, the poor are often victims of government monopolies. Some prerequisites for financial assistance, such as reduced implicit taxation of subsistence farmers, reduced government monopolies, and reduced trade barriers, may be more beneficial to the poor in African countries than the financial assistance itself.

## CONCLUSION

The dispute settlement system that evolved from Article XXIII of GATT and was formalized by the DSU gives the WTO a unique ability to enforce obligations. This capacity is shared by only a few other international institutions.[35] While member countries may have concerns about the implications of the DSU on their sovereignty, they are also aware of the merits of predictable trade rules and disciplined trading partners. Moreover, one might also argue that the agreement simply enforces obligations to which contracting parties themselves agreed. Even with its imperfections and apparent asymmetrical effectiveness between countries, it promotes a sense of obligation and discipline and, thus, a more predictable trade environment. This is conducive to long-term trade commitments and investment.

Although developed countries sometimes use their leverage with no regard for poor countries, the DSU system creates a buffer to curb such abusive tendencies because it operates in a multilateral setting. What limits African countries most from participation in WTO dispute settlement proceedings is the preferential treatment accorded to them. This leads to a lack of strong disputable cases and fosters a reticence to antagonize countries which provide the preferential treatment (and assistance). Beyond this, the low level of participation by

---

[35] Others include the U.N. Security Council and the International Court of Law, which are more known by the public and arguably more important in international affairs.

African countries in the dispute settlement mechanism can be attributed to the availability of more effective ways of working (or dealing) with developed countries and prohibitively high legal costs.

In general, developed countries are open to products from African countries far more than they must be to fulfill their WTO obligations. In situations where developed countries implement policies that are inconsistent with the WTO rules, they can use their leverage as preference-giving nations to pre-empt cases or retaliation against them, as the United States demonstrated with Brazil in the cotton subsidies case. While this can be interpreted as abuse of power by developed countries, it is also a reminder that developing countries need to weigh the costs against the benefits of being preference recipients. Moreover, the margin of preference is eroding over time, and supply constraints often limit the ability of African countries to take advantage of preferential access to markets in developed countries.[36]

African countries should continue using the general WTO forum to voice their concerns and bring cases only when there is a clear violation, as was the situation with the cotton case. To the extent that African countries signed the WTO agreements at the conclusion of the Uruguay Round of GATT without fully understanding them, they should use the rulings of DSU cases as a guide to determine which agreements need to be revisited. Likewise, they should be clear about any new agreements being proposed. The DSU system gives the WTO an enforcement power that was not coherent under GATT and is still unavailable to most other international organizations. This phenomenon encourages some countries to try to integrate agreements reached by other international institutions into the WTO, by categorizing them as "trade related" (as if there is much that is not trade related), as was done

---

[36] For an empirical study addressing whether it is worth it for African countries to ask for more trade preferences and whether they should reform their own trade policies, see Yu and Jensen (2005).

with the TRIPS Agreement, to gain the legal authority to enforce those agreements.

To help address the high cost of bringing cases to the DSU, the ACWL provides legal training and highly subsidized services in dispute settlement proceedings, as discussed in the case below. African countries should support the ACWL with membership and ideas and take full advantage of its services.

The WTO should evaluate carefully the proposal for monetary compensation for the economic damage incurred by the complainant in cases where the panel finds the trade policies in question to be inconsistent with the WTO agreements. The WTO should also deliberate about damage caused by threats of trade barriers, as credible threats can be just as damaging as actual trade barriers. For African countries, even a threat of suspending preferential treatment by a developed country can be detrimental to attracting and retaining investment.

Considering the many challenges that African countries face and their vulnerability, it is only appropriate that their situation be carefully taken into account. But African countries walk a fine line when they push for swifter and stricter enforcement measures in the face of WTO violations against them. The time will come when African countries no longer have the luxury of (or the complacency stemming from) long transitional periods or the luxury of being asked to do very little in terms of trade liberalization through the WTO. When that time comes, there is nothing to suggest that African countries or least-developed countries will be less likely to violate WTO obligations than developed countries. Anticipating that, the African Group and the LDC Group have proposed further special and preferential treatment for developing countries, because the stricter enforcement measures they have proposed, if agreed upon, would eventually be applied to them.

One proposal by the LDC Group requests that least-developed countries not be subject to demands for compensation or retaliation. "In the alternative it could be recognized 'a least-developed country Member against whom a case has been determined shall be expected to withdraw the offending measure'" (WTO, 2002c: 5). The proposal aims at preventing demands for compensation from least-developed countries or retaliating against them, even if those countries are found to be in violation of their obligations. It is likely that the proposals of African countries for effective retaliation and compensation would carry more weight if these countries showed more commitment to move toward trade liberalization, instead of simply asking for leniency. Moreover, benefits from trade come not only from access to foreign markets, but also from an efficient internal allocation of resources resulting from opening one's own market. That is probably where the genius of the DSU system lies. A country that loses a case is compelled to meet its WTO obligations to freer trade, thereby allowing a better allocation of its resources. Thus, even the country that loses a case should end up "winning" in the long run.

### CASE: THE ADVISORY CENTER ON WTO LAW[37]

The need for an institution like the Advisory Center on WTO Law (ACWL) was clear from the very beginning of the negotiations for the Dispute Settlement Understanding (DSU). The ACWL was conceived of in conjunction with other suggestions to augment the technical capacity of least-developed and developing countries and to increase their participation in the WTO and their potential to benefit from WTO agreements.

The ACWL was established in 2001 to provide legal advice, training, and assistance in dispute settlement proceedings to least-developed countries and eligible developing countries. ACWL membership falls into three distinct categories of countries:

---

[37] This case study is based on information provided to the author by officials from developing countries (mostly African countries) based in Geneva and connected to the WTO; reports by the Advisory Center on WTO Law (ACWL 2005, 2006); and other information at the ACWL website (www.acwl.ch).

least-developed countries, developing countries (other than least-developed countries), and developed countries. All least-developed countries that are members of the WTO or have observer status in the WTO are automatically eligible for services of the ACWL. Although least-developed countries are invited to become ACWL members, there is no membership pre-requisite for them to have access to the services of the ACWL. Other developing countries must be members of the ACWL to be eligible for its services. As for developed country members, they are major contributors to the ACWL but do not receive its services.

As of December 2006, none of the least-developed countries were paying members of the ACWL and only four African countries were members – Egypt, Kenya, Mauritius, and Tunisia, as shown in Table 2.9. In total, the ACWL had thirty-seven members: ten developed countries and twenty-seven developing countries (entitled to ACWL services), as shown in Table 2.9. Altogether, there were sixty-nine countries eligible for ACWL services, including forty-two least-developed countries.

The ACWL is a shining example of how technical assistance can and should be delivered. It stands out not simply because of its uniqueness but, most importantly, because of its excellent management and adherence to its goals, as testified to by representatives of developing countries to the WTO with whom the author had the opportunity to speak.

The budget for the ACWL is funded by contributions from developed country members with a minimum contribution of $1 million each. In addition, developing country members make contributions, the minimum amounts of which are determined by their world trade shares and income per capita. Developing countries are divided into three categories, A, B, and C. For membership, each developing country contributes a minimum of $300,000, $100,000, or $50,000, respectively, according to its category. Supplementing membership contributions are fees paid for legal services for least-developed countries and eligible developing countries.

TABLE 2.9  Membership in the ACWL: December 2006

| | Developed Countries | Members Entitled to the Services of the ACWL (Category in Parentheses)* |
|---|---|---|
| Signatories to the Agreement Establishing the ACWL | Canada Denmark Finland Ireland Italy Netherlands Norway Sweden United Kingdom | Bolivia (C) Colombia (B) Dominican Republic (C) Ecuador (C) Egypt (B) Guatemala (C) Honduras (C) Hong Kong, China (A) India (B) Kenya (C) Nicaragua (C) Pakistan (B) Panama (C) Paraguay (C) Peru (C) Philippines (B) Thailand (B) Tunisia (C) Uruguay (B) Venezuela (B) |
| ACWL Members By Accession | Switzerland | Chinese Taipei (A) El Salvador (C) Indonesia (B) Jordan (C) Mauritius (B) Oman (B) Turkey (B) |
| In the Process of Accession | | Costa Rica (C) Georgia (C) |

* *Developing countries are divided into three categories – A, B, and C – according to their world trade shares and income per capita. Countries in category C are the poorest.*

In theory, the ACWL should not succeed. Consider these practical challenges. Why would a developed country contribute to an institution that subsidizes its potential opponents in dispute cases? How autonomous can an institution be if it is supposed to assist least-developed and developing countries, when major contributions are expected to come from developed countries? How would such an institution handle cases where both the complainant and the defendant are countries eligible for the institution's services?

The fact that the ACWL is not only surviving but meeting its obligations ardently reflects the ingenuity of the architects of the ACWL, the strong commitment of developed country members, the attentive guidance of the ACWL Management Board, and the outstanding leadership of the ACWL's Executive Director, Frieder Roessler, and his Deputy, Leo Palma.

When developed countries provide assistance to developing countries, they do so sometimes at the risk of making recipient countries their potential rivals in trade. Contributing to an institution that would subsidize your potential adversaries could be reckless, from a political point of view. Therefore, it should not be a surprise that many developed countries, including the United States, have not (yet) become members of the ACWL.

It is not hard to imagine the condescending editorials some U.S. newspapers would run if the United States were a contributing member of the ACWL, and a country subsidized by the ACWL were to bring a dispute case against the United States. This is all the more reason why those developed countries that have contributed to ACWL are notable for their generosity and commitment to such an institution. The World Bank has also made contributions to the ACWL.

The autonomy of the ACWL was of the utmost importance to the signatories of the agreement establishing it. An ACWL that was an extension of developed countries' hegemony would have been worse than not having one at all. There is no evidence to indicate that the independence of the ACWL has been compromised by any country. It also helps that members are only obliged to make a one-time contribution or installments over a 5-year period, rather than pay perennial dues for membership. An institution that relies on annual dues can be held hostage by its major contributors, a painful experience that even the United Nations has endured. Having completed its transitional period of 5 years, the ACWL's main sources of funds are the revenue from its endowment fund and fees for its legal services.

No amount of ingenuity would have allowed the ACWL to represent two eligible opposing parties on a single case simultaneously. However, both parties receive equally subsidized legal services. In such a situation of potential conflict, the ACWL represents whichever party seeks its services first. The ACWL maintains a roster of private law firms from which opposing parties can select legal counsel and receive the same rates and conditions as those of the ACWL. However, an official from a developing country member of the ACWL that has the experience of having received direct services from both the ACWL and one of the private firms maintains that the ACWL services were far superior. This is both an affirmation for the ACWL, as well as a challenge.

Ironically, it is a blessing in disguise for the ACWL that not all developing countries have opted to become members. The more developing country members there are, the more likely eligible members would face each other in dispute cases and, in turn, the greater would be the need to engage the services of private firms. Of course, many other important services to members, apart from dispute settlement, are provided directly only by the ACWL. The ACWL (2005) has reported the progress it has made in its four years of operation; Table 2.10 shows highlights of this report.

The African Group contends that the ACWL is not enough to address "all institutional and human capacity constraints of developing countries. [The ACWL's] terms of reference are equivocal, and it does not cover all developing countries" (WTO, 2002a: 2). No single institution can be an answer to all capacity constraints

TABLE 2.10 Summary of Services Rendered by the ACWL: July 2001–December 2006

| | | Charge (Hourly Rate), Swiss Francs (CHF) | |
| | | Members and LDCs | Developing Countries Not Members of the ACWL |
| Service | Summary | | |
| --- | --- | --- | --- |
| Legal Advice | For the period 2002–2006, 264 legal opinions to: 40 individual countries, including 12 African countries; the LDC Group as a whole; and the African Group as a whole. | Free: While the ACWL Management Board may, at its discretion, fix the maximum number of hours, to date, it has not done so. | Category A – CHF567<br>Category B – CHF486<br>Category C – CHF405 |
| WTO dispute settlement | Directly represented 17 countries in 26 disputes. (Thailand was represented in 6 disputes.) Of the 17 countries, 2 were LDCs, Bangladesh and Chad (as a third party). Provided assistance through external legal counsel to 5 countries in 2 disputes. | Category A – CHF324<br>Category B – CHF243<br>Category C – CHF162<br>LDCs – CHF40 | Category A – CHF567<br>Category B – CHF486<br>Category C – CHF405 |

(continued)

TABLE 2.10 (*continued*)

| Service | Summary | Charge (Hourly Rate), Swiss Francs (CHF) | |
| --- | --- | --- | --- |
| | | Members and LDCs | Developing Countries Not Members of the ACWL |
| Training Activities | 6- Month training courses | A regular annual training course consisting of 6 months of weekly, 2-hour seminars. Four of these courses were held in the period 2002–2006. A total of 169 individuals have participated and 95 have received certificates based on their level of participation. | Free for Members: Non-member developing countries invited when there is space available. They do not pay fees. |
| | Seminars and Speaker Programs | *Ad hoc* seminars by experts in WTO law on topics of interest to LDCs and developing countries. Collaboration with other organizations such as the United Nations Conference | Free for Members: Non-member developing countries invited when there is space available. They do not pay fees. |

| | | |
|---|---|---|
| The Secondment Program | on Trade and Development (UNCTAD) to broaden the reach of ACWL services. A 9-month program to provide training for up to 3 government lawyers from LDCs and/or eligible developing countries. The trainees join the ACWL staff for the period of their training. The program started in 2005. In September 2005, 2 trainees joined: one from Lesotho, the other from Paraguay. In September 2006, 2 trainees joined: one from Malawi, the other from Egypt. | The ACWL pays for salaries and all expenses. (The Secondment Program is supported by contributions from Canada, Denmark, Ireland, Norway, and Sweden.) |
| Outreach | Various communications and activities to increase awareness of ACWL services to LDCs and developing countries, including those WTO Members and Observers that do not have missions in Geneva. | |

*Sources: ACWL (2005 and 2006) and www.acwl.ch*

in developing countries. To the extent that all developing countries are welcome to become members of the ACWL, the contention that the ACWL does not cover all developing countries does not carry much weight. Automatic services for all developing countries would be unsustainable. Any income-based, assistance system that is not sensitive to income differences among developing countries is bound to fail. First, it would violate its basic principle of providing assistance according to need. Second, it would reduce funds and, thus, assistance to least-developed countries. No matter what recommendations might be made regarding a standing fund or increasing the capacity of the ACWL, all developing countries (that are not least-developed countries) still must be willing to become members and, thus, contribute to the ACWL endowment.

The concern by the African Group that the ACWL cannot address all capacity constraints of developing countries is not a criticism of the ACWL. If anything, it is an appeal for more institutions with equal integrity and expertise. A WTO diplomat from Latin America made the point to the author more explicitly by wishing that the ACWL model could be replicated by regional blocs and bilateral agreements, a recommendation also made by Mosoti (2006).

The summary presented in Table 2.10 reveals some of the ACWL's attributes. By providing legal opinions and representation in dispute cases, it addresses the immediate capacity deficiency problem suffered by least-developed countries and many developing countries, and by providing seminars and training, is building the future capacity of those countries. The ACWL is preparing least-developed and developing countries to be less dependent on ACWL services in the future. In fact, the long-term success of the ACWL is going to be measured, in part, by the rate at which countries graduate from different ACWL services as a result of the training they have received.

Even in the few years since it was established, the ACWL has proven that it is a dynamic institution willing to, and looking for new ways to, broaden its outreach to least-developed countries. Of course, the ACWL must be careful not to expand too fast or broaden its scope too much. Given its success, it is likely that some well-meaning WTO members may want to utilize the ACWL to provide services not necessarily central to WTO law. To remain effective, the ACWL must refrain from such pressures or temptations.

# 3 TRADE-RELATED ASPECTS
# OF INTELLECTUAL PROPERTY RIGHTS

AMONG THE AGREEMENTS THAT BECAME EFFECTIVE AT the establishment of the WTO in 1995 was the Agreement on Trade-Related Aspects of Intellectual Property Rights (TRIPS). The TRIPS Agreement sets a minimum uniform standard to protect intellectual property rights in eight areas: copyright and related rights; trademarks; geographical indications; industrial designs; patents; layout-designs (topographies) of integrated circuits; protection of undisclosed information; and control of anti-competitive practices in contractual licenses.

Under the TRIPS Agreement, patents provide protection for twenty years "for any inventions, whether products or processes, in all fields of technology, provided they are new, involve an inventive step and are capable of industrial application" (Article 27:1). Certain provisions give governments some discretion to refuse to grant patents for public health reasons.

The signing of the TRIPS Agreement was a celebrated achievement for developed countries, the main producers of technological knowledge. African and other developing countries, on the other hand, had all along been opposed to and wary of an agreement that might adversely affect their access to generic and cheaper medicines and hamper their adoption of new technology. But concerted pressure from developed countries (Abbott, 2002) and promises that national emergencies and the need to protect public health would override the TRIPS Agreement rules brought developing countries to the signing table, although reluctantly.[1] Moreover, Article 7 of the TRIPS Agreement gave developing countries some assurance with its stipulation that:

The protection and enforcement of intellectual property rights should contribute to the promotion and to the transfer and dissemination of technology, to the mutual advantage of producers and users of technological knowledge and in a manner conducive to social and economic welfare, and to a balance of rights and obligations.

This commitment was reiterated in 2001 at the launching of the Doha Round of negotiations, in the "Declaration on the TRIPS Agreement and Public Health," in which WTO members stated:

We recognize the gravity of the public health problems afflicting many developing and least-developed countries, especially those resulting from HIV/AIDS, tuberculosis, malaria and other epidemics. (paragraph 1)
We agree that the TRIPS Agreement does not and should not prevent Members from taking measures to protect public health. Accordingly, while reiterating our commitment to the TRIPS Agreement, we affirm that the Agreement can and should be interpreted and implemented in a manner supportive of WTO Members' right to protect public health and, in particular, to promote access to medicines for all. (paragraph 4)
We recognize that WTO Members with insufficient or no manufacturing capacities in the pharmaceutical sector could face difficulties in making effective use of compulsory licensing under the TRIPS Agreement. We instruct the Council for TRIPS to find an expeditious solution to this problem and to report to the General Council before the end of 2002. (WTO, 2001: paragraph 6)

Given these stipulations and others of this kind in the TRIPS Agreement, were the fears of African countries well-founded? Has the agreement so far been implemented in a manner that demonstrates the spirit of Article 7 and the declarations of the Doha

[1]  Developing countries felt even added pressure as countries had to sign off on all agreements under the "single undertaking" approach that required them to accept all the results of the Uruguay Round if they wanted to be WTO members.

Round? Are the policy options available to developing countries meaningful and sufficient for African countries to avoid adverse effects of the agreement on public health and development, and perhaps even benefit from the agreement? Is the extension of the transitional period for the least-developed countries to 2016 long enough? The discussion in this chapter sheds some light on these and other questions. The focus is on the minimum standard to protect intellectual property rights on patents.

## A THEORETICAL PERSPECTIVE ON PATENTS

A patent is ideally a legal intervention used to correct for market failures. It offers producers of technological knowledge the legal right to exclude potential *free riders* from producing goods that are embodiments of the knowledge they produce.

Because of the external benefits associated with the production of new technology, the market, without intervention, does not produce a socially optimal amount of technology. In fact, some types of technology have the characteristics of *public goods*. The private sector on its own cannot produce an optimal amount of public goods. Public goods have the characteristics of non-rivalry and non-exclusion in consumption. A good is non-rival in consumption if consumption by one person does not "use up" anything, that is, it does not diminish the consumption possibilities of the good by others. For example, once the knowledge to produce aspirin is available, any number of pharmaceutical companies can use it without reducing the amount of the technical knowledge available.

The non-exclusion characteristic of public goods refers to the situation where it is prohibitively costly for the market to confine consumption only to the paying customers. This would be the case if, say, a pharmaceutical company that developed the technology to produce aspirin could not confine the use of that technology to itself and its licensees.

Where external benefits are prevalent and/or *free riding* is a problem, government intervention is arguably important. It is partly due to the external benefits of technology that public funds are used in research and development (R&D). A U.S. government study describes the rationale for public funds for R&D as follows:

The rationale for government funding of basic scientific research is that if such research were left solely to the private sector, too little of it would be done, in the sense that the benefits to society from doing additional basic R&D is limited to its own expected returns. In the case of basic research and development, those returns can be particularly low compared with the social benefits, because it can be difficult for private companies to capture more than a small fraction of the total social value of their basic research. (U.S. Congressional Budget Office, 2006)

The same study reports that spending on R&D by the National Institutes of Health (NIH) – the primary recipient of government funding for health-related research – increased steadily from $5.8 billion in 1970 to $28.5 billion in 2004 (using 2005 dollars). On average, from 1994 to 2004, the annual spending by the NIH on R&D was about 40 percent of the aggregate spending by the Pharmaceutical Research and Manufacturers of America (PhRMA) members and the NIH on R&D.[2]

Patents are used to provide exclusion that is important, if not essential, if individuals, companies, and institutions are to invest in R&D programs. The patent system is used to motivate invention. This "invention motivation" theory of patents (Mazzoleni and Nelson, 1998) has been the most widely used argument by pharmaceutical companies in their relentless lobbying for the TRIPS Agreement.

The logical conclusion of this argument is that in the absence of patents, there would be little or no innovation and that the more

---

[2] Annual spending by PhRMA members on research and development increased gradually from $3.5 billion in 1970 to $38.5 billion in 2004 (using 2005 dollars).

stringent the patent system is, the more innovations a country will experience. This was how developed countries justified the TRIPS Agreement to developing countries. They asserted that the TRIPS Agreement is good for poor countries – that it will promote innovations and development in those countries.

When considering the benefits of patents, attention must also be given to the inefficiency that comes from the monopoly power created. Although patents give a pharmaceutical company an incentive to invest in R&D, they also limit the diffusion of knowledge. Patents create an inefficient use of knowledge because patents exclude some potential users of that knowledge. Understandably, developing countries were concerned that the TRIPS Agreement would increase the cost of acquiring technology from developed countries and increase the prices of consumer products, including essential drugs (Khor, 2002).

TECHNOLOGY AND TRADE

While the TRIPS Agreement may be an incentive for innovation, it has the potential to undermine trade dynamics. Trade patterns are indeed dynamic, and technology plays an important role in determining those dynamics, as explained below.

Basic trade theory informs us that a country's comparative advantage (or disadvantage) in relation to its trading partners partly determines a country's trading pattern. Comparative advantage refers to lower relative opportunity cost. Producers in one country have a comparative advantage in producing a good or service if their opportunity cost in its production is lower than that of producers in another country. Comparative advantage is determined by various factors, including differences in factor endowments and differences in technology, as demonstrated by the Heckscher–Ohlin model and the Ricardian mosdel, respectively.[3]

---

[3]  For an explanation of these models, refer to any international economics textbook.

For example, African countries have a comparative advantage in some minerals with which they have been endowed and some crops such as cocoa, coffee, cotton, and sugar because they have been endowed with the appropriate climate and soil for the production of these commodities. African countries have a comparative *dis*advantage in processed and manufactured goods compared to developed countries, because of developed countries' advanced technology. It is important to add, however, that some comparative advantage revealed by trading patterns is a result of trade policies, such as production and export subsidies.

Trading patterns are dynamic because comparative advantage is dynamic. Relative abundances of endowments of a country such as minerals change over time, either due to depletion or the discovery of similar minerals in that country or in other countries. However, the most important source of changes in comparative advantage and trade patterns is the change in technology. The *technological gap* and the *product cycle* models outlined, respectively, by Posner (1961) and Vernon (1966) capture the dynamics of comparative advantage emanating from the development and assimilation of technology.

The *technological gap* model explains comparative advantage based on the development of new products or new processes of production. The role of technology in determining and shifting comparative advantage is sketched and empirically estimated in a collection of articles in Fagerberg, et al. (1997). While the TRIPS Agreement may be an incentive for innovation, it may also shield comparative advantage by giving the innovating firms temporary monopoly power. In other words, the TRIPS Agreement has the potential to undermine trade dynamics.

The *product cycle* model reveals the interconnectedness between trade and technology. It outlines technological assimilation and the standardization of the production process facilitated by trade. It also reveals the potential for trade to be an incentive for developing new products and new production processes. This is particularly the case for countries whose domestic markets are too small to allow producers to take advantage of economies of scale. The new products and production processes are disseminated through trade and/or foreign direct investment. Over time the production process becomes standardized, requiring relatively less skilled labor than when the product was first introduced. According to the *product cycle* model, comparative advantage for new products moves gradually from developed countries to developing countries, eventually leading to a change in the patterns of production and trade (Flam and Helpman, 1987). This has been the case with the production of textiles, radios, TV sets, and cars.

By strengthening intellectual property rights between countries with significant economic differences, the TRIPS Agreement may reduce the potential for African countries to acquire new technology and penetrate the world market. Glass (1997) developed a general equilibrium model that supports this view. Among the many factors that contributed to the successful industrialization of Asian countries such as Singapore and South Korea was their ability to use technology from developed countries. African countries need even more access to technology because, unlike the Asian countries with which they are often compared and contrasted, they are undertaking export-led policies disadvantaged by a very narrow range of export products (primarily, unprocessed commodities).

## DEVELOPED AND DEVELOPING COUNTRIES' PERSPECTIVES ON PATENTS

Countries try to strike a balance between appropriation (exclusive use) and diffusion (spreading) of technology by considering various domestic development factors and goals. Due to the wide economic gap between developed and developing countries, there is an obvious conflict of interest between these groups of countries. Developed countries, the main producers of technological knowledge, tilt the pendulum more to the appropriation side.

Historically, in their early stages of development, countries invariably give highest priority to diffusion. Appropriation becomes "affordable" only gradually as a country develops and is able to compete with the rest of the world. For example, even the United States, a staunch advocate for and enforcer of intellectual property rights, refused copyright protection until 1891, with the argument that it needed to educate its people (Subramanian, 2003; Piccioto, 2002: 226; Pretorius, 2002: 184).

A lot of criticism has been leveled against India, Brazil, Argentina, Mexico, and other developing countries for passing laws in the 1970s that weakened their patent laws in the pharmaceutical area. However, the action by these countries was not without precedent. For example, in 1919, realizing Germany's competitiveness in the chemical industry, the United Kingdom reformed its patent laws to remove patents of chemical compounds (Drahos, 2002: 165). Pharmaceutical products – a major source of contention between developed and developing countries with respect to the TRIPS Agreement – became patentable as recently as 1967 in France and West Germany, 1976 in Japan, 1977 in Switzerland, 1979 in Italy, and 1992 in Spain. These countries waited until they felt they could compete with their trading partners in producing patentable pharmaceutical products before they granted patent protection to those products.

Thus, while there is a theoretical and practical basis for patents, the spread of knowledge has always been of paramount importance when it comes to arrangements with countries that have superior technology. The TRIPS Agreement has changed that and has placed the least-developed countries and the richest countries in the world under the same general umbrella.

Correa (2000) provides some reasons why global international property rights were given such a high priority by developed countries in the Uruguay Round of GATT. Among the reasons was the growing importance of technology in determining comparative advantage, the increasing non-exclusivity of new technologies, and the growing power of multinational corporations that want direct access to developing countries' markets without having to share their technology with local firms. Pharmaceutical companies have, in particular, been the major force behind the TRIPS Agreement in the area of patents. Developed countries also used the inclusion of the agricultural and textile industries into the WTO as bargaining chips for the TRIPS Agreement.

African countries are not categorically averse to intellectual property rights; all are members of the World Intellectual Property Organization (WIPO). Analogous to the focused mandate of the International Labor Organization (ILO) on labor issues and the World Health Organization (WHO) on health issues, the WIPO deals only with intellectual property rights issues. This is a good forum for African countries for various reasons.

Given that the WIPO deals exclusively with intellectual property rights, representatives to the meetings, wherever they are from, usually possess a relevant technical background. In the WTO, in contrast, there are usually many varied and complex agreements being negotiated simultaneously. Whereas developed countries can afford specialists for each area of negotiation, African countries typically have very limited technical and diplomatic representation. As Pacón (1996: 353) noted:

The modest negotiating strength of the developing countries was revealed in the TRIPS negotiations of the Uruguay Round. Although a North-South conflict was to be expected, the success of the negotiations depended more on the settlement of a number of differences among industrialized countries themselves. This was compounded by the fact that in many cases the experts from the developing countries were hardly ever involved.

In the WIPO, it is also easier for developing countries to coordinate their arguments and strategies and work as a coalition. The fact that the WTO deals with such a wide range of issues makes it much harder for a coalition of developing countries on any single issue to be sustained, with the case of cotton subsidies (discussed in Chapter 4) providing a rare exception. The varied interests and goals of developing countries on various agreements make these countries natural prey to the "divide and rule" phenomenon. Moreover, in the WTO, more so than in the WIPO, developed countries can leverage and coerce developing countries into accepting unfavorable agreements by promising technical assistance and other relatively favorable agreements (such as agriculture and textile and apparel) or by threatening to use trade barriers (Piccioto, 2002: 226).[4]

Another important reason why developed countries wanted intellectual property rights to be incorporated into the WTO is enforcement. The TRIPS Agreement brought into the WTO many of the existing rules and agreements reached under three WIPO conventions: the *Paris Convention* for the protection of industrial property, the *Berne Convention* for the protection of literary and artistic works, and the *Rome Convention* for the protection of performers, producers of phonographs, and broadcasting organizations. Under the WIPO, member countries can choose conventions to which to subscribe, as shown in Table 3.1.

Membership in the WTO means subscribing to all of its agreements with very few exceptions, like the Agreement on Government Procurement, discussed in Chapter 5. More importantly, WTO agreements are enforceable by the *WTO Understanding on Rules and Procedures Governing the Settlement of Disputes*, discussed in Chapter 2. (This understanding is referred to in the TRIPS Agreement in Article 64.) It is worth noting that under the WIPO, disputes can be brought to the International Court of Justice (ICJ). However, the authority of the ICJ does not apply to WIPO members that do not recognize the court's jurisdiction.[5]

---

[4]  For a good discussion on U.S. coercion in negotiating the TRIPS Agreement, see Drahos (2002).
[5]  For more information about enforcement of the TRIPS Agreement, see Lee and Lewinski (1996) and Dreier (1996).

TABLE 3.1 Members of the WTO and Signatories to the Paris, Berne, and Rome Conventions*

| Country | WTO | Paris Convention | Berne Convention | Rome Convention |
|---|---|---|---|---|
| Algeria | o | x | x | |
| Angola | x | | | |
| Benin | x | x | x | |
| Botswana | x | x | x | |
| Burkina Faso | x | x | x | x |
| Burundi | x | x | | |
| Cameroon | x | x | x | |
| Cape Verde | x | | x | |
| Central African Republic | x | x | x | |
| Chad | x | x | x | |
| Congo, Dem. Rep. of | x | x | x | |
| Congo, Rep. of | x | x | x | x |
| Côte d'Ivoire | x | x | x | |
| Djibouti | x | x | x | |
| Egypt | x | x | x | |
| Equatorial Guinea | o | x | x | |
| Ethiopia | o | | | |
| Gabon | x | x | x | |
| Gambia | x | x | x | |
| Ghana | x | x | x | |
| Guinea | x | x | x | |
| Guinea-Bissau | x | x | x | |
| Kenya | x | x | x | |
| Lesotho | x | x | x | |
| Liberia | | x | x | |
| Libya | o | x | x | |
| Madagascar | x | x | x | |

(*continued*)

TABLE 3.1 *(continued)*

| Country | WTO | Paris Convention | Berne Convention | Rome Convention |
|---|---|---|---|---|
| Malawi | x | x | x | |
| Mali | x | x | x | |
| Mauritania | x | x | x | |
| Mauritius | x | x | x | |
| Morocco | x | x | x | |
| Mozambique | x | x | | |
| Namibia | x | | x | |
| Niger | x | x | x | x |
| Nigeria | x | x | x | |
| Rwanda | x | x | x | |
| São Tomé and Principe | o | x | | |
| Senegal | x | x | x | |
| Seychelles | o | x | | |
| Sierra Leone | x | x | | |
| South Africa | x | x | x | |
| Sudan | o | x | x | |
| Swaziland | x | x | x | |
| Tanzania | x | x | x | |
| Togo | x | x | x | |
| Tunisia | x | x | x | |
| Uganda | x | x | | |
| Zambia | x | x | x | |
| Zimbabwe | x | x | x | |

*An "x" identifies member governments and an "o" identifies observer governments.
*Sources: WTO and World Intellectual Property Organization (WIPO) websites*
*http://www.wto.org/english/thewto_e/whatis_e/tif_e/org6_e.htm,*
*http://www.wipo.int/treaties/documents/english/word/d-paris.doc,*
*http://www.wipo.int/treaties/documents/english/word/e-berne.doc,*
*http://www.wipo.int/treaties/documents/english/word/k-rome.doc.*

HEALTH INDICATORS IN AFRICA

A glance at health indicators can help explain the apprehension of African countries about the TRIPS Agreement. The dire economic states in which most African countries operate is reflected vividly by the health indicators of those countries. For example, life expectancy at birth has fallen or remained constant since the 1990s in many Sub-Saharan African countries, as shown in Table 3.2. On average, life expectancy at birth in Sub-Saharan Africa fell by 6 percent between 1990 and 2004. Likewise, the number of physicians available to populations in Sub-Saharan Africa is very small, as shown in Table 3.2. From these statistics alone, one can appreciate that these countries need all the support they can get to address public health challenges, and not additional obstacles introduced by WTO agreements.

The TRIPS Agreement was negotiated in the early 1990s when the HIV/AIDS pandemic was gaining ground in Sub-Saharan Africa. At the same time, although HIV antiretroviral drugs were proving to be effective, they were far too expensive for the vast majority of HIV patients in developing countries. Partly due to the confluence of these factors, the debate over and the implications of the TRIPS Agreement are often presented in the context of the HIV/AIDS epidemic.

Although Sub-Saharan Africa has 10 percent of the world population, it is home to over 60 percent of the people in the world living with HIV/AIDS. Estimates by the Joint United Nations Program on HIV/AIDS (UNAIDS) indicate that the adult HIV prevalence rate in some southern African countries is over 20 percent, as shown in Table 3.3.[6] Not surprisingly, there is a high

---

[6]  Co-sponsors of UNAIDS include the Office of the United Nations High Commissioner for Refugees, the United Nations Children's Fund, the United Nations World Food Program, the United Nations Development Program, the United Nations Population Fund, the United Nations Office on Drugs and Crime, the International Labor Organization, the United Nations Educational, Scientific and Cultural Organization, the World Health Organization, and the World Bank.

TABLE 3.2  Life Expectancy at Birth and Physicians per 1,000 People

| Country | Life Expectancy at Birth | | | Physicians per 1,000 People | |
|---|---|---|---|---|---|
| | 1990 | 2004 | Change (Percent) | 1990 | 1997–2004* |
| Algeria | 67 | 71 | 6.0 | 0.9 | 1.1 |
| Angola | 40 | 41 | 2.5 | 0.0** | 0.1 |
| Benin | 53 | 55 | 3.8 | 0.1 | 0.0** |
| Botswana | 64 | 35 | (45.3) | 0.2 | 0.4 |
| Burkina Faso | 48 | 48 | 0.0 | 0.1 | 0.3 |
| Burundi | 44 | 44 | 0.0 | 0.1 | 0.0** |
| Cameroon | 52 | 46 | (11.5) | 0.1 | 0.2 |
| Central African Republic | 48 | 39 | (18.8) | 0.0** | 0.1 |
| Chad | 46 | 44 | (4.3) | 0.0** | 0.0** |
| Congo, Dem. Rep. of | 46 | 44 | (4.3) | 0.3 | 0.2 |
| Congo, Rep. of | 54 | 52 | (3.7) | 0.3 | 0.2 |
| Côte d'Ivoire | 52 | 46 | (11.5) | 0.1 | 0.1 |
| Egypt | 63 | 70 | 11.1 | 0.8 | 0.5 |
| Eritrea | 48 | 54 | 12.5 | n.a. | 0.1 |
| Ethiopia | 45 | 42 | (6.7) | 0.0** | 0.0** |
| Gabon | 60 | 54 | (10.0) | 0.5 | 0.3 |
| Gambia | 50 | 56 | 12.0 | n.a. | 0.0** |
| Ghana | 56 | 57 | 1.8 | 0.0** | 0.2 |
| Guinea | 47 | 54 | 14.9 | 0.1 | 0.1 |
| Guinea-Bissau | 42 | 45 | 7.1 | n.a. | 0.1 |
| Kenya | 58 | 48 | (17.2) | 0.0** | 0.1 |
| Lesotho | 57 | 36 | (36.9) | 0.0** | 0.0** |
| Liberia | 43 | 42 | (2.3) | n.a. | 0.0** |
| Libya | 68 | 74 | 8.8 | 1.1 | 1.3 |
| Madagascar | 51 | 56 | 9.8 | 0.1 | 0.3 |
| Malawi | 46 | 40 | (13.0) | 0.0** | 0.0** |
| Mali | 46 | 48 | 4.3 | 0.1 | 0.1 |

*(continued)*

TABLE 3.2 (*continued*)

| Country | Life Expectancy at Birth | | | Physicians per 1,000 People | |
|---|---|---|---|---|---|
| | 1990 | 2004 | Change (Percent) | 1990 | 1997–2004[*] |
| Mauritania | 49 | 53 | 8.2 | 0.1 | 0.1 |
| Mauritius | 69 | 73 | 5.8 | 0.8 | 1.1 |
| Morocco | 64 | 70 | 9.4 | 0.2 | 0.5 |
| Mozambique | 43 | 42 | (2.3) | 0.0[**] | 0.0[**] |
| Namibia | 62 | 47 | (24.2) | 0.2 | 0.3 |
| Niger | 40 | 45 | 12.5 | 0.0[**] | 0.0[**] |
| Nigeria | 46 | 44 | (4.3) | 0.2 | 0.3 |
| Rwanda | 31 | 44 | 41.9 | 0.0[**] | 0.0[**] |
| Senegal | 53 | 56 | 5.7 | 0.1 | 0.1 |
| Sierra Leone | 39 | 41 | 5.1 | n.a. | 0.0[**] |
| Somalia | 42 | 47 | 11.9 | n.a. | 0.0[**] |
| South Africa | 62 | 45 | (27.4) | 0.6 | 0.8 |
| Sudan | 53 | 57 | 7.5 | n.a. | 0.2 |
| Swaziland | 57 | 42 | (26.3) | 0.1 | 0.2 |
| Tanzania | 53 | 46 | (13.2) | n.a. | 0.0[**] |
| Togo | 57 | 55 | (3.5) | 0.1 | 0.0[**] |
| Tunisia | 70 | 73 | 4.3 | 0.5 | 1.3 |
| Uganda | 46 | 49 | 6.5 | 0.0[**] | 0.1 |
| Zambia | 46 | 38 | (17.4) | 0.1 | 0.1 |
| Zimbabwe | 59 | 37 | (37.3) | 0.1 | 0.2 |
| World | 65 | 67 | 3.1 | 1.6 | 1.5 |
| Low-income countries | 56 | 59 | 5.4 | 0.5 | 0.4 |
| Sub-Saharan Africa | 49 | 46 | (6.1) | n.a. | 0.1 |
| South Asia | 59 | 63 | 6.8 | 0.5 | 0.5 |

[*]Data are for the most recent year available.
[**]Less than 0.05.
n.a., not available.
*Source*: *World Bank (2006)*.

TABLE 3.3  HIV/AIDS Estimates: 2005

| Country | Estimated Number of People Living with HIV/AIDS | | | Estimated Total AIDS Deaths (2005) |
| | Adults and Children | Adults (Age 15 +) | Adult Rate (Percent) | |
| --- | --- | --- | --- | --- |
| Algeria | 19,000 | 19,000 | 0.1 | <500 |
| Angola | 320,000 | 280,000 | 3.7 | 30,000 |
| Benin | 87,000 | 77,000 | 1.8 | 9,600 |
| Botswana | 270,000 | 260,000 | 24.1 | 18,000 |
| Burkina Faso | 150,000 | 140,000 | 2.0 | 12,000 |
| Burundi | 150,000 | 130,000 | 3.3 | 13,000 |
| Cameroon | 510,000 | 470,000 | 5.4 | 46,000 |
| Central African Republic | 250,000 | 230,000 | 10.7 | 24,000 |
| Chad | 180,000 | 160,000 | 3.5 | 11,000 |
| Comoros | <500 | <500 | <0.1 | <100 |
| Congo, Dem. Rep. of | 1,000,000 | 890,000 | 3.2 | 90,000 |
| Congo, Rep. of | 120,000 | 100,000 | 5.3 | 11,000 |
| Côte d'Ivoire | 750,000 | 680,000 | 7.1 | 65,000 |
| Djibouti | 15,000 | 14,000 | 3.1 | 1,200 |
| Egypt | 5,300 | 5,200 | <0.1 | <500 |
| Equatorial Guinea | 8,9000 | 8,000 | 3.2 | <1,000 |
| Eritrea | 59,000 | 53,000 | 2.4 | 5,600 |
| Gabon | 60,000 | 56,000 | 7.9 | 4,700 |
| Gambia | 20,000 | 19,000 | 2.4 | 1,300 |
| Ghana | 320,000 | 300,000 | 2.3 | 29,000 |
| Guinea | 85,000 | 78,000 | 1.5 | 7,100 |
| Guinea-Bissau | 32,000 | 29,000 | 3.8 | 2,700 |
| Kenya | 1,300,000 | 1,200,000 | 6.1 | 140,000 |
| Lesotho | 270,000 | 250,000 | 23.2 | 23,000 |
| Madagascar | 49,000 | 47,000 | 0.5 | 2,900 |
| Malawi | 940,000 | 850,000 | 14.1 | 78,000 |

*(continued)*

TABLE 3.3 *(continued)*

| Country | Estimated Number of People Living with HIV/AIDS | | Adult Rate (Percent) | Estimated Total AIDS Deaths (2005) |
|---|---|---|---|---|
| | Adults and Children | Adults (Age 15+) | | |
| Mali | 130,000 | 110,000 | 1.7 | 11,000 |
| Mauritania | 12,000 | 11,000 | 0.7 | <1,000 |
| Mauritius | 4,100 | 4,100 | 0.6 | <100 |
| Morocco | 19,000 | 19,000 | 0.1 | 1,300 |
| Mozambique | 1,800,000 | 1,600,000 | 16.1 | 140,000 |
| Namibia | 230,000 | 210,000 | 19.6 | 17,000 |
| Niger | 79,000 | 71,000 | 1.1 | 7,600 |
| Nigeria | 2,900,000 | 2,600,000 | 3.9 | 220,000 |
| Rwanda | 190,000 | 160,000 | 3.1 | 21,000 |
| Senegal | 61,000 | 56,000 | 0.9 | 5,200 |
| Sierra Leone | 48,000 | 43,000 | 1.6 | 4,600 |
| Somalia | 44,000 | 40,000 | 0.9 | 4,100 |
| South Africa | 5,500,000 | 5,300,000 | 18.8 | 320,000 |
| Sudan | 350,000 | 320,000 | 1.6 | 34,000 |
| Swaziland | 220,000 | 210,000 | 33.4 | 16,000 |
| Tanzania | 1,400,000 | 1,300,000 | 6.5 | 140,000 |
| Togo | 110,000 | 100,000 | 3.2 | 9,100 |
| Tunisia | 8,700 | 8,600 | 0.1 | <100 |
| Uganda | 1,000,000 | 900,000 | 6.7 | 91,000 |
| Zambia | 1,100,000 | 1,000,000 | 17.0 | 98,000 |
| Zimbabwe | 1,700,000 | 1,500,000 | 20.1 | 180,000 |
| World | 38,600,000 | 36,300,000 | 1.0 | 2,800,000 |
| Sub-Saharan Africa | 24,500,000 | 22,400,000 | 6.1 | 2,000,000 |
| South and Southeast Asia | 7,600,000 | 7,400,000 | 0.6 | 560,000 |

*Source:* UNAIDS *(2006: Annex 2). The report is available at http://www.unaids.org/en/ HIV_data/2006GlobalReport/default.asp.*

correlation between the HIV prevalence rate and the decline in life expectancy at birth. The correlation between these two variables is −0.81. The correlation is −0.87 when Rwanda, a clear outlier given its genocide history, is removed. This correlation is also portrayed in Figure 3.1, where HIV prevalence and the percentage change in life expectancy are roughly mirror images of each other.

Since the early 2000s, there has been an impressive increase in the number of people receiving antiretroviral therapy in Sub-Saharan Africa as a percent of those who require the therapy. In December 2003, only about 100,000 people received antiretroviral drugs in Sub-Saharan Africa. As of June 2006, that number had increased over ten-fold to 1,040,000. As a percent of people who need HIV treatment, the increase was from 2 percent in 2003 to 23 percent in 2006 (WHO, 2006).

As encouraging as these numbers are, the distribution of this progress is noticeably uneven. The proportion of people receiving antiretroviral therapy among those who need it is over 50 percent in countries such as Botswana, Namibia, and Uganda, but less than 10 percent in almost half of the Sub-Saharan African countries, as shown in Table 3.4. While it is not shown in Table 3.4, in 2002 only three countries – Gabon, Senegal, and Uganda – had reached the range of 10 to 24.9 percent. All the rest were below 10 percent. The uneven distribution of the progress reflects the impact of a myriad of factors, the explanation of which is beyond the scope of this study. Suffice it to say that the overall success is a result of concerted efforts within individual countries, coordinated programs by philanthropists, NGOs, international organizations, and developed countries, and, of course, cheaper drugs.

In December 2003, the WHO and UNAIDS launched an ambitious initiative with the goal of providing treatment to 3 million people in developing countries living with HIV/AIDS by the end of 2005, thus the "3 by 5" slogan (WHO, 2006a). While the "3 by 5" initiative did not reach its goal, it has achieved commendable

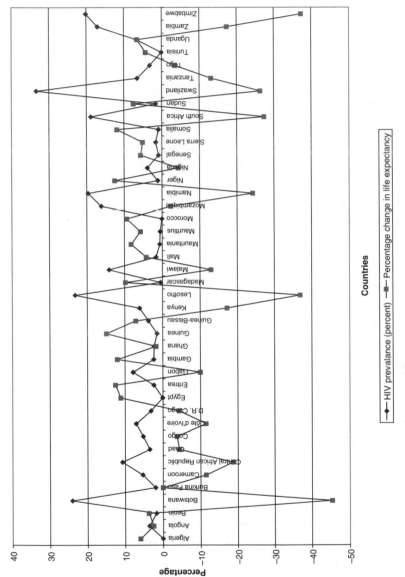

FIGURE 3.1 HIV Prevalence in 2005 and Change in Life Expectancy between 1990 and 2005.

TABLE 3.4 People Receiving Antiretroviral
Therapy as a Percent of Those in Need: 2005

| | |
|---|---|
| Angola | <10 |
| Benin | 25–49.9 |
| Botswana | 75–100 |
| Burkina Faso | 10–24.9 |
| Burundi | 10–24.9 |
| Cameroon | 10–24.9 |
| Central African Republic | <10 |
| Chad | 10–24.9 |
| Congo, Dem. Rep. of | <10 |
| Congo, Rep. of | 10–24.9 |
| Côte d'Ivoire | 10–24.9 |
| Djibouti | 10–24.9 |
| Equatorial Guinea | <10 |
| Eritrea | <10 |
| Ethiopia | <10 |
| Gabon | 10–24.9 |
| Gambia | <10 |
| Ghana | <10 |
| Guinea | <10 |
| Guinea-Bissau | <10 |
| Kenya | 10–24.9 |
| Lesotho | 10–24.9 |
| Liberia | <10 |
| Madagascar | <10 |
| Malawi | 10–24.9 |
| Mali | 25–49.9 |
| Mauritania | 25–49.9 |
| Mozambique | <10 |
| Namibia | 50–74.9 |
| Niger | <10 |
| Nigeria | <10 |
| Rwanda | 25–49.9 |
| Senegal | 25–49.9 |

(*continued*)

TABLE 3.4 *(continued)*

| Sierra Leone | <10 |
|---|---|
| Somalia | <10 |
| South Africa | 10–24.9 |
| Swaziland | 25–49.9 |
| Tanzania | <10 |
| Togo | 25–49.9 |
| Uganda | 50–74.9 |
| Zambia | 25–49.9 |
| Zimbabwe | <10 |

*Source: WHO (2006a).*

results and continues to be an important catalyst toward universal treatment.[7] This initiative is an important factor in the progress witnessed in Sub-Saharan Africa. The ultimate goal of the initiative is to provide universal access to treatment.

The reduction in the prices of drugs (partly attributable to the "3 by 5" initiative) has also been a reason for increased treatment. Between 2003 and 2005, the average price of first-line medication decreased between 37 percent and 53 percent. The decrease is in part explained by increased competition among products prequalified by the WHO, an increased scale of purchases, and negotiations between the William J. Clinton Foundation and major generic manufacturers (WHO, 2006a).

OPTIONS AVAILABLE TO AFRICAN COUNTRIES
UNDER THE TRIPS AGREEMENT

When the WTO took effect in 1995, the agreements that were expected to have the most direct and immediate significance to

---

[7] In December 2003, there were about 400,000 people receiving antiretroviral therapy in developing countries. That number increased to 1.3 million in December 2005 and 1.6 million in June 2006. Approximately 6.8 million people in developing countries living with HID/AIDS in 2006 required antiretroviral therapy (WHO 2006, 2006a).

Africa were those on agriculture and textiles and apparel. However, the TRIPS Agreement was soon also of great interest to policy makers, researchers, and NGOs. The impetus for this interest and concern was what was perceived by some as the abuse of the TRIPS Agreement by pharmaceutical companies who had filed a lawsuit against the South African government.

This lawsuit, filed in 1998 by the Pharmaceutical Manufacturers Association of South Africa, highlighted how trade policy and public health policy intertwine and the extent to which the profit motive can influence decision making. The association, representing thirty-nine pharmaceutical companies, challenged a South African law aimed at easing access to AIDS drugs through the use of parallel importing and compulsory licensing. Parallel importing is permitted by Article 6 of the TRIPS Agreement. Compulsory licensing is permitted by Article 31 of TRIPS, which "allows for other use of the subject matter of a patent without the authorization of the right holder."

Parallel imports are products resold by a third party without the approval of the patent holder. For example, suppose Profitmax pharmaceutical company sells a patented drug to Uganda and Zimbabwe, but sells it at a lower price in Uganda. If another company buys it in Uganda and sells it in Zimbabwe at a price lower than the price charged by Profitmax, such action would constitute parallel importing. Parallel importing is permitted under TRIPS to allow price competition and to give developing countries access to the lowest drug prices available (Abbott, 2002: 41–45).

Compulsory licensing takes place when a government allows a third party to produce a patented product without the consent of the patent holder. This provision is allowed under certain conditions, including a public health emergency. Any objective assessment of South Africa's situation would have concluded that the country was experiencing a serious health care crisis. South Africa had the fastest growing HIV epidemic in the 1990s. According to UNAIDS data, the HIV prevalence for adults in South Africa shot up from about 1 percent in 1990 to almost 20 percent in 1998 when the lawsuit was filed.

The South African laws were arguably permissible under TRIPS in the face of urgent public health care needs. Nonetheless, the U.S. government and the EU sided with the pharmaceutical companies in pressuring the South African government to amend its law allowing parallel importing and compulsory licensing (Abbott, 2002: 52–54; Pretorius, 2002: 190–193). Paradoxically, the TRIPS Agreement that was expected to prevent unilateral actions by developed countries (Correa, 2000: 11–12) became the basis for unilateral pressures from the United States and the EU. Although the WHO did not want to be directly involved in the legal standoff, it supported the South African drugs legislation and the rationale of the law, which was to provide affordable medicines to its people, explaining that essential drugs were not ordinary commodities. After a three-year legal battle, the Pharmaceutical Manufacturers Association withdrew its court case against the South African government in April 2001.

Considering the potentially negative impact of the TRIPS Agreement on developing countries, calls to remove the TRIPS Agreement from the WTO altogether may not be outrageous.[8] However, the political reality and power structure in the WTO completely eliminate that as a viable option to pursue. Moreover, the United States and the EU already argue that the TRIPS Agreement does not go far enough. In negotiating bilateral agreements with other countries, they each have a version of "TRIPS Plus," which they use to demand that countries protect intellectual property rights more than what is required by the multilateral TRIPS Agreement (Pretorius, 2002: 191–195). Therefore, African countries are "stuck" with the TRIPS Agreement and, depending on the spirit in which it is interpreted, they may also be "tripped up" by it in the long run.

---

[8]  See Stiglitz and Charlton (2005). For a review of Stiglitz and Charlton (2005), see Lawrence (2007).

While parallel importing and compulsory licensing are policy options available to developing countries under the TRIPS Agreement, they are of little direct importance to most African countries. Twenty-six of the thirty-three least-developed countries that are currently members of the WTO are African countries. While drug prices in these countries are still too high relative to purchasing ability, these prices tend to be lower, in absolute terms, than prices in other countries. Therefore, if there is any parallel importing, it would be from, rather than to, these countries. In fact, to help ensure the flow of relatively cheap drugs to African countries, these countries should be assuring pharmaceutical companies that they will not be party to parallel *exporting* and that they will work diligently to prevent the smuggling of drugs *from* Africa. It would be unwise and irresponsible of African countries to re-export cheap drugs to other countries, just because parallel importing is allowed (under certain circumstances) under the TRIPS Agreement.

As for compulsory licensing, it is a viable option if a country has the capacity to produce and market generic drugs. Most African countries do not have that capacity. Considering opportunity costs, even where such capacity could be built, it may not be the best use of resources. For many African countries, this provision is thus useful only if they can import from other countries such as India and Brazil that can themselves take advantage of compulsory licensing to produce generic drugs. However, the TRIPS Agreement stipulated that any use of compulsory licensing "shall be authorized predominantly for the supply of the market of the Member authorizing such use" (Article 31(f) of the TRIPS Agreement); that is, compulsory licensing was to be authorized primarily for the "domestic market." Thus, while the agreement established compulsory licensing as a legal option under certain conditions, one of those conditions – that it be used primarily for the domestic market – posed a significant problem for countries that lacked production capacity.

At the same time, the TRIPS Agreement, adopted in 1995, gave developing countries until January 1, 2006, to comply with its provisions. In 2002, the WTO extended the deadline to January 1, 2016, for least-developed countries to begin to provide patent protection for pharmaceuticals. During the transitional period, least-developed countries are not even required to provide "mailbox" protection, specified in Article 70 of the TRIPS Agreement. "Mailbox" protection describes a situation whereby a pharmaceutical company can register a patent application for a new product in a country that does not provide patent protection, so that the company receives exclusive marketing rights when the country does begin to grant patent protection. By exempting least-developed countries from giving such exclusive marketing rights, it means only products developed after the transitional period will receive patent protection in those countries.

Other developing countries, however, were still bound by the original deadline. That meant that although India, for example, could still utilize the compulsory licensing provision to produce generic drugs, as of January 1, 2006, it could not export them. Although a least-developed country like Tanzania (still under the extended transitional period) would theoretically have been allowed to import generic drugs from India, India would have been bound by the TRIPS Agreement not to export the drugs. Tanzania would have had to either produce the drugs itself or find another least-developed country that produced the drugs.

### AFRICAN COUNTRIES' PROPOSALS AND KEY ISSUES
### REGARDING COMPULSORY LICENSING

Aware of what this predicament meant for Africa, the African Group in the WTO pushed for two main changes to the compulsory licensing provisions under TRIPS: (1) a waiver that would allow countries that make use of compulsory licensing to export their drugs to countries with insufficient or no manufacturing capacity, and

(2) a broader definition of "domestic market." The African Group requested that "domestic market" refer not only to a single country's market, but also to a free trade area or a customs union. Thus, if South Africa, for example, were able to produce a generic product under the compulsory licensing provision, the product could be sold to all members of the Southern African Development Community (SADC), of which South Africa is a member.

One may wonder whether the second request would be redundant if the first were granted. However, classifying a free trade area as a "domestic market" may not only be important for intra-regional trading; imports of drugs by a free trade area as a single market would allow for bulk purchases and discounted prices. For example, SADC would tend to get a better price for drugs imported from India or Brazil than would any individual member of SADC.

For most African countries, the capacity to produce pharmaceutical drugs is very limited at best. Yet they are plagued by a wide array of diseases and public health problems. Therefore, it was important that their modest requests be dealt with quickly. Moreover, NGOs were watching closely the developments of the TRIPS Agreement debate. It became apparent that this issue would be a sticking point at the Cancun Ministerial Meetings and could derail other discussions. Strategically, on August 30, 2003, less than two weeks before the Cancun Meetings, the General Council of the WTO reached a decision on the implementation of paragraph 6 of the Doha Declarations, intended to find expeditious solutions to the problems countries may face in making use of compulsory licensing.

The August 30, 2003 decision waived Article 31(f) of the TRIPS Agreement.[9] This meant that countries that utilized compulsory

---

[9] The following countries declared that they would not use the system outlined by the August 2003 decision as importing countries: Australia, Austria, Belgium, Canada, Denmark, Finland, France, Germany, Greece, Iceland, Ireland, Italy, Japan, Luxembourg, Netherlands, New Zealand, Norway, Portugal, Spain, Sweden, Switzerland, United Kingdom, and the United States.

licensing to produce generic drugs were no longer constrained to their domestic markets; they could now export them to eligible importing countries or regional trading blocs.

Article 31(f) of the TRIPS Agreement shall be waived to the extent necessary to enable a pharmaceutical product produced or imported under a compulsory licence in that Member to be exported to the markets of those other developing or least developed country parties to the regional trade agreement that share the health problem in question. (WTO, 2003h: 4)

Eligibility of an importing country is based on its lack of capacity to produce the drug and its public health crisis.

Apparently, the decision was adopted in light of the statement by the General Council chairperson Carlos Pérez del Castillo, the Ambassador from Uruguay, that members must use the waiver in good faith to protect public health. He warned against using the system as a loophole to undermine patent protection.[10]

In a letter to Mexico's Foreign Minister (the host of the Cancun Meetings), Director-General of the WTO, Supachai Panitchpakdi, hailed the decision as an:

historic and significant event. We believe that this evidence that the WTO system is working, and can produce important results on critical issues of particular interest to developing countries, will give us all added confidence in dealing with the challenges we face in other areas. (http://www.ictsd.org/ministerial/cancun/docs/coverletter.pdf)

The decision may not have been historic; however, it was an important interim decision from which African countries expected that a more permanent solution could be reached. While the decision brought some temporary relief to the TRIPS debate, it continued to be a source of frustration for African countries, as reflected by

---

[10] The August 30, 2003, decision and the Chair's statement can be found, respectively, at: http://www.wto.org/English/tratop_e/trips_e/implem_para6_e.htm and http://www.wto.org/english/news_e/news03_e/trips_stat_28aug03_e.htm.

their proposals. Some of those proposals pre-date the August, 30, 2003 decision, but were not addressed by the decision (Southern and Eastern African Trade Information and Negotiations Institute (SEATINI), 2005).

The African Group's proposals identified several key issues to be addressed regarding compulsory licensing, including (1) the capacity to utilize compulsory licensing, (2) coverage, (3) safeguards, (4) the Chair's Statement, and (5) predictability.

## Capacity to Utilize Compulsory Licensing

As discussed, while African countries – Sub-Saharan African countries in particular – are characterized by ubiquitous health epidemics, most of them lack the capacity to produce generic drugs, even if given the green light to do so. Some lack even the physical infrastructure and institutional framework required to effectively distribute and administer medicines when they are available.

African countries have continually favored fewer restrictions on the exportation of generic drugs to countries facing public health crises. As long as a generic drug was exported to an importing country with a health epidemic, the African Group demanded that the public health situation in the exporting country should have no bearing on that country's permission to produce and export it. In other words, they make the strong argument that even pure exporters should be allowed to engage in compulsory licensing, as long as the product is to be exported solely to eligible importers. This would be the typical situation for developed countries that pass domestic legislation to implement the WTO provision allowing compulsory licensing.

Reducing constraints on exports of generic drugs is undeniably a commendable achievement because it puts the spotlight where it should be – on the urgent need for relatively cheaper generic drugs in developing countries. There are economic and social rationales for this action. Allowing pure exporters to make use of compulsory licensing increases the competition among producers of generic drugs, thus lowering the price for eligible importing countries, which is the primary reason behind compulsory licensing. Moreover, the domestic market alone, even in the face of a health epidemic, may not be large enough to justify the cost of domestic production. Furthermore, even if production was initially mainly for domestic consumption, the need for that drug in the producing country may eventually decrease to the point where the drug is no longer needed, as the country lifts itself out of the health care crisis. If compulsory licensing were to be constrained to domestic use only, even countries with the capacity to produce generic drugs and the domestic need for those drugs due to a health epidemic, might be too hesitant to invest in production. In that scenario, compulsory licensing would not be useful. It would fail to meet its social goal to make medicines more accessible in poor areas of the world with health care crises.

In addition, manufacturing capacity must be considered not simply in terms of the actual ability and technical know-how to produce a generic drug. It must also be considered in terms of the opportunity costs of domestic production versus importing. Even the least-developed countries could establish the capacity to produce a generic drug if they were sufficiently determined to do so. However, at what opportunity cost? In this sense, a lack of capacity should not be based on income per capita or some other statistic, but rather on the simple fact that there is no domestic production. For the WTO, an organization whose main objective is to promote production based on market forces and an efficient allocation of resources, it would be a contradiction to deny a country access to an imported generic drug on the grounds that the country should have had the capacity to produce it itself. Considering that a country is looking to find the cheapest medicines available to alleviate whatever public health crisis it is facing, its declaration that it lacks the capacity to produce a drug should be taken at face value. Otherwise, an unnecessary burden on exporting and importing countries is created as exporting countries are required to confirm "that the eligible importing Member in question, other than a least-developed country Member, has established that it has insufficient or no manufacturing capacities" (WTO, 2003h).

Where does this leave the commitment to promote technical assistance and capacity building in the pharmaceutical sector in least-developed countries? Article 66.2 of the TRIPS Agreement and paragraph 7 of the Doha Declaration on the TRIPS Agreement affirm the commitment of the governments of developed countries to provide incentives to their enterprises and institutions to promote and encourage the transfer of knowledge to least-developed countries (WTO, 2001). Not surprisingly, the call for transfer of technology and assistance for capacity building for developing countries is incorporated into all WTO agreements. Nonetheless, support for developing countries cannot be distributed evenly among recipient countries or uniformly among sectors within a given country. Lack of a specific technology or capacity, say to produce drugs, in a given country, even coupled with a severe public health crisis in that country, is not sufficient for that country to receive assistance to build a pharmaceutical industry. The transfer of knowledge and capacity building must be guided by the opportunity costs involved. Based on opportunity costs and access to imported generic drugs, certainly not all least-developed countries that qualify for assistance in general would qualify for specific assistance to introduce the capacity to produce generic drugs. Tackling the public health crisis in a given country does not necessarily require that the country become self-sufficient in the production of drugs, but rather that it be able to acquire the drugs it needs, whether through imports and/ or domestic production.

The provision in the TRIPS Agreement permitting compulsory licensing should always be implemented in the spirit that (a) not all countries have the capacity to produce generic drugs; and (b) not all countries are at the point where they should *develop* such capacity. Reinforcing the latter point is the fact that the August 30, 2003 decision accepted the call from the African, LDC, and ACP Groups to treat as a single market those regional economic blocs that are composed of developing and/or least-developed countries, thus enabling those countries to make the most of compulsory licensing.

## Coverage

Another issue on which the African Group has been persistent involves the products and diseases covered by compulsory licensing. The Group warns against applying a narrow and rigid definition of pharmaceutical products and having an *a priori* list of diseases. African countries want "pharmaceutical products" to include medicines and vaccines for treatment and prevention, active ingredients needed to manufacture generic drugs, and kits and equipment needed for diagnosis and administering treatment. A narrow definition that only allows compulsory licensing for generic drugs would certainly have very limited impact when dealing with a public health crisis. Providing public health care is a process in which the effectiveness of each link depends on the availability of other links in the chain.

Preparing an *a priori* list of specific diseases is both myopic and unnecessary. The grounds for utilizing compulsory licensing must continue to be a public health crisis, irrespective of the underlying disease. In fact, preparing an *a priori* list would render the August 30, 2003 decision a perpetual temporary waiver, notwithstanding the fact that, as will be discussed, it is expected to become a permanent amendment to the TRIPS Agreement. Any time a disease not on the list causes a public health crisis, the afflicted country would have to undertake the diplomatic agony of WTO negotiations to seek special permission for the disease to be placed on the list.

The experience of the United States in dealing with the anthrax scare in 2001 suggests that countries should have great latitude (in collaboration with the WHO) in determining what constitutes a health care crisis or national health emergency. In 2001, five people died in the United States after being exposed to mail contaminated with anthrax bacteria. The anthrax attack started only a week after the September 11, 2001 attacks, when the United States was nervous and on highest alert. The bioterrorism nature of the anthrax attacks was treated as a national emergency, and the United States had the right to handle it as such. The apparent need to stockpile millions of doses (tablets) in a short period found the United States, the ardent defender of patent law, weighing whether to use compulsory licensing. The WTO could not have stopped the United States from using compulsory licensing had the United States chosen to do so, although other countries might well have criticized the United States for hypocrisy. The point is that each country should be able to classify a situation as a national health crisis or national emergency as they understand it. As the anthrax scare in the United States demonstrated, it is not always a question of how many people die or have been infected; circumstances surrounding those occurrences and the potential for more infections and deaths must also be considered in the determination of what constitutes a health care crisis or national health emergency.

## Safeguards

Having generic versions of patented drugs that can only be sold to a subset of countries creates a two-tier market system with the potential for a serious smuggling problem. The price disparity opens many doors for triangular trans-shipment of generic drugs; that is, generic drugs could be exported by a country producing them under the compulsory licensing provision to an eligible importing country and then re-exported to a non-eligible country.

For example, Glaxo's AIDS drugs that were sold in Sub-Saharan Africa at an 80 to 90 percent discount were illegally re-exported to Europe (Crouch, 2002; Naik, 2002).

To prevent such trans-shipment, or at least to be able to detect it easily and quickly when it happens, the WTO established conditions and requirements for eligible exporting and importing countries (WTO, 2003h). These include the following:

- the eligible importing Member(s) has made a notification to the Council for TRIPS, that specifies the names and expected quantities of the product(s) needed;
- only the amount necessary to meet the needs of the eligible importing Member(s) may be manufactured under the licence and the entirety of this production shall be exported to the Member(s) which has notified its needs to the Council for TRIPS;
- products produced under the licence shall be clearly identified as being produced under the system set out in this Decision through specific labelling or marking. Suppliers should distinguish such products through special packaging and/or special colouring/shaping of the products themselves, provided that such distinction is feasible and does not have a significant impact on price; and
- before shipment begins, the licensee shall post on a website the following information: the quantities being supplied to each destination … and the distinguishing features of the product(s). (WTO, 2003h: 2–3)

The WTO Agreement on Technical Barriers to Trade (TBT) allows technical regulations for the prevention of deceptive practices and to achieve other legitimate objectives. It is only appropriate that the safeguard measures pass the criteria set by Article 2.2 of the Agreement on TBT, which include ensuring "that technical regulations are not prepared, adopted or applied with a view to or with the effect of creating unnecessary obstacles to international trade." However, the African Group was wary that the safeguard measures might create an undue burden on eligible users of compulsory licensing. In the spirit of freer trade and in light of the public health crises in their countries, the African Group proposed removing many of the procedural requirements.

## The Chair's Statement

Countries that use compulsory licensing to produce generic drugs were allowed, under the August 30, 2003 decision, to export those drugs to eligible importing countries. That decision was tied in with a statement by the Chair of the General Council announcing the decision. The statement urged members to use the decision in good faith and warned them against using it as an instrument to pursue industrial or commercial policy. Furthermore, the statement elaborated on the need and ways for transparency, notification, and product differentiation to prevent diversion of products to non-eligible countries. The statement was later added to the decision as a footnote.

The Chair's statement brought comfort to countries that were concerned that the decision, as it stood, could adversely compromise the protection of patents. However, it faced resistance from the African Group, which viewed it as making the procedures and regulations for exporting and importing generic drugs more cumbersome. In addition, the African Group objected to making the statement a part of the amendment, because by doing so its legal status was inappropriately elevated.[11] Interestingly, the Chair of the General Council at the time (August 2003) was an ambassador from a developing country, Uruguay. Likewise, in December 2005, when the WTO members approved making the August 2003 temporary waiver a permanent decision, it was accompanied by a similar Chair's Statement; the Chair this time was from the African Group, the Kenyan Ambassador to the WTO. This phenomenon

---

[11] For details, see the Communication from Rwanda on Behalf of the African Group titled "Legal Arguments to Support the African Group Proposal on the Implementation of Paragraph 11 of the 30 August 2003 Decision," in SEATINI (2005).

suggests that regardless of the nationality of the chair of the General Council, a responsible individual in that position can and will take into account the interests of different constituencies.

## Predictability

The August 30, 2003 decision was a temporary decision. In addition to proposing further amendments to remove what they perceived to be the shortcomings of the decision, the African Group pushed for a subsequent and appropriate decision to be made permanent and, thus, predictable. It was too risky for businesses to make long-term investments in the production of generic drugs (for exports to eligible importers) on the basis of a temporary waiver that could be rescinded at any time. Partly due to the temporary nature of the decision, countries did not move quickly to amend their domestic patent laws to allow pharmaceutical companies to produce generic drugs for export. The exceptions were Canada and Norway, followed by the Netherlands.

Calling for the removal of some procedural requirements and at the same time pressing for a permanent decision meant that the African Group was treading a thin line. Debate over procedures could delay making the decision a permanent one. At the same time, there was a real risk of making permanent a decision that fell short of the ideal.

As negotiations progressed and it became clear that the decision was either going to remain temporary in perpetuity or made officially permanent, more countries started the process of adjusting their domestic laws to be able to make effective use of the August 30, 2003 decision. This included Switzerland, a source and host country of major patent-holding pharmaceutical companies.

On December 6, 2005, the WTO members agreed to make the August 30, 2003 decision, which was a temporary waiver, a permanent amendment to the TRIPS Agreement. This must be considered a victory for the African Group, which clearly demonstrated its tenacity and ingenuity in the WTO TRIPS Council. When two-thirds of the WTO members ratify the changes, this will be formally built into the TRIPS Agreement. Assuming the waiver does become a permanent amendment, as expected, it will be the first time a core WTO Agreement has been amended. Initially the WTO gave itself a deadline of December 1, 2007 to achieve this. Later, in October 2007, with only 11 out of 152 countries having ratified the amendment, the WTO extended the deadline to the end of 2009 (ICTSD, 2007b).

No sooner had the WTO members agreed to make the waiver permanent, than U.S. Senator Patrick Leahy introduced a bill titled, "The Life-Saving Medicines Export Act of 2006."[12] The bill proposed amending U.S. law to allow U.S. companies to produce generic drugs for patented medicines for export to poor countries that face public health crises but have no capacity to produce the drugs for themselves. Senator Leahy has been a consistent voice of conscience in the United States, advocating for more health care support from the United States and other wealthy nations to impoverished countries. Although the bill failed to pass the committee level, the WTO approval to make its August 30, 2003 waiver permanent will continue to invigorate those in the United States and around the world who argue for increased aid for health care for poor countries.

In 2007, Rwanda became the first country to notify the WTO that it was going to apply the compulsory licensing provision to import HIV/AIDS generic drugs from Canada (ICTSD, 2007). However, given the cumbersome administrative and legal procedures involved, it took a year before the export of generic drugs from Canada to Rwanda actually started. As of September 2008, only one Canadian drug maker, Apotex, was participating in the Canada-Rwanda deal (ICTSD, 2008). It is important to note that Rwanda already receives some assistance for HIV/AIDS drugs

---

[12] The proposed bill is available at http://www.govtrack.us/data/us/bills.text/109/s/ s3175.pdf.

through other initiatives, thereby reducing the urgency of the Canada-Rwanda deal.

CONCLUSION

There is a Swahili expression, *kuuma na kupuliza*, literally "to bite and to soothe." This is a technique that developed countries seem to have applied with regard to the TRIPS Agreement. They persuaded developing countries to sign an agreement that was certainly going to prove painful. Then, as if the pain of the developing countries was unexpected, developed countries tried to soothe that pain by agreeing (though reluctantly) to the August 30, 2003 decision.[13] This decision waived Article 31(f) of the TRIPS Agreement, thus enabling countries that used compulsory licensing for the production of generic drugs, to export them to eligible importing countries or regional trading blocs. The temporary nature of this decision was not sufficient, and eventually approval was given to make it a permanent amendment to the TRIPS Agreement, pending ratification by at least two-thirds of the WTO members.

It is unfortunate that African countries have had to expend so much of their meager diplomatic resources fighting for access to cheap medicines. Nonetheless, the approval to amend the TRIPS Agreement is a victory, albeit modest, for the African Group. The outcome shows how slow the WTO can be in making genuine changes, as well as how important it is to be persistent with justifiable demands.

WTO Agreements cannot be amended on a whim if they are to guide long-term trade policies and be applied to the filing and settlement of trade disputes. However, the WTO's rigidity in making corrections even in such a clear case as that involving

[13] As one reviewer suggests, it could be that developed countries themselves did not understand fully the implications of the initial agreement; that is, there was learning to be done by all.

compulsory licensing discussed above, makes African countries instinctively and, perhaps, justifiably hesitant about any proposed new agreements.[14]

Most African countries are in an awkward situation because the constraints imposed by various agreements are often not directly aimed at them. The constraints are usually targeted at large developing countries, such as Argentina, Brazil, China, India, and South Africa. Such countries are typically capable of taking advantage of any available loopholes. Of course, South Africa is in the African Group, and for various strategic, historical, and institutional reasons, the African Group tends to be in coalitions with other developing countries, even if their interests are not completely in harmony.

Nonetheless, the TRIPS Agreement gave the African Group a unique opportunity to show its maturity and shrewdness in negotiations at the WTO. The experience the African Group acquired and the coalitions it forged in the process are assets transferable to other endeavors. The African Group did not achieve all of its objectives, particularly in the area of reducing procedural requirements. However, given other pressing demands in the WTO, it is not clear that the African Group should continue to spend its resources on the issue of procedures. It should focus its scant resources on other battles. Moreover, considering various initiatives by the WHO and, in particular, the AIDS Medicines and Diagnostics Service (AMDS) network, procedural requirements can be readily facilitated. AMDS provides procurement services and acts as a clearinghouse for drugs for HIV/AIDS, tuberculosis, and malaria.[15]

---

[14] See Chapter 5.

[15] AMDS was launched in December 2003, with its secretariat hosted by the HIV/ AIDS Department of WHO. AMDS partners include: Centrale Humanitaire Médico-Pharmaceutique, the Clinton Foundation, Commonwealth Pharmaceutical Association, Crown Agents, the Global Fund to Fight AIDS, Tuberculosis and Malaria, Ecumenical Pharmaceutical Network, Ensemble pour une Solidarité Thérapeutique Hospitaliè En Réseau, International Pharmaceutical Federation, International Dispensary Association HIV/AIDS Group, IDA Solutions, John Snow Inc/DELIVER, Management Sciences for Health/RPM-Plus, Missionpharma, Partnership for Supply

The reluctance of developed countries to permit what seems to them to be extensive use of compulsory licensing is understandable. Although Africa is not an important market for expensive, patent-protected medicines, widespread use of compulsory licensing will increase the number of producers of generic drugs that will enter the overall medicine market as soon as the patent period expires. Compulsory licensing not only creates competition for a patented medicine during the life of the patent, it also increases competition afterward. That is, compulsory licensing does pose a threat to existing pharmaceutical companies.

The assertion that the August 30, 2003 decision should not be used as an instrument to pursue industrial or commercial policy does not provide patent holders much comfort. In fact, such an assertion is a rhetorical contradiction, touted about only in diplomatic and political circles. Regardless of what the primary purpose of compulsory licensing might be, the reality is that its use advances a country's industrial capacity. Producing generic drugs is a stepping stone to the production of patent-protected medicines. The contradiction of the statement is even more apparent when one considers the call in Article 66.2 of the TRIPS Agreement for technical assistance:

Developed country Members shall provide incentives to enterprises and institutions in their territories for the purpose of promoting and encouraging technology transfer to least-developed country Members in order to enable them to create a sound and viable technological base.

Moreover, while the August 30, 2003 decision allows the use of compulsory licensing for exports to eligible importers, the

Chain Management System, ReMed-Réseau Médicaments et Développement, UNAIDS, the United Nations Development Program, the United Nations Children's Fund, the United Nations Population Fund, United States Agency for International Development, WHO Essential Health Technology, WHO HIV/AIDS Department, WHO Medicines Policy and Standards, WHO Technical Cooperation for Essential Drugs and Traditional Medicine, and the World Bank. For more information about AMDS, see http://www. who.int/hiv/amds/en/.

preference for the developed countries has been to have developing countries use it primarily for their domestic markets. Given the common knowledge that developed countries have been reluctant to allow exports of generic drugs, developing countries have all the more incentive to develop their capacities to produce pharmaceutical products.

Patent holders are also concerned about the potential for illegal trade of generic drugs. While procedural measures to prevent illegal trade have been outlined, it may not be possible to prevent such trade altogether. Thus, the fight to contain the use of compulsory licensing (and parallel importing) will not end. Pharmaceutical companies in the United States, for example, have successfully lobbied their government to establish more stringent arrangements regarding the use of compulsory licensing in negotiating agreements for free trade areas (Abbott, 2005). The United States, a formidable power to contend with in any setting, has much more leverage in bilateral negotiations than in the WTO. Therefore, any prediction of the extent to which the amendment of the TRIPS Agreement will ease exports of generic drugs must take into account various bilateral arrangements, which are often more restrictive regarding intellectual property rights.

For several reasons, some developed countries have been advocating strict measures for the protection of intellectual property rights. At best, they may be genuinely concerned about the potential negative long-term impact of relaxed intellectual property rights on research and development in the pharmaceutical industry worldwide. From a narrower point of view, they must be concerned about the potential loss of profits by their pharmaceutical companies and the decreased government revenues that would follow. They may also believe that relaxing intellectual property rights is not the best way to deal with public health crises. Whatever the reasons for advocating stringent rules on intellectual property rights, it would be unfair to categorically describe these countries as being indifferent to human suffering.

While the progress in Sub-Saharan Africa in providing anti-retroviral therapy to HIV patients can be attributed to cheaper drugs, another important explanation is the financial support from developed countries. Governments of developed countries help African countries address public health challenges directly and through international organizations. For example, in 2003 the U.S. President's Emergency Plan for AIDS Relief (PEPFAR) committed $15 billion, to be disbursed over a period of five years (2004–2008), to fight HIV/AIDS in fifteen focus countries.[16] According to the WHO, the U.S. initiative is the largest ever undertaken by one country to address a single disease. In 2008, President Bush and the U.S. Congress approved an additional $48 billion to PEPFAR over an additional five years (2009–2013).

The major contributors to the Global Fund to Fight AIDS, Tuberculosis and Malaria are Canada, the EC, France, Germany, Italy, Japan, the Netherlands, the United Kingdom, the United States, and the Bill and Melinda Gates Foundation. In 2005, the G8 countries agreed to write off $40 billion in debt owed by eighteen low-income countries, mostly in Africa, to allow these indebted countries to direct more resources to health services (WHO, 2006a). The beneficiary countries were Benin, Bolivia, Burkina Faso, Ethiopia, Ghana, Guyana, Honduras, Madagascar, Mali, Mauritania, Mozambique, Nicaragua, Niger, Rwanda, Senegal, Tanzania, Uganda, and Zambia. Through their partnership with the AMDS network, developed countries also provide African countries with information that enables them to get the most competitive prices for the WHO-approved drugs.

In terms of long-term goals for health care, African countries must try to implement policies that would encourage acquisition

---

[16] The countries are Botswana, Côte d'Ivoire, Ethiopia, Guyana, Haiti, Kenya, Mozambique, Namibia, Nigeria, Rwanda, South Africa, Tanzania, Uganda, Vietnam, and Zambia.

and dissemination of new technologies and new services. These include establishing appropriate systems for national intellectual property rights. It also involves a holistic approach – investment in human capital, health care education, investment in health care and other infrastructure, and appropriate macroeconomic policies.

Acquisition of new technology must not be confused with the technical assistance often sought by African countries. Technical assistance may be one of the means by which to acquire the technology, but it is not an end in itself. While most technical assistance is valuable and leads to greater independence, it can itself be a form of pressure on, or incentive for, African countries to sign agreements before they fully understand them. For example, African countries and other developing countries were pressured to sign the TRIPS Agreement with the promise that they would be assisted in amending their existing legislation and enacting new laws to conform to the agreement. However, such assistance does not necessarily eliminate or reduce the potentially negative impact of an agreement; it simply speeds up the process of countries' implementation of the agreement.

As discussed above, the WTO extended the deadline for least-developed countries to provide patent protection for pharmaceuticals from January 1, 2006 to January 1, 2016. If the focus is on preparing and enacting laws and regulations to protect intellectual property rights, the extension of the transitional period from 2006 to 2016 for least-developed countries might be sufficient, especially considering that developed countries would be more than willing to provide technical assistance to develop the appropriate legal mechanisms. However, if part of the rationale for the extension is to give least-developed countries ample time to build their technical pharmaceutical base, the time allotted is too short and appears almost arbitrary. These countries have quite underdeveloped manufacturing bases. Given the pre-requisites for establishing a manufacturing base, the planning and time it takes to harmonize those pre-requisites, and the host of challenges least-developed countries face, it will take much longer for them to develop their manufacturing bases than the additional ten years they have been given. Needless to say, proposals to extend the deadline should be expected when 2016 approaches.

African countries must continue to work with other nations, international organizations, NGOs, and multinational corporations that demonstrate interest in Africa's development. At the same time, they should cooperate with pharmaceutical companies that seem to understand the health care crisis in Africa. Although sometimes NGOs and members of civil society do not fully appreciate the advantages of freer trade, African countries need to work with them. NGOs have been quite effective in articulating the negative impact of the TRIPS Agreement for developing countries. They played a pivotal role in the lawsuit that was brought by pharmaceutical companies against South Africa.

Although the lawsuit brought by the 39 pharmaceutical companies was without merit, it was not legal argumentation that brought about the withdrawal of the lawsuit. The lawsuit was dropped because a coalition of NGOs in and outside South Africa brought public attention to the situation, exposing the public health impact of the industry action. (Abbott, 2002: 54)

Finally, it is important to note that access to cheap drugs is only part of the equation for dealing with the health care crisis in Africa. The amendment of the TRIPS Agreement to allow exports of generic drugs, while significant, must be understood in its proper context. For some African countries, the most effective way to improve health care would be the cessation of civil war and the achievement of political stability.

## 4 AGRICULTURE IN THE DOHA ROUND

T HE AGRICULTURAL SECTOR IS THE MOST IMPORTANT economic sector in Africa. It was brought under the WTO in 1995, when the Agreement on Agriculture took effect. The Agreement's objectives are, ostensibly, to increase market access and to reduce domestic support and export subsidies. Given how much leeway countries were given, though, it was clear early on that no significant liberalization could be expected. Further negotiations would have to take place to set the agricultural sector en route to more meaningful liberalization.

The Doha Round of negotiations was launched at the WTO Ministerial Conference in 2001 with this in mind. It was launched with the hope of bringing the agricultural sector into greater harmony with the development objectives of developing countries. Two years earlier, the WTO had failed to produce a round of trade negotiations (in Seattle, Washington, U.S.), in part due to the dissatisfaction of developing countries. The Doha Round was declared to be a development round and, indeed, has come to be known by many as the "Doha Development Round." This round was acceptable to African countries because of its uniquely explicit development agenda and its attention to agriculture.

Trade liberalization has typically been associated with development in an indirect way through its potential positive impact on economic growth. In the Doha Round, trade liberalization was to be guided directly by the development goals of developing countries.

In the world of political rhetoric, it would appear that this was a significant achievement for developing countries.

Moreover, the title – Doha *Development* Round or Doha *Development* Agenda – resonates with the United Nations' ambitions summarized in its declaration on Millennium Development Goals. The language of the Doha Round was clearly pro-developing countries, as suggested by the following excerpt.

International trade can play a major role in the promotion of economic development and the alleviation of poverty. We recognize the need for all our peoples to benefit from the increased opportunities and welfare gains that the multilateral trading system generates. The majority of WTO members are developing countries. We seek to place their needs and interests at the heart of the Work Programme adopted in this Declaration. Recalling the Preamble to the Marrakesh Agreement, we shall continue to make positive efforts designed to ensure that developing countries, and especially the least-developed among them, secure a share in the growth of world trade commensurate with the needs of their economic development. In this context, enhanced market access, balanced rules, and well targeted, sustainably financed technical assistance and capacity-building programmes have important roles to play. (WTO, 2001a: paragraph 2)

Yet the Doha Round of negotiations has suffered a number of setbacks, mainly due to disagreement between developed and developing countries and between developed countries themselves over agricultural subsidies. Even among developing countries, there is often disagreement on what should be done regarding agricultural subsidies in the Organization for Economic Co-operation and Development (OECD) countries. The following discussion will highlight the importance of agriculture to Africa and consider agricultural policies in African countries. The focus will then shift to those agricultural subsidies in OECD countries and how reducing them, in the presence of special and differential treatment extended by these countries, would affect African (and other developing) countries differently.

## THE IMPORTANCE OF AGRICULTURE IN AFRICA

Given its emphasis on development, the Doha Round had to give agriculture special attention (WTO, 2001a: paragraph 13). Agriculture remains the most important sector in most African countries, as data in Table 4.1 suggest. For some countries, such as Burundi, Cameroon, Ethiopia, Guinea-Bissau, Niger, Sierra Leone, Tanzania, and Togo, agriculture contributes at least 40 percent of the GDP. For Benin, Burkina Faso, Burundi, Côte d'Ivoire, Ethiopia, Gambia, Ghana, Guinea-Bissau, Lesotho, Madagascar, Malawi, Rwanda, Sierra Leone, Tanzania, and Uganda, agricultural exports generate at least 50 percent of the foreign exchange. The importance of the agricultural sector is even more pronounced when one considers that 65 percent and 50 percent of the populations of Sub-Saharan Africa and North Africa, respectively, live in the rural areas relying primarily on farming and livestock production. The countryside supplies raw materials to factories and food products to the cities.

While plantations for major commodities can be found, farming in Africa for both food and export crops is generally done on a small scale and is quite labor intensive. Hand tools are still the basic equipment used for farming by most people. The major agricultural exports from Africa are cocoa, coffee, cotton, tea, tobacco, wood, sugar, fish, and spices. These commodities generate income for farmers as well as revenue for the government. Due to various factors, including agro-ecological conditions, the residual impact of colonialism, and agricultural and other policies, African countries tend to specialize in one or two agricultural export commodities. As a result, any sharp decreases or wild swings in the prices or output of agricultural commodities can have a detrimental effect not only on farmers but also on the economies as a whole.

African countries produce a variety of food crops, most of which are non-exportables. Within the limits of soil, the whims of nature, and the spacing and crop husbandry required for the export crop, small farmers normally intercrop the major crop such as coffee

TABLE 4.1  Agriculture in Africa: 2004

| Country/Region | Agriculture as Percent of GDP | Agriculture as Percent of Exports | Agriculture as Percent of Imports |
|---|---|---|---|
| Algeria | 10 | 0 | 24 |
| Angola | 9 | .. | .. |
| Benin | 37 | 90 | 29 |
| Botswana | 3 | 3* | 15* |
| Burkina Faso | 31 | 88 | 13 |
| Burundi | 51 | 93 | 10 |
| Cameroon | 44 | 43 | 20 |
| Cape Verde | 17** | .. | .. |
| Central African Republic | 56 | 27 | 28 |
| Chad | 64 | .. | .. |
| Comoros | 53** | .. | .. |
| Congo, Dem. Rep. of | 58 | .. | .. |
| Congo, Rep. of | 6 | .. | .. |
| Côte d'Ivoire | 22 | 65 | 23 |
| Djibouti | 3** | .. | .. |
| Egypt | 15 | 17 | 27 |
| Equatorial Guinea | 18** | .. | .. |
| Eritrea | 15 | .. | .. |
| Ethiopia | 47 | 88 | 22 |
| Gabon | 8 | 11 | 25 |
| Gambia | 32 | 70 | 40 |
| Ghana | 38 | 82 | 22 |
| Guinea | 25 | 3 | 24 |
| Guinea-Bissau | 63 | .. | .. |
| Kenya | 27 | 52 | 12 |
| Lesotho | 18 | .. | .. |
| Liberia | 43 | .. | .. |
| Madagascar | 29 | 67 | 14 |
| Malawi | 39 | 83 | 14 |
| Mali | 36 | 59 | 18 |
| Mauritania | 18 | 10 | .. |

TABLE 4.1 *(continued)*

| Country/Region | Agriculture as Percent of GDP | Agriculture as Percent of Exports | Agriculture as Percent of Imports |
|---|---|---|---|
| Mauritius | 6 | 27 | 20 |
| Morocco | 16 | 21 | 14 |
| Mozambique | 22 | 25 | 12 |
| Namibia | 10 | 49 | 16 |
| Niger | 40 | 34 | 38 |
| Nigeria | 17 | 0 | 16 |
| Rwanda | 41 | 59 | 16 |
| Sao Tomé and Principe | 29** | .. | .. |
| Senegal | 17 | 38 | 30 |
| Seychelles | 4** | .. | .. |
| Sierra Leone | 53* | 93 | 31 |
| South Africa | 3 | 11 | 6 |
| Sudan | 39 | 16 | 17 |
| Swaziland | 13 | 23 | 20 |
| Tanzania | 45 | 66 | 17 |
| Togo | 41 | 40 | 19 |
| Tunisia | 13 | 12 | 12 |
| Uganda | 32 | 79 | 19 |
| Zambia | 21 | 26 | 8 |
| Zimbabwe | 18 | 47 | 21 |
| Sub-Saharan Africa | 16 | 21 | 13 |
| Middle E. and North Africa | 12 | 7 | 20 |
| South Asia | 21 | 12 | 12 |
| High-income countries | 2 | 8 | 9 |
| World | 4 | 9 | 9 |

*Data are for 2003.
**Data are for 2002 or most recent year available.
*Sources: World Bank (2004, 2005a, 2006).*

with minor food crops and vegetables to minimize the likelihood of a bad return, to have a variety of foods used in traditional cuisine, and to preserve the biological diversity of the land.

While some African countries export food commodities such as maize (corn), wheat, rice, barley, fish, and meat, Africa is clearly a net importer of food. According to the United Nations (2004a), in 2003 Africa exported and imported, respectively, $9.6 billion and $15 billion worth of food products.[1] For a few individual agricultural commodities, Africa exports a noticeable percentage of the world's total volume. These include cocoa (43 percent), tea (16 percent), cotton (17 percent), tobacco (14 percent), coffee (8 percent), and sugar (8 percent). (The percentages given are annual averages of Africa's contribution to the world exports for the period 2000–2003.) In aggregate, however, Africa plays a relatively small role in the world market, contributing less than 4 percent of the world exports of all agricultural products.

Domestically, agriculture is not as important to high-income countries as a source of employment or foreign currency as it is to African countries. In high-income economies, agriculture contributes, on average, about 2 percent of the GDP and about 9 percent of foreign exchange. Likewise, their imports of agricultural products constitute only 9 percent of their total imports. Nonetheless, these seemingly small percentages translate into much more significant percentages in the world market. On average, for the period 2000

---

[1] The food items included are those classified under division 00–06 by the Standard International Trade Classification (SITC):
00 Live animals other than animals in division 03
01 Meat
02 Dairy products
03 Fish
04 Cereal (maize, wheat, rice, barley, etc.)
05 Vegetables and fruits
06 Sugar and honey
The following divisions are not included:
07 Beverages (coffee, cocoa, tea) and spices
08 Feeding stuff for animals

to 2003, two-thirds of world exports for all food items were supplied by high-income countries and two-thirds of world imports were bought by high-income countries.

## AGRICULTURAL POLICIES IN AFRICAN COUNTRIES[2]

African leaders have always proclaimed the urgent need to increase agricultural production to reduce poverty, malnutrition, and reliance on food imports (sometimes described as food insecurity). Following independence, they promised to provide farmers with credits and subsidies. In actual practice, many of these leaders were more concerned about power than about the development and welfare of their people (Ake, 1996). Even where leaders had good intentions, as in Tanzania and Zambia, they failed to provide policies that would effectively help small farmers.

In broad terms, the income distribution impact of these policies was to tax small farmers heavily through price controls on their crops. At the same time, the policies subsidized food consumption by the people in the cities, few in number but politically powerful. Most countries turned the cooperative societies and marketing boards established during the colonial era into legal monopolies (sole legal providers of inputs) and monopsonies (sole legal buyers of crops). In countries that leaned toward socialism, marketing boards became convenient tools for governments to tax farmers. Because any profits earned by marketing boards were collected by the government, producer prices, set by the government, were only a fraction of the already declining world prices. (See the case at the end of this chapter about Benin and cotton exports.)

Marketing boards were notoriously inefficient in providing inputs and collecting crops. Even when crops were collected on time, small farmers would receive promissory notes in lieu of actual payments. These pieces of paper had to be held until such time as both money

---

[2] Some of the discussion in this section is drawn from Mshomba (2000).

and a cashier were available. Because it was not always clear when the money would be available, farmers would go to the payment stations every day with the hope of being paid. Sometimes they had to wait more than a month. Thus, instead of the marketing boards giving agricultural credits as they were designed to do, they were actually borrowing from the farmers and increasing transaction costs to the farmers. Due to inflation, this delay in payment was also an indirect tax on farmers, who were also taxed implicitly through overvalued domestic currencies. Furthermore, because inputs such as seeds, fertilizers, and pesticide were under the monopoly control of the government and inputs for other crops were rarely available, the potential for diversification was limited.

The agricultural sector in African countries went through varying degrees of liberalization in the 1980s and 1990s under structural adjustment programs, allowing farmers to receive a larger fraction of the world price for their products. The New Partnership for Africa's Development (NEPAD), a framework envisioned by the African Union, also has focused on ways to improve the agricultural sector in Africa. NEPAD published a comprehensive development program that highlighted the pivotal role of the private sector in production and marketing for the agricultural sector, with the government primarily playing a supporting role (NEPAD, 2003). It also outlined the importance of the agricultural sector to Africa, impediments to its growth, and measures that could be taken to develop the sector.

Impediments include poor political and economic governance under which the rural poor have little or no voice in decisions affecting their livelihood, technological stagnation, scarcity of managerial and entrepreneurial skills, lack of land ownership by the poor and women (the principal users of land in Africa), the HIV/AIDS epidemic, and political unrest. Measures to enhance the agricultural sector include promoting effective dialogue between governments and farmers, cultivating technical and entrepreneurial capacities in the private sector, orderly land reform that would give women access to and control of land, adequate health and education services, political solutions to civil and cross-border conflicts, a sound macroeconomic environment with liberalized trade and financial markets, an efficient physical infrastructure with increased irrigation capacity, the removal of obstacles to cross-border trade, and improved agricultural research and information dissemination.

The list is long and each country has to determine its own priorities. For example, land reform is a major priority in South Africa. In eastern and southern African countries, the HIV/AIDS epidemic is a serious public health problem in itself, but also a significant challenge to agricultural production and land rights for widows and orphans (Drimie, 2003). Zimbabwe's main challenge has been Mugabe's dictatorial political control and pervasive economic mismanagement, which plunged the country into a horrific macroeconomic nightmare with hyperinflation that reached an astounding rate of 231 *million* percent (annual rate) in July 2008. For some countries, such as Chad, Central African Republic, Democratic Republic of Congo, Côte d'Ivoire, Eritrea, Ethiopia, Sudan, and Uganda, addressing cross-border conflicts and political unrest must be a priority. Whatever the issues, political commitment at the highest levels of government is imperative to formulate and facilitate the implementation of appropriate policies to enhance agricultural development in Africa (FAO, 1996).

Although domestic policies and supply constraints are arguably the most important factors in determining the course of agricultural production in Africa, one cannot underestimate the role of agricultural policies in developed countries. African countries are highly dependent on OECD countries, both as consumers of African exports and suppliers of African imports. About 75 percent and 68 percent of Sub-Saharan Africa's exports and imports, respectively, of agricultural products are destined to and originate from OECD countries (Mshomba, 2000).

The agricultural sector in OECD countries reflects a long history of protection and domestic support. It has been protected by quotas, tariffs, voluntary export restraints, seasonal prohibitions of imports, and so on. The sector has also been supported by a variety of instruments such as price floors, subsidized credit, payments for not growing, and payments to supplement market prices when those prices are below certain target levels, that is, deficiency payments. In addition, the agricultural sector has been supported with export subsidies, which in many countries were a consequence of domestic supports.

### THE AGREEMENT ON AGRICULTURE

The Uruguay Round of GATT and the establishment of the WTO led to the Agreement on Agriculture. The Agreement has three main elements: increasing market access, reducing domestic support, and reducing export subsidies. The implementation period was set to be 1995 to 2000 for developed countries and 1995 to 2004 for developing countries.

From the very beginning, analysts realized that the Agreement on Agriculture left countries with so much leeway that no significant liberalization could be expected. The choice of a base period when protection was relatively high, the use of a simple average to calculate tariff reductions, and the renaming of protection and subsidy instruments meant developed countries could maintain most of their protection at the pre-Uruguay Round level or even raise protection to a higher level. Least-developed countries were hardly required to do anything except bind their tariffs at whatever level they chose. Nonetheless, the Agreement on Agriculture was greeted with enthusiasm because it brought the agricultural sector under the WTO, setting it en route to trade liberalization in the future.

### THE DOHA ROUND

The Doha Round, launched in 2001, was envisioned to move the agricultural sector on a trajectory toward more meaningful trade liberalization.

Building on the work carried out to date and without prejudging the outcome of the negotiations we commit ourselves to comprehensive negotiations aimed at: substantial improvements in market access; reductions of, with a view to phasing out, all forms of export subsidies; and substantial reductions in trade-distorting domestic support. We agree that special and differential treatment for developing countries shall be an integral part of all elements of the negotiations and shall be embodied in the schedules of concessions and commitments and as appropriate in the rules and disciplines to be negotiated, so as to be operationally effective and to enable developing countries to effectively take account of their development needs, including food security and rural development. (WTO, 2001a: paragraph 13)

If the expectation was that attention to agriculture would reduce some of the controversies between developing and developed countries, it has been a disappointment. Considering the negotiations that have taken place since the Doha Round was launched, it appears that eventually the outcome will be some watered-down commitments and, again, promises for further liberalization in the future. To put the discussion in context, an examination of some of the elements contained in the initial draft proposal will be helpful (WTO, 2003a). The draft is referred to as the Harbinson draft proposal, after Stuart Harbinson, who was the chair of the WTO agricultural negotiations group, Stuart Harbinson. This is not to suggest that the final agreement (when it is achieved) will necessarily resemble the initial draft; moreover, the draft has already been revised several times, which was to be expected. Nonetheless, the Harbinson draft proposal raises certain important discussion points that will persist no matter what the final version includes.

Table 4.2 has a summary of some of the key elements in the draft. On aggregate, they reveal that developed countries are expected to have deeper and faster liberalization, and developing countries are to continue to receive special and differential treatment. Developed countries are expected, with caution, to open their markets to products with long-standing preferences. For example, Mauritius has

TABLE 4.2 Summary of Key Elements of the Harbinson Draft Proposal

| Subject | Trade Barrier | Liberalization | Implementation Period | Base |
|---|---|---|---|---|
| Tariffs (t) | t > 90% | DC | Reduce by a simple average of 60% Minimum reduction per tariff line – 45% | 5 years | Final bound tariffs under Uruguay Round |
| | 90% ≥ t > 15% | | Reduce by a simple average of 50% Minimum reduction per tariff line – 35% | | |
| | 15% ≥ t | | Reduce by a simple average of 40% Minimum reduction per tariff line – 15% | | |
| | Tariff affecting long-standing preferences | | Three-year grace period; Reductions as above | 8 years | |

| | DVC | 10 years | Final bound tariffs under Uruguay Round |
|---|---|---|---|
| t > 120% | Reduce by a simple average of 40% <br> Minimum reduction per tariff line –30% | | |
| 120% ≥ t > 60% | Reduce by a simple average of 35% <br> Minimum reduction per tariff line – 25% | | |
| 60% ≥ t > 20% | Reduce by a simple average of 30% <br> Minimum reduction per tariff line – 20% | | |
| 20% ≥ t | Reduce by a simple average of 25% <br> Minimum reduction per tariff line – 5% | | |
| Tariff on Special Products | Reduce by a simple average of 10% | | |

*(continued)*

TABLE 4.2 *(continued)*

| Subject | Trade Barrier | Liberalization | | Implementation Period | Base |
|---------|---------------|----------------|---|----------------------|------|
| | | | Minimum reduction per tariff line – 5% | | |
| Tariff Quota Volume* | At least 5% | DC | At least 10% of domestic consumption | 5 years | 1999/2001 |
| | Varies | DVC | At least 6.6% of domestic consumption | | 1999/2001 |
| | Tariff quota on SPs | DVC | Not required to expand tariff quota volumes | | |
| Export Competition | | | | | |
| Export Subsidies | | DC | Reduce spending by 50% | 5 years | Final bound levels under Uruguay Round |
| | | | Remaining 50% eliminated | 9 years | |
| | | DVC | Reduce spending by 50% | 10 years | Final bound levels under Uruguay Round |

| Domestic Support | Aggregate Measure of Support (AMS) | DC | Remaining 50% eliminated | 12 years | Final bound levels under Uruguay Round |
| --- | --- | --- | --- | --- | --- |
| | | | Reduce by 60% | 5 years | |
| | | DVC | Reduce by 40% | 10 years | Final bound levels under Uruguay Round |

DC, developed countries; DVC, developing countries; SPs, special products.

*A tariff quota volume of at least 5 percent implies that imports equivalent to at least 5 percent of domestic consumption are allowed in at tariffs low enough to compete with domestic producers.

*Sources:* http://www.wto.org/English/tratop_e/agric_e/negoti_modistdraft_e.htm#thepaper and http://www.agtradepolicy.org/output/resource/NEGOTIATIONS_ON_AGRICULTUREFIRST_DRAFT_OF_M_2.pdf.

been a long-time beneficiary of special access to the EC market. Because sugar exports account for at least 20 percent of Mauritius' merchandise exports, Mauritius would be able to ask the EC to delay liberalization of the sugar market by three years. In addition, the EC would be encouraged (not required, just as preferential treatment is not an obligation) to assist Mauritius in diversifying its economy, presumably away from its reliance on sugar.

Developing countries would have the privilege and flexibility to declare some of the agricultural products to be "special products." The selection would be based on the importance of those products for food security, livelihood security, and rural development, as determined by developing countries themselves. Developing countries would have additional transitional periods or no obligations at all (especially for least-developed countries) to liberalize their markets or reduce production support for those products. Another element of special treatment in the proposal is a provision for a "special safeguard mechanism." This provision could potentially allow developing countries to impose tariff rates above the bound rates to curb import surges for some agricultural crops deemed to be sensitive.

It is clear that it will be very difficult to forge a meaningful commitment to liberalize the agricultural sector. For example, what practical criteria are to be used to determine eligibility for "special products" or a "special safeguard mechanism"? The proposed criteria, that is, food security, livelihood criteria, and rural development, could be subject to very broad interpretations that could result in every product being given the status of "special." Consider this description of "livelihood security" proposed by the G-33 in 2005[3]:

---

[3]  G-33 is a group of over forty developing countries in the WTO that have made their voices heard on the issues of special products and a special safeguard mechanism. Other major "groupings" in agriculture negotiations are the EC, the United States, G-10, G-20, the Cairns Group, the ACP Group, the African Group, and the LDC group. A number of African countries belong to the last three groupings and the G-33 group (Chomthongdi, 2005).

Livelihood security relates to the adequate and sustainable access to resources or assets (i.e. education, land, capital, social networks, etc.) by households and individuals to realize a means of living. Moreover, alternative employment opportunities are simply not available to illiterate, aged and/or unskilled people, and agriculture presents almost the only option, including in developing countries with high levels of rural illiteracy as well as those which do not have adequate safety-nets. The situation becomes aggravated in the case of perennial crops as opposed to annual crops.

Another crucial characteristic that defines livelihood security in developing countries is that low income or resource poor, disadvantaged or uncompetitive farmers have very low risk thresholds, and it is not possible for them to shift from their traditional product to another easily since this involves both considerable resources as well as high levels of risk. Therefore, it is not so much a question of the importance of a particular product in the total production structure in agriculture, but the characteristic of farmers producing the product that drive agricultural policy in developing countries in this case. (G-33, 2005: 2)

While this description has merit, it would fit all agricultural products in Africa – those produced by subsistence farmers and also those produced by big farmers who employ unskilled labor. G-33 has proposed to make at least 20 percent of all agricultural tariff lines eligible for the special products status. According to the WTO Secretariat, that would allow some developing countries to shield more than 90 percent of their farm products from Doha tariff cuts (ICTSD, 2006). G-33, the African Group, the ACP Group, and the LDC Group want provisions that would make all agricultural goods eligible for the special safeguard mechanism (ACP, 2005; G-33, 2005a; WTO, 2006a). This proposal not only puts African countries at odds with the United States and the EC, but also with other developing countries that view this proposal, if accepted, as a threat to South-South trade.

The difficulty in attaining effective commitments can be appreciated even if the discussion is limited to the dilemma faced by African countries and the seemingly contradictory positions they take.

African countries want OECD countries to eliminate agricultural export subsidies; those subsidies depress the world prices of agricultural commodities from which the African countries derive their foreign exchange. At the same time, African countries are worried about a proposal that would lead to an increase in their food import bill. They also want to be equipped with the flexibility afforded by a special safeguard mechanism, so they can increase protection to limit imports of agricultural crops. In addition, they want preferential treatment preserved for their exports to OECD countries, although some of the preferential treatment is linked to the OECD agricultural export subsidies. The following statement by the African Union captures some of the dilemma and contradictions:

While the current "Doha Development Round" provides an opportunity to reduce distortions in international agricultural markets through further strengthening of disciplines on trade distorting support and protection, appropriate account needs to be taken of the development and food security needs of our people through special and differential treatment under trade rules. Our countries need flexibility and policy space under WTO multilateral trade rules, to choose the most effective strategy appropriate to our situation. The effective and expeditious reduction in subsidies by developed countries in cotton, sugar and all other commodities of interest to developing countries would be a welcome development, while taking into account the interest of preference receiving countries. (African Union, 2005: paragraph 14)

This apparent dilemma results from the different economic interests among African countries. For example, South Africa, a net exporter of food products, is most interested in the reduction of subsidies in OECD countries. That is also the position of cotton-exporting African countries, as demonstrated by a campaign against OECD cotton subsidies launched jointly by Benin, Burkina Faso, Chad, and Mali in 2003. Net food-importing least-developed countries are uneasy about the potential increase in food prices. Flexibility to increase protection is like an insurance policy – every country would like to have it. Countries like Burkina Faso, Malawi,

Mauritius, and Mozambique do not want to lose preferential access to the EU high prices for their sugar exports, even though this preference is tied to OECD export subsidies that hurt sugar producers in other developing countries.

As the above discussion suggests, a dilemma exists even within individual countries, depending on what a country exports and imports. For example, a country like Burkina Faso wants OECD subsidies to cotton growers to be removed. At the same time, it wants preferential access preserved for its sugar exports to the EU market, even though that would imply subsidies to EU sugar growers would continue.

In making their proposals, African countries seem to want all their needs – collectively and as individual countries – to be addressed. Sometimes it appears African countries are asking for customized commitments that would fit each one of them perfectly. They seem to want commitments that would bring benefits without entailing any sacrifice because, as the argument typically goes, African countries are poor and have suffered enough already from the unfair global trading system.

Given how African countries were steered to signing agreements at the conclusion of the Uruguay Round without fully understanding their ramifications, it is easy to understand their current assertiveness, apprehension, and even defiance. However, their contradictory demands (or their desire for everything at once) will make it difficult for an effective commitment to be reached. It is important to note that it would be inaccurate to conclude from the discussion here that African countries are the main detractors of the negotiations. One would have to study carefully all groupings to be able to make any such determination, something that is beyond the scope of this study. Likewise, a full analysis of all positions taken by African countries would be unwieldy and lead to a discussion that goes in circles. Instead, the focus in the discussion below is on agricultural subsidies in OECD countries, in the context of preferential treatment for African countries.

## OECD SUBSIDIES AND SPECIAL AND DIFFERENTIAL
## TREATMENT

The history and size of agricultural subsidies in OECD countries are well documented in many studies.[4] In 2002 and 2003, total OECD agricultural support was $310 billion and $350 billion, respectively (OECD, 2005). During the Uruguay Round of GATT, a great deal of attention was given to the negative impact of these subsidies on African countries (and other developing countries), because they depress world prices of agricultural products. Reducing agricultural subsidies would benefit African countries that export agricultural products. At the same time, however, net food-importing countries would see their food bills rise and African countries with preferential market access would face erosion in the margin of preference. Some provisions were included in the Harbinson proposal to address these concerns of net food-importing countries and the potential loss by African countries with preferential market access. Nonetheless, these concerns did not receive substantial attention.

More than ten years after the establishment of the WTO, OECD subsidies are still a major concern for African countries. However, there is growing acknowledgment that some of these subsidies may actually be good for some African countries, especially when linked to preferential access extended to African exports. This acknowledgment is the result of a closer look at the operation of subsidies and their impact; it is also the result of some relatively new preferential arrangements that favor African countries. Two in particular stand out – the U.S. African Growth and Opportunity Act (AGOA) and the EU's Everything But Arms (EBA) initiative. AGOA took effect in May 2000 and increased U.S. openness to African products in a preferential way beyond the preferential treatment given under the Generalized System of Preferences (GSP). EBA took effect in 2001, removing quotas and tariffs on all products

---

[4]  See, for example, OECD (2004) and Sanderson (1997).

(except weapons and ammunition) coming from forty-nine least-developed countries, including thirty-four African countries.

Because of these and other preferential arrangements and the fact that least-developed countries are net food-importing countries, some economists find it a fallacy to assert that agricultural subsidies of developed countries hurt poor countries. Panagariya (2005), building on Bhagwati and Panagariya (2002), makes many important points that warrant a lengthy review and analysis. Panagariya (2005) lists and debunks what he considers to be fallacies associated with protection and export subsidies in developed countries and their impact on least-developed countries. These are:

Fallacy 1: Agricultural border protection and subsidies are largely a developed country phenomenon.

Fallacy 2: Developed-country agricultural subsidies and protection hurt the poorest developing countries most.[5]

Fallacy 3: Developed-country subsidies and protection hurt poor, rural households in the poorest countries.

Fallacy 4: Developed-country agricultural protection and subsidies constitute the principal barrier to the development of the poorest developing countries.

Fallacy 5: Agricultural protection reflects [a] double standard and hypocrisy on the part of the developed countries.

Fallacy 6: What the donor countries give with one hand (aid), they take away with the other (farm subsidies). In effect, the benefits of aid to the poorest countries are more than offset by the losses from the developed-country subsidies. (Panagariya, 2005: 1278–1279)

Panagariya astutely debunks these fallacies step by step and two main points emerge. One is that protection (applied tariff rates and coverage) in agriculture is higher in developing countries than it

---

[5]  Stiglitz and Charlton (2005: 47) are among those who argue that agricultural subsidies in OECD countries hurt the poorest developing countries the most. For an insightful review of Stiglitz and Charlton (2005), see Lawrence (2007).

is in developed countries. Second, agricultural subsidies in developed countries help, instead of hurting (Fallacy 2), least-developed countries. This second point needs to be explained. However, first consider a short specific comment on the first fallacy and a general comment on all the fallacies.

Regarding the first fallacy, various sources would confirm that, in general, developed countries are relatively less protectionist than developing countries.[6] However, it is important to point out that policies of developed countries (and a few developing countries) have an impact on world prices, whereas most developing countries are price takers for almost all products. Moreover, some trade barriers in least-developed countries are not instituted primarily as trade barriers, but rather as sources of government revenues. In addition, developed countries have been fervent promoters of free trade, and they have thus put their trade barriers in the limelight. For these reasons, or perhaps simply because rich countries are expected to set a good example for freer trade, developed countries are usually held to higher standards when it comes to trade barriers and subsidies. An analogy might be how multinational corporations might be criticized for paying low wages in developing countries, while local firms in those countries might get away with paying even lower wages.

Part of what Panagariya (2005) is responding to is the exaggeration that has become common even among academics, not to mention international institutions and NGOs whose presentations include campaign-style advocacy. In an environment where there are so many voices and where some groups focus on narrow issues, exaggeration becomes a way one hopes to be heard, whether through catchy titles, sound bites, or selective data. For example, what Panagariya presents as the fourth fallacy cannot be taken seriously, especially when applied to all least-developed

---

[6] See, for example, the levels of tariff barriers for various countries in any issue of *World Development Indicators* published by the World Bank.

countries. This fallacy is an exaggeration, not unlike focusing on any one of the following as if it were the principal barrier to development in Africa as a whole: HIV/AIDS, malaria, the debt crisis, poverty, corruption, structural adjustment programs, the legacy of colonialism, or civil wars and cross-border conflicts.

Regarding what Panagariya (2005) lists as the second fallacy, that developed-country agricultural subsidies and protection hurt the poorest developing countries, he asserts that in fact such subsidies help them. How could this be if agricultural subsidies depress world prices of agricultural products? The answer has to do with export subsidies (an important subset of agricultural subsidies) and their impact both on the domestic (OECD) market price and on the preferential market access that poor countries have to those domestic (OECD) markets.

In effect, an export subsidy is a monetary reward for selling a product in the world market. In the subsidizing country, export subsidies cause an increase in domestic production and exports. Because sellers are subsidized only for the volume they export, these subsidies also cause an increase in the domestic price of the relevant product. That is, the domestic price ends up being the sum of the world price and the subsidy rate. If the subsidizing country or region is large, as are the United States, the EU, Japan, and, of course, developed countries in aggregate, the increases in exports cause the world price to fall. To prevent an influx of imports (into the subsidizing country) that are cheaper at the world price, usually an export subsidy is accompanied by trade protection.

Figure 4.1 illustrates the impact of an export subsidy by a large country.[7] Panel (A) represents a large country. SS and DD are initial domestic supply and demand lines, respectively. Panel (W) represents the world market. EX and IM are initial export supply

---

[7] This is just an illustration. In reality, the subsidizing country and the rest of the world would engage in both exporting and importing due to product differentiation, varying harvesting seasons, and transportation costs.

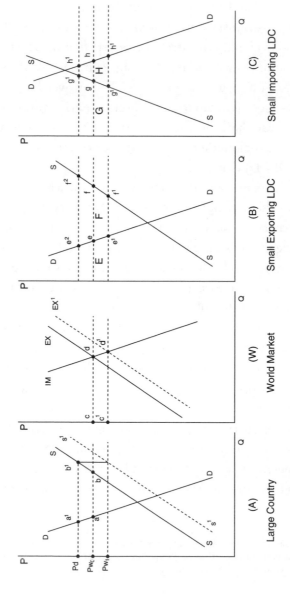

FIGURE 4.1 Impact of an Export Subsidy by a Large Country

and import demand lines, respectively. Panel (B) represents a small exporting least-developed country. SS and DD are domestic supply and demand lines, respectively. Panel (C) represents a small importing least-developed country. SS and DD are domestic supply and demand lines, respectively. Under free trade (no subsidies), the world price is $Pw_0$. (This and other prices are marked on panel (A); they apply to all the panels.) Country A exports a-b, country B exports e-f, and country C imports g-h. The world volume of exports equals the volume of imports, c-d. A subsidy by country A causes the supply line in country A to shift to $S^1$ $S^1$ and the world export supply to shift to $EX^1$. The world price falls to $Pw_1$ and the domestic price in country A increases to Pd. The difference between Pd and $Pw_1$ is the subsidy rate. Country A's exports increase to $a^1$-$b^1$; country B's exports decrease to $e^1$-$f^1$; and country C's imports increase to $g^1$-$h^1$. The world volume of exports (imports) increases to $c^1$-$d^1$.

In country B, consumer surplus increases by area E and producer surplus decreases by the sum of areas E and F, resulting in a net loss of area F.[8] In country C, consumer surplus increases by the sum of areas G and H and producer surplus decreases by area G, resulting in a net gain of area H. Thus, net importers of food products, like country C, benefit from country A's export subsidy. If country A removes the subsidy, country C will be hurt.

However, how about a net importing country that would become a net exporter when subsidies are removed? This would be the case for countries that have been pushed by the subsidies to become importers. Figure 4.2 shows what happens to a small country that is a net importer because of subsidies in developed countries. When

---

[8]   Consumer surplus is the difference between the maximum amount consumers are willing and able to pay for a given product and the actual amount that they pay. Geometrically, it is the area below the demand line and above the price line. Producer surplus is the difference between the amount sellers are paid for a given product and the minimum acceptable amount. It is the area above the supply line and below the price line.

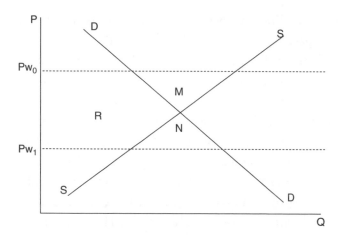

FIGURE 4.2 Impact on a Small Country of Removing Export Subsidies in OECD Countries

subsidies are removed, the world price increases from $Pw_1$ to $Pw_0$. Producer surplus increases by areas R and M. Consumer surplus decreases by areas R and N. If area M is greater than area N, the country will experience a net gain.

For least-developed countries, however, Panagariya (2005) dismisses the likelihood that those that were net importers would become net exporters. For those countries, removal of subsidies would actually *reduce* their export price, rather than increase it. The explanation for this seemingly counterintuitive occurrence is that under the EU's Everything But Arms (EBA) initiative, least-developed countries have preferential access to the EU market at the domestic EU price. In other words, when least-developed countries export their agricultural products to the EU, they receive the high domestic prices that prevail in the EU. The same could be said for ACP countries and their preferential market access under the Cotonou Agreement. There is an overlap between least-developed countries and ACP countries, and usually countries that qualify for both EBA and the Cotonou Agreement choose the most favorable preferential scheme.

To illustrate this point using Figure 4.1, countries B and C would be allowed to export to country A at its domestic price, Pd. In this scenario, country B would export more, $e^2$-$f^2$. Country C would still not be able to compete successfully in country A's market. Note that removing subsidies would reduce the price in country A from Pd to $Pw_0$. Panagariya's conclusion is that if a least-developed country (country C) cannot export to a subsidizing country at that high price of Pd when subsidies are in place, it certainly would not be able to export at the lower price of $Pw_0$. Panagariya concludes that least-developed countries would lose from a reduction or elimination of subsidies, whether the least-developed country is a net importer or a net exporter. In either case, their terms of trade deteriorate. A least-developed country that is a net exporter would see its export price falling from Pd to $Pw_0$. In fact, it can even be pushed from being a net exporter to being a net importer. A least-developed country that is a net importer will see its import price rising from $Pw_1$ to $Pw_0$.

Some African countries benefit from OECD subsidies on two fronts. As discussed above, given preferential market access, they export their agricultural products to the subsidizing countries at a higher price (that is, the domestic price in the subsidizing country) than the free trade price. In addition, they import food at a lower price than what the free trade price would have been. Removing OECD subsidies would, therefore, be a double strike against them.

African countries (most of which are net food-importers) have always raised concerns regarding the erosion of preferential margins and increases in their food import bill. For example, in the Cairo Declaration, the African Union (2005a) emphasized:

[t]he urgent implementation of the Marrakech Decision on NFIDCs [net food-importing developing countries] and LDCs [least-developed countries] and a clear reflection of the special and differential treatment component of any disciplines to be developed on export credits in accordance with paragraph 4 of the Decision. (3)

Paragraph 4 of the Marrakech Decision declares that:

*Ministers* further *agree* to ensure that any agreement relating to agricultural export credits makes appropriate provision for differential treatment in favour of least-developed and net food-importing developing countries. http://www.wto.org/english/docs_e/legal_e/35-dag_e.htm

For a real-world example of his point that OECD subsidies benefit some exports from some developing countries, Panagariya (2005) cites the sugar dispute case in the WTO against the EC that was brought and won by Brazil. (Similar cases against the EC were brought by Australia and Thailand.) Complainants argued that export subsidies provided by the EC exceeded subsidy commitments. The EC imports raw sugar from ACP countries at the EC's internal high price, refines it, and re-exports it with the help of export subsidies.[9] ACP countries saw the WTO ruling as hurting their interests. Gibb (2004) estimates that southern Africa as a region receives a net transfer of about €220 to €266 million a year from the EC's preferential sugar program.[10] (€1 was, on average, equivalent to $1.25 in 2004.) Mauritius and Swaziland, the greatest beneficiaries in Gibb's study, receive an income transfer equal to 5 percent of their gross national income. The WTO ruling and EC reforms became effective July 2006. The reforms will lead to a reduction of the guaranteed price for ACP countries for unrefined brown sugar by 36 percent by 2010, from €632 to €404 per ton (Haley, 2006; Harman, 2006).

Another example that highlights welfare gains to African countries from agricultural subsidies in the EU is the banana case, discussed in Chapter 2. The EC's import regime, which favored ACP countries, was found to be inconsistent with the EC's obligations.

---

[9] For more detail, see Gibb (2004).
[10] The countries included in the study are Angola, Democratic Republic of Congo, Malawi, Mauritius, Mozambique, South Africa, Swaziland, Tanzania, Zambia, and Zimbabwe.

In that regard, the African Union (2005a) made the following appeal in its Cairo Declaration.

We note that an arbitration procedure is going on in the WTO, initiated by non-African countries that are banana producers. This procedure, which doesn't fully associate African countries, may lead to an enormous loss of market shares and advantages hitherto enjoyed by African countries [in] traditional European markets. As a result of this situation, we are strongly requesting that the rights of African countries be preserved and their market shares be protected. (African Union, 2005a: 5)

To summarize, Bhagwati and Panagariya (2002) and Panagariya (2005) conclude that least-developed countries benefit from agricultural subsidies in OECD countries. Unless one were willing to argue that not only is their conclusion wrong but African countries *also* got it all wrong, their conclusion cannot be dismissed as theoretical conjecture or economic lunacy, as labeled by Sharma (2005). OECD subsidies and preferential access for least-developed countries' exports give least-developed countries a competitive advantage. When OECD subsidies are reduced, the margin of preference for least-developed countries decreases. Such acknowledgment is important because it might lead to the formation of effective programs to assist least-developed countries when OECD countries are compelled to reduce agricultural subsidies.

It is important to know what Bhagwati and Panagariya (2002) and Panagariya (2005) are not saying. They are not advocating for subsidies. Instead, they are pointing out the impact on least-developed countries (and ACP countries) of removing agricultural subsidies in developed countries, regardless of whether the least-developed countries (and ACP countries) are net-importing or net-exporting countries. Nor are they saying that the removal of those subsidies would hurt all developing countries. In fact, they make it clear that middle-income countries with comparative advantage in agriculture, such as South Africa, would benefit from a reduction of subsidies in developed countries. Gibb (2004) estimates that South

Africa loses €39 to €75 million a year from the EC sugar program. In addition, Panagariya (2005) does not argue that broader liberalization of all merchandise (agricultural and manufactured products) would hurt least-developed countries. With broader liberalization, the negative impact of the reduction of subsidies discussed above would be offset by an increase in exports of non-manufactured products (Anderson et al., 2006).

OECD SUBSIDIES FROM A LONG-TERM PERSPECTIVE

As sound as the argument might be that some African countries benefit from the agricultural policies of developed countries, it has its limitations, especially in the long run. Important considerations in evaluating the long-term benefits of those subsidies include: (1) their long-term impact on demand; (2) the goal to diversify African economies; (3) food security; (4) the uncertainty of OECD policies; (5) the cost of compliance and of being preferred; (6) the ability to utilize preferential treatment; (7) building coalitions with other developing countries; and (8) the cotton case.

*Long-term Impact on Demand*

Although OECD subsidies (coupled with preferential treatment) benefit least-developed countries in the short run, they may cause long-term structural changes that are damaging to least-developed countries. The high price of sugar in developed countries, for example, contributed to rapid substitution of high fructose corn syrup for sugar, especially in the 1970s and 1980s (Barros, 1992; Moss and Schmits, 2002). The world demand for sugar in developed countries did not grow as fast as it would have, had there been no sugar subsidy programs in the United States and the EU. Although currently exports of sugar from least-developed countries may have preferential access to developed countries at a particular price (Pd in Figure 4.1), this price might be lower than what the free trade price would have been, had the sugar market in developed countries never been protected.

## Diversification

The long-term goal of all African countries since independence has been to diversify the agricultural sector and the economy in general. Various initiatives have been tried to achieve this goal, including import substitution policies and provisions for diversification under international commodity agreements. Yet at the same time, African countries seem to sacrifice the goal of diversification for the short-term benefits of preferential treatment for a given commodity. This is not an indictment of preferential treatment *per se*, but rather of its utilization by preference-receiving countries. When utilized strategically and with a long-term vision, preferential treatment can be used successfully to move a country toward diversification, as Mauritius has done with preferential access to the EU and the United States. (See Subramanian and Roy, 2003.)

However, for most African countries, preferential treatment often creates complacency and dependency on a single commodity or on the single use of a commodity. This is not only the case in African countries, but in other developing countries as well. After depending on sugar exports for centuries, it took the EC's forced reforms of the sugar industry for Jamaica to have a serious strategic plan to diversify into producing a variety of products from sugar, such as molasses, rum, and ethanol. While such diversification incurs high short-term costs and may even require financial aid, it creates a relatively more stable economy. According to the head of the Jamaica Office of the British Department of International Development, "the EU sugar reforms could end up as positive for the region, with Caribbean countries eventually developing more robust, diverse economies" (Harman, 2006).

Preferential treatment seems to create political inertia regarding diversification. Therefore, the benefits of preferential treatment for African countries must be adjusted by the long-run costs of delayed diversification (attributed to preferential treatment) to the extent that diversification reduces the vulnerability of African economies to exogenous shocks.[11] In a study of twenty African countries, Berthélemy and Söderking (2001) show that diversification is an important determinant of long-term growth.

## Food Security

Another long-term goal of African countries has been food security. A country is considered to have attained food security when its population has effective access to enough food to meet daily nutritional requirements. The food supply may be achieved through domestic production and/or imports, depending on various factors that determine the opportunity cost of food production.

Table 4.3 shows the value of food exports and imports for 2003 for African countries for which data were available. The food items included are those classified under division 00–06 by the Standard International Trade Classification (SITC): live animals, meat and meat preparations, dairy products and eggs, fish, cereals and cereal preparations, vegetables and fruits, and sugar and honey. Beverages (coffee, cocoa, tea) and spices are not included. It is clear that most African countries are net importers of food. Only ten of forty countries listed in the table had their value of food exports exceed the value of food imports. Of course, being a net food importer (or a net food exporter) does not necessarily mean that the country is doing poorly (or well) in terms of food security.

However, domestic policies for food security always include efforts to increase domestic production so as to decrease dependency on

---

[11] In computing the economic vulnerability index, UNCTAD uses the following indicators which are proxies for the level of economic diversification: the share of manufacturing and modern services in GDP, the merchandise export concentration index, the agricultural production instability index, and the goods and services instability index (UNCTAD, 2005: 9).

TABLE 4.3  Food Exports and Imports: 2003 or Latest Year
for Which Data Were Available (Millions of Dollars)

| Country | Exports | Imports | (Exports/ Imports)* 100 |
|---|---|---|---|
| Algeria | 0 | 2241 | 0 |
| Benin | 61 | 138 | 44 |
| Botswana | 137 | 337 | 41 |
| Burkina Faso | 15 | 86 | 17 |
| Burundi | 2 | 9 | 22 |
| Cameroon | 75 | 306 | 25 |
| Cape Verde | 0 | 51 | 0 |
| Central African Republic | 0 | 17 | 0 |
| Comoros | 0 | 13 | 0 |
| Côte d'Ivoire | 397 | 608 | 65 |
| Egypt | 427 | 1885 | 23 |
| Eritrea | 36 | 138 | 26 |
| Ethiopia | 62 | 465 | 13 |
| Gambia | 5 | 50 | 10 |
| Ghana | 128 | 408 | 31 |
| Kenya | 385 | 207 | 186 |
| Lesotho | 9 | 124 | 7 |
| Madagascar | 193 | 104 | 186 |
| Malawi | 126 | 47 | 268 |
| Mali | 5 | 106 | 5 |
| Mauritius | 430 | 315 | 137 |
| Morocco | 1678 | 865 | 194 |
| Mozambique | 114 | 100 | 114 |
| Namibia | 447 | 127 | 352 |
| Niger | 53 | 108 | 49 |
| Nigeria | 0 | 945 | 0 |
| Rwanda | 0 | 21 | 0 |
| Sao Tomé and Principe | 0 | 8 | 0 |
| Senegal | 310 | 480 | 65 |

(*continued*)

TABLE 4.3 *(continued)*

| Country | Exports | Imports | (Exports/ Imports)*100 |
|---|---|---|---|
| Seychelles | 14 | 40 | 35 |
| Sierra Leone | 1 | 62 | 2 |
| South Africa | 2084 | 430 | 485 |
| Sudan | 183 | 321 | 57 |
| Swaziland | 107 | 108 | 99 |
| Tanzania | 285 | 158 | 180 |
| Togo | 28 | 61 | 46 |
| Tunisia | 267 | 426 | 63 |
| Uganda | 36 | 130 | 28 |
| Zambia | 52 | 126 | 41 |
| Zimbabwe | 219 | 133 | 165 |

*Source*: United Nations (2004 and 2004a).

food imports. Because we live in a world of uncertainties, no country wants to be totally dependent on imports when it comes to food, no matter what trade theory might suggest. India is certainly an example of a country that has been consistent and arguably successful in its initiatives toward self-sufficiency in food. African countries face a conflict between the short-term benefits of cheap food imports and the long-term benefits of increased domestic food production.

Net food-importing countries are concerned that elimination of agricultural subsidies in OECD countries will increase their food import bill and endanger their food security, which is already tenuous to begin with. At the same time, they want to achieve food security that is less dependent on imports (IFPRI, 2004). In 1996, speaking on the need to formulate a framework for food security in Africa, Vijay Makhan, Assistant Secretary-General of the Organization of African Unity (OAU), remarked:[12]

[12] The OAU was established in 1963. It was succeeded by the African Union in 2002.

More recently, the development and production of native grains have been further undermined by the importation and distribution at subsidized prices of millions of tons of cereals, particularly rice and wheat. The promotion of native grains must be the cornerstone of our food security strategy because such grains are better adapted to the environmental and ecological conditions, as well as to the vagaries of weather in Africa. (FAO, 1996)

The short-term benefits of importing food at a lower price because of export subsidies in OECD countries must be weighed against the long-term benefits of increased domestic food production and food security. This is especially important because the majority of African workers are subsistence farmers. An increase in food production will translate directly into increased calorie intake.

## The Uncertainty of OECD Policies

There is uncertainty associated with OECD policies that have been producing these cheap food imports. The duration of, and the conditions and eligibility for, preferential treatment can change haphazardly. The same can be said of the magnitude of preference, given sporadic changes in the most favored nation tariffs and the trade agreements OECD countries establish with other countries. As such, long-term investment planning in African countries based on preferential treatment is often difficult.

No matter how OECD subsidies are structured, they are primarily meant to benefit domestic producers in OECD countries. The fact that net food-importing countries benefit from these subsidies is only incidental. Even preferential treatment that has benefited ACP countries through their sugar exports to the EU, for example, is a by-product of a system to support domestic producers. Domestic pressure will continue to be the dominant factor in determining how, how much, and how long developed countries continue to subsidize their farmers. African countries must therefore work to be less dependent on a system whose future they do not control.

## The Cost of Compliance and of Being Preferred

To qualify for preferential treatment, goods must be certified by authorities agreed upon by respective trading partners. The fees and transaction costs involved are part of the reason some exporters simply do not care to go through the process necessary for their products to be certified. Complicating the situation is the heterogeneity of preference schemes offered by different countries and the complexity of multiple preferences offered by individual countries or regions. For example, for African exports to the EU, there is the GSP program, the Cotonou Agreement (which evolved into Economic Partnership Agreements), the EBA, and some individual commodity protocols from which to choose. Exporters must constantly calculate which preference works to their best advantage at what time of the year and for which commodities. Brenton and Ikezuki (2005) highlight the complexity of the EU preference scheme for ACP countries for fruits and vegetables; the scheme varies depending on the time of the year.

For those who are able to take advantage of preferential access to markets in the OECD countries, their benefits cannot be measured by simply taking the difference between the preferential price and the world price. The cost of compliance must be factored in; otherwise, the benefits of preferential treatment will be exaggerated. Moreover, some of the preference premium is captured by importers in OECD countries, depending on their monopsony power (Olarreaga and Özden, 2005).

Asking for preference treatment involves other costs in terms of the diplomatic resources that must be utilized for this purpose. Moreover, in a giver-recipient relationship, the recipient incurs the intangible costs of weakened bargaining power in other areas of negotiations. It also weakens the recipient's privilege to bring cases against the preference-giving countries, as discussed in Chapter 2.

## The Ability to Utilize Preferential Treatment

African countries are often unable to take advantage of preferential treatment due to domestic supply constraints, institutional constraints, and conditions imposed by the preference-giving countries, such as rules regarding country of origin. Likewise, non-trade barriers, such as unnecessarily stringent sanitary and phytosanitary standards and labeling requirements, limit the amount of African exports that could potentially receive preferential treatment (Mutume, 2006). For example, the EU applies higher aflatoxins standards than the ones set by the Codex Alimentarius Commission (CAC), a joint commission of the Food and Agriculture Organization (FAO) and the WHO. A study by Otsuki et al. (2001) finds that the EU standard decreases African exports of cereals, dried fruits, and nuts by 64 percent or $670 million compared to the standard set by the CAC. It should be noted that Otsuki et al. (2001) suggest that the EU standards would reduce health risks by only 1.4 deaths per billion people per year. Fox and Vorley (2004) indicate that higher EU food safety standards that were to be enforced in 2005 had the potential of reducing Kenya's annual exports of fruits and vegetables by $400 million (€325 million).

## Building Coalitions With Other Developing Countries

Not all African countries benefit from the preferential access of the EBA or AGOA. Likewise, among other developing countries, not all benefit from these programs either. Although targeted to poor countries, these programs have the potential to weaken the coalitions of African countries in particular and developing countries in general.

Given complaints against OECD agricultural subsidies, one would have thought that African countries would unconditionally support the complete elimination of these subsidies. However, as unlikely as it may seem, OECD farmers and some African countries are now united (without direct collaboration) in their petitions to delay removal of some of the agricultural subsidies. Meanwhile, other developing countries have pressed for the removal of the subsidies and preferential market access, as exemplified by the sugar and banana cases. In both cases, the complainants won and the EC was asked to reform its preferential programs. Of course, that does not mean the EC will not be able to find an excuse to retain some of its challenged subsidies and preferential treatment. Moreover, having some very poor countries on its side, the EC could try to make a *moral* argument for extending subsidies.

No matter what the EC and other developed countries decide to do, African countries would do better to form stronger coalitions with other developing countries. African countries have much more in common with themselves and with other developing countries and must be careful not to alienate those developing countries that do not benefit from preferential treatment. Moreover, whether OECD subsidies are removed now or later, the reduction process that has begun will not be substantially reversed.

## The Cotton Case

Finally, supporting some agricultural subsidies undermines the credibility of Africa's legitimate criticism of the OECD cotton subsidies. Unlike the situation with sugar, all African cotton-exporting countries are hurt by cotton subsidies. OECD cotton subsidies will continue to be in the spotlight for the next few years, given the importance of cotton to West African countries. The case at the end of this chapter about the cotton producers in Benin that are squeezed by domestic policies and OECD subsidies, sheds light on the importance of cotton to Benin and the impact of the confluence of domestic policies and OECD subsidies.

In short, African countries must be careful to assess the potential negative long-run impact of agricultural subsidies in developed countries, even if they benefit from them in the short run.

CONCLUSION

Agriculture was brought under the WTO when the Agreement on Agriculture came into effect in 1995. The agreement has three main elements: increasing market access, reducing domestic support, and reducing export subsidies. From the outset, though, analysts realized that no significant liberalization could be expected, given how much leeway countries were given. It was understood that the agreement would be revisited, to set the agricultural sector en route to more meaningful liberalization. That is in part what the Doha Round is trying to accomplish.

As to be expected, the negotiations on agriculture in the Doha Round are fraught with complications. One of the issues is the special and differential arrangements in favor of developing countries. Of course, regardless of their magnitude and utilization, these arrangements help to keep alive the discussion about the role of trade in economic development. These preferences are an acknowledgment of the income disparity between nations and serve as testimony to the fact that developed countries have a responsibility to support poor nations, even though developed countries do it partly in their self-interest. Trade preferences are also a form of support that has the potential to increase economic activity more than some types of direct aid. With the preferential market access that least-developed countries and ACP countries have, they are able to export agricultural products to OECD countries at a higher price than the free trade price, due to OECD agricultural subsidies.

These arrangements in favor of developing countries complicate the Doha Round negotiations, as every poor country tries to garner special treatment that is most suitable for its conditions. African countries complain about the gradual decline in the margin of preference, even when this decline could and should have been anticipated and prepared for. In fact, in some cases, the deterioration in the margin of preference should actually be welcome as it forces those countries that have been complacent to diversify their exports. Moreover, when one considers the long run, these special and differential arrangements may not be as beneficial as they might otherwise appear.

Complicating the negotiations further is the sentiment of many African countries that opening their own markets more would hurt their economies. They want to be equipped with the flexibility afforded by a special safeguard mechanism to be able to increase protection to limit imports of agricultural crops. For them, negotiations are successful if African countries are left to maintain their protective measures and developed countries are asked to open their markets discriminatorily, that is, in favor of exports from African and other ACP countries.

Perpetual subsidies in developed countries have also been a major obstacle in the negotiations. Some African countries want OECD countries to eliminate agricultural export subsidies because those subsidies depress the world prices of the agricultural commodities that African countries export. Other African countries are concerned about the negative impact of removing the OECD subsidies, such as an increase in the food import bill for poor countries. As discussed, removing these subsidies would also mean that some countries would lose out on the higher prices they have been getting when exporting agricultural products to OECD markets, given their preferential market access. Yet African countries are united in their legitimate opposition to cotton subsidies.

Another complicating factor is that the Doha Round of negotiations has been called a *development* round. By characterizing it as such, the intention was to focus on the salient features and needs of developing countries. However, it also meant the WTO was trying to be something it cannot be. The WTO is not a development agency – it is a trade organization. Even when development is the primary goal of international trade, the link is indirect. Development is determined in large part by a number of domestic factors which simply do not fall under the purview of the WTO.[13]

Faizel (2005) identifies four elements of development relevant to the WTO: fair trade, capacity building, balanced rules, and good governance. There is no question that these basic elements of development should guide any round of negotiation. However, while calling it a *development* round might challenge the multilateral system to be more cognizant of development issues, it also creates the potential for the WTO to intrude in areas that should be left to domestic policies.

Consider a fair trading system as articulated by Faizel (2005: 378) that "would remove the obstacles that developing countries experience in exporting their products to developed [countries'] markets and create opportunity for them to advance their development." Suppose the obstacles, or perceived obstacles, to exporting, and thus to development, are internal policies. What should then prevent the WTO from intervening in the name of development?[14] Regardless of how useful the WTO might be in formulating uniform trade policies for its members, countries still need policy space to take into account their own unique development goals and interests.

Incidentally, while Faizel's description of a fair trading system is useful, one could argue that to make trade truly fair and pro-development, developing countries must also reduce trade barriers. This is because imports (especially of inputs and technology) also play a key role in fostering development.

Regardless of the good intentions, words like "development" and "poverty" usually come with a price because they are open to

---

[13] For a discussion of some of the causes of the lack of development in least developed countries, see Collier (2007). Rodrik (2007) develops a case for the critical role of domestic institutions in dealing with development challenges. He makes the point that these institutions may be quite different between countries and may not necessarily be created on the basis of free trade.

[14] In fact, this kind of outside intervention or intrusion is already associated with preferential treatment received by developing countries, which typically stipulates various preconditions for eligibility.

very broad interpretations. It seems almost anything can be done in the name of "development" or reducing "poverty." In 1999, in their efforts to improve their image, the International Monetary Fund and the World Bank came up with a "new" mechanism for issuing loans which they called *Poverty* Reduction Strategy Papers (PRSPs). With "poverty" being the operative term, the IMF and World Bank secured the right to be even more engaged in policy formation in developing countries, notwithstanding that PRSPs are supposed to be country-driven.

Yet the challenge of the term "development" can cut both ways. Calling it a "development" round means developing countries, as well, can support or object to any proposition in the name of "development." That is part of the reason why African countries, for example, stepped up to support Brazil in the cotton case, but moved against Brazil in the sugar case, even though both cases involve OECD subsidies. As soon as "development" is the litmus test, each and every argument becomes a development argument, and even the basic principles of free trade can be conveniently abandoned. In short, the "development" argument can be used to support or object to just about any proposition.

Of course, if the adjective "development" were to be *officially* removed now from the "Doha Development Round," as it is sometimes called, that would be interpreted as the WTO no longer caring about development. In fact, it was a cosmetic proposition meant to appease developing countries or made in the euphoria of the WTO finally being able to launch its first round of multilateral trade talks since failing to do so two years earlier in Seattle. As should have been anticipated, the Doha Round of negotiations came to be held hostage by its own rhetoric. The Doha Round of negotiations was suspended for six months, from July 2006 to February 2007, mainly due to disagreements between developed and developing countries and between developed countries themselves over agricultural subsidies. When negotiations resumed, the agricultural sector continued to be the most contentious area of negotiations, and as of mid-2008 it was still not possible to predict when the round might be concluded.

Some of the challenges in negotiating policy reforms in agricultural trade are unique to the sector. Agriculture is by far the most important economic sector in most developing countries and, therefore, it receives the most attention. In addition, the agricultural sector, in developed and developing countries alike, exhibits entrenched domestic policies that contradict the spirit of free trade the WTO promotes. It should be noted, though, that many of the challenges in negotiating agreements in the WTO apply to all sectors to varying degrees. Negotiating any enforceable agreement among 152 WTO members – the least developed, the rich, and everyone in between – is a daunting task.

It seems reasonable to predict that the Doha Round will not produce an agreement that will significantly change the landscape of agricultural subsidies in developed countries or trade barriers in African countries, except, presumably, for cotton subsidies.[15] It is not that developed countries do not know the advantages of removing subsidies; rather, they do not have the political will to remove them, given the political strength of their farmers. Developing countries and certainly least-developed countries will be exempted from most obligations. This means most African countries will be able to maintain their protective agricultural domestic policies with hardly any infringement, taking advantage of a nebulous "special products" provision.

It can be expected that the debate over OECD subsidies and the special and differential treatment governing agricultural trade is here to stay. Yet no amount of rhetoric or WTO agreements can

---

[15] Although the upward trend of food prices that began in 2005 weakens developed countries' argument for subsidies and developing countries' argument for trade barriers on food imports, the high food prices may also create inertia in the WTO. Rising world food prices would automatically reduce OECD subsidies and also force developing countries that are net food importers to reduce import barriers on food imports. These temporary developments may give WTO members more breathing room and even a way out of demanding meaningful changes to agricultural policies.

bring development to African countries if their domestic initiatives are not in line with their development goals.

African countries developed a comprehensive program in 2003 to promote the agricultural sector, focusing on supply-side constraints (NEPAD, 2003). The program highlights the need for cultivating the technical and entrepreneurial capacities of the private sector, orderly land reform that would give women greater access to and control of land, adequate health and education services, political solutions to civil and cross-border conflicts, a sound macroeconomic environment with liberalized markets for exchange rates and trade, an efficient physical infrastructure with increased irrigation capacity, the removal of obstacles to cross-border trade, and improved agricultural research and information dissemination. Africa should live up to this program.

The diverse nature of these initiatives requires coordination of various ministries, something that is often hard to create and sustain. Nonetheless, as comprehensive as these initiatives may seem, they are only a sub-set of the initiatives needed for an all-inclusive development agenda. It is precisely the diverse and intricate nature of such initiatives that places development in the domestic domain.

The trajectory of the agricultural sector in African countries will be determined primarily by domestic policies and not so much by changes in policies in developed countries. Developed countries are already quite open to African products through AGOA, EBA, and other arrangements, and the issue of agricultural subsidies is a complex one. Given the latitude that African countries have to meet the WTO obligations (as illustrated by how high their bound tariffs are compared to their applied tariffs, for example), African countries are in a position to take charge of their own development. However, they should be careful not to confuse the latitude to maintain barriers as a justification to maintain them. Any comprehensive development program must include the careful and deliberate removal of trade barriers.

CASE: COTTON PRODUCERS IN BENIN SQUEEZED
BY DOMESTIC POLICIES AND OECD SUBSIDIES

Leaders in both developed and developing countries talk fervently about the omnipresent high poverty rates in rural Africa and the Millennium Development Goals. Yet talk is cheap. While rich farmers in developed countries are paid well above the world price, poor farmers in African countries receive only a percentage of the world price for their commodities.

Consider cotton producers in Benin. For many years, they have been taxed heavily by their own government, which controlled the agricultural sector and set producer prices below 50 percent of the world price. Their competitors in large cotton-producing countries, notably the United States, China, and those in the EU, receive generous subsidies from their governments and, thus, are paid above the world price. Those subsidies increase production and reduce the world price of cotton; as such, they are implicit taxes on cotton growers in Benin. This is not a matter of African cotton growers being jealous. It is rather a case of domestic and external agricultural policies directly hurting cotton farmers in Benin.

Benin is a small country located in West Africa. It attained its independence from France in 1960. Benin is one of the least-developed countries in the world, with a gross domestic income per capita of $440 in 2003. Its population in 2004 was 7 million people. Benin is well integrated into the world economy, as indicated by the trade ratios shown in Table 4.4. (Trade ratios are exports and imports as a percentage of GDP.)

Agriculture is the backbone of Benin's economy, contributing 36 percent of GDP and over 90 percent of export revenue. The agricultural sector supports the rural population, which is about 55 percent of the total population.

Cotton occupies a dominant role in Benin's economy. It contributes about 40 percent of export revenue. About a quarter of the population relies almost solely on cash earnings from cotton (Goreux

TABLE 4.4   Basic Economic Indicators for Benin: 2002 and 2003

|  | 2002 | 2003 |
|---|---|---|
| GDI ($ millions) | 2,500 | 3,000 |
| GDI per capita ($ Atlas) | 380 | 440 |
| GDI per capita ($ purchasing power parity – PPP) | 1,060 | 1,110 |
| Merchandise exports ($ millions) | 365 | 541 |
| Merchandise imports ($ millions) | 653 | 758 |
| Export/GDP ratio | 14 | 16 |
| Import/GDP ratio | 24 | 21 |
| Agricultural output as percent of GDP | 36 | 36 |
| Agricutural exports as a percent of merchandise exports | 94 | 92 |
| Percent of population below poverty line* | | |
| Rural | 25 | 33 |
| Urban | 29 | 23 |

*GDI, Gross Domestic Income.*
*\*The data are for 1995 and 1999, respectively.*
*Source: World Bank, World Development Indicators, 2004 and 2005.*

and Macrae, 2003). Cotton production is concentrated in the central and northern parts of the country, where substitution with other crops and opportunities for non-farm employment are lower than in other places in the country (Minot and Daniels, 2002).

Benin's trade pattern is almost a classic illustration of the Heckscher–Ohlin model, importing a myriad of manufactured products and exporting a small range of commodities based on its endowments and comparative advantage.[16] Benin has specialized in what it is good at – producing and exporting cotton. A survey by the International Cotton Advisory Committee (ICAC, 2001) suggested that the per-unit cost of production of cotton in Benin was

---

[16]   For an explanation of this model, refer to any textbook on international economics.

less than half of that in the United States. Note, though, that the ICAC cautions against any comparisons among countries because of differences in production practices, extension services, financial support to farmers, and input supply systems.

While production of cotton in Benin has fluctuated, presumably due to diseases, pests, inconsistent weather conditions, and changes in prices, there has been a remarkable upward trend, with production climbing from an annual average of 16,000 metric tons of fiber in 1970/1971 to 1974/1975 to an annual average of 145,000 metric tons in 1998/1999 to 2002/2003 (Baffes, 2004). The increase in output is the result of an increase in the area under cotton cultivation and productivity.

Like many African countries in the 1970s and 1980s, the agricultural sector in Benin was under direct government control. Following the establishment of a Marxist regime in 1974, the government established a state-owned National Agricultural Promotion Company – *Societé Nationale pour la Promotion Agricole* (SONAPRA). SONAPRA had pure monopoly power in the provision of inputs and processing and pure monopsony power as the single official buyer of cotton.

The increase in cotton production was due partly to SONAPRA's promotion of production through extension work and its provision of agricultural credits. The increase was also partly the result of SONAPRA's monopoly power, which limited the supply of resources for other crops. In effect, SONAPRA dictated what was to be produced and the price paid to farmers. Because of its monopsony power, SONAPRA was able to set prices far below the world price and, thus, to pay for its operational costs and its inefficiency and to generate revenues for the government.[17]

With pressure from the World Bank and after self-assessment, Benin started earnest reforms in 1992, reducing the monopoly and monopsony powers of SONAPRA by allowing some competition

---

[17]  A monopsony refers to a buyer which is the sole buyer in a market.

from the private sector. Producer prices, as a percent of world prices, adjusted for subsidies and bonuses, increased from an annual average of about 46 percent in 1994/1995 to 1997/1998 to an annual average of 53 percent in 1999/2000 to 2001/2002 (Goreux and Macrae, 2003).[18] While internal reforms have produced a modest increase in the proportion of revenue channeled to farmers in Benin, it is still a long way from being a system that can be classified as efficient and farmer-friendly.

The low remuneration to cotton growers in Benin is not only due to internal factors; the continual decline of the world price of cotton is another factor. The world price of cotton (in real terms) has declined by an annual average of 0.9 percent between 1960 and 1984 and by an annual average of 0.2 percent between 1985 and 2003 (Baffes, 2004). Among the reasons for the fall in the price of cotton are the subsidies given to domestic producers of cotton in the United States, China, and the EU, that together account for about 90 percent of all cotton subsidies[19] (see Table 4.5). Due to these subsidies, the fall in the world price of cotton has received so much attention since the early 2000s that it nearly overshadows the internal deficiencies in African countries.

The following discussion focuses on the U.S. subsidies, for several reasons. First, the U.S. government is currently the largest subsidizer in terms of total spending. Second, the United States is the world's largest exporter of cotton and has substantial influence on the world price of cotton. Third, information about U.S. subsidies is much more readily available than that for Chinese subsidies, for example. (Ironically, it is the good quality of information provided by U.S. government agencies that sometimes makes the United States an easy target.) In addition, the United States has a

---

[18] In 1998/1999, the producer price as a percent of the world price was almost 71 percent. This number was not included in calculating the change in annual averages, because it was an outlier.

[19] Other reasons include increased consumption of synthetic fibers, increased productivity, and the relatively low price and income elasticities of demand for cotton.

TABLE 4.5 Government Assistance to Cotton Producers (Millions of Dollars)

| Country/ Region | 1997/1998 | 1998/1999 | 1999/2000 | 2000/2001 | 2001/2002 | 2002/2003 |
|---|---|---|---|---|---|---|
| U.S. | 597 | 1,480 | 2,056 | 1,020 | 3,001 | 1,920 |
| China | 2,013 | 2,648 | 1,534 | 1,900 | 1,196 | 750 |
| EU | 870 | 864 | 795 | 716 | 980 | 957 |
| *U.S. assistance per kilogram* | | | | | | |
| US$ | 0.15 | 0.49 | 0.56 | 0.27 | 0.61 | 0.54 |
| Percent of price | 9 | 38 | 48 | 22 | 75 | 44 |

*Source: Baffes (2004:70).*

long history of advocating for free markets, so any deviation from that position draws attention. Finally, the United States is a leader rather than a follower and, therefore, its policies set the tone for others.

Domestically, cotton production is not nearly as important in the United States as a source of employment and foreign currency as it is in Benin. In 2003, cotton production employed almost 173,500 people, about 0.12 percent of the civilian labor force, on about 31,400 farms.[20] Cotton exports generated an annual average of 0.25 percent of the total U.S. merchandise exports for the period 2000 to 2003 (or about 3.3 percent of total agricultural exports).[21] However, in the world market, the United States is the leading exporter of cotton, supplying 30 to 40 percent of total cotton exports. (Benin contributes about 2.5 percent of the world's exports of cotton.)

As a large exporter, U.S. domestic policies on cotton production and exports are of great interest to the world. Those policies are of even greater interest to Benin and other cotton-dependent countries. It is for that reason developing countries have always wanted the agricultural sector to be brought under multilateral rules.

At the conclusion of the Uruguay Round of GATT, the agricultural sector was integrated into GATT/WTO under the Agreement on Agriculture, setting the sector en route toward trade liberalization. However, even at the outset, many analysts viewed with skepticism the so-called commitments by developed countries to increase market access and reduce production subsidies and export subsidies. Commitments were characterized by elusive definitions of various agricultural subsidies, the choice of an "outlier" period as a base period for reducing subsidies, the calculation of tariff reductions based on a simple average, and, of course, safeguard measures which were themselves *safeguarded* by arbitrariness.

---

[20] U.S. cotton data are reported by the National Cotton Council of America at: http://www.cotton.org/econ/world/detail.cfm?year=2003.

[21] The percentage was calculated using data from the U.S. Census Bureau, U.S. Department of Commerce, *Statistical Abstract of the United States: 2004–2005*, 124th Edition.

Agricultural subsidies and protection for politically-sensitive agricultural crops are not new in the United States and other developed countries.[22] What is frustrating for African farmers is the fact that, in spite of the Agreement on Agriculture, not only do these subsidies not seem to be decreasing, they have actually been reinforced for some commodities. The U.S. cotton subsidies highlight this situation. The United States supports cotton growers through several channels specified in the 1996 Farm Bill: decoupled payments (production flexibility contract payments), market price payments, crop insurance payments, export subsidies, and emergency funding introduced in 1998 (Gillson et al., 2004; Baffes, 2004; Oxfam, 2002).

*Decoupled payments* are an example of renaming a subsidy instrument under the pretense of being consistent with the Agreement on Agriculture. Prior to the 1996 Farm Bill, one of the instruments for supporting domestic cotton growers (and other farmers) was what was called "deficiency payments," that is, payments made to farmers to supplement market prices when those prices were below a certain target price. The 1996 Farm Bill, which set the target price at $1.59 per kilogram of cotton, "eliminated" deficiency payments and replaced them with *decoupled* payments meant to compensate farmers for the loss of deficiency payments!

By supposedly "decoupling" these payments from production, the United States was claiming that these subsidies do not provide an incentive for production, do not distort prices, and, therefore, should be permissible. Moreover, the United States set out to engage in legal maneuvering from the very beginning, at the incorporation of the agricultural sector into the WTO. When the United States was establishing its commitment regarding its aggregate measure of support (AMS) in agriculture, it included deficiency payments in the base period level from which reductions were to

---

[22] See Baffes (2004: 68–69) for a chronology of the U.S. commodity programs with cotton provisions dating back to the Agricultural Marketing Act of 1929.

be made. However, when calculating its AMS to verify that it has actually met its commitment, the deficiency payments were *not* included, as stated below. (The dollar amounts refer to the whole agricultural sector and not only to cotton.)

The commitment entered into by the United States requires it to reduce its total AMS from the base period level of $23.9 billion to a final bound level at the end of the implementation period of $19.1 billion. Deficiency payments accounted for almost US$10 billion during the base period and have been included in the base and final bound commitments. However, they are excluded from the current annual total AMS calculations. The result is a drop in current total AMS of such magnitude that the US need not contemplate any further change in policy in order to meet its AMS commitment. There are, therefore, likely to be virtually no policy changes required in response to AMS commitments in the US during the implementation period of the Agreement. (OECD, 1995: 40)

*Market price payments* include market assistance loans and loan deficiency payments. The loan rate ceiling and floor are, respectively, $1.14 and $1.10 per kilogram of cotton. Suppose a farmer takes out a loan at a rate of $1.12 per kilogram. The farmer is guaranteed at least the price of $1.12 per kilogram, regardless of what the world price might be. The government pays the difference between the loan rate and the world price, when the latter is lower. Eligible farmers do not even have to take out loans to receive this subsidy.

*Crop insurance payments* are meant to protect farmers against weather-related shortfalls in yield and revenues. *Export subsidies* (also called step 2 programs) are supposed to make U.S. cotton exporters competitive when the domestic price of cotton exceeds the world price. *Emergency payments* are supposed to be a "safety net" against potentially low world prices. Note that given the various channels and justification for requesting subsidies, U.S. cotton growers can receive subsidies regardless of what the world price might be.

The 2002 Farm Bill secured more subsidies for U.S. cotton growers. It replaced production flexibility contract payments (decoupled payments) with direct payments that were set at about $0.15 per kilogram of cotton ($0.0667 per pound). Emergency payments were made permanent and re-classified as counter-cyclical payments, issued when the effective price of a commodity is below a certain target price. The target price for cotton for 2002/2003 to 2006/2007 was $1.60 per kilogram ($0.724 per pound).[23] Counter-cyclical payments to U.S. cotton farmers amounted to $1.26 billion in 2002/2003 (Baffes, 2005: 265).

The 2002 Farm Bill was the impetus for the complaint by Brazil and the ongoing outcry about U.S. subsidies from West African countries. In his op-ed piece, Kristof referred to them as "subsidies that kill":

Could there be a worse indictment of American agricultural policy, rendered even more scandalous by the new $180 billion [2002] farm bill signed by President Bush? Actually, there is a worse indictment. By inflating farm subsidies even more, Congress and the Bush administration are impoverishing and occasionally killing Africans whom we claim to be trying to help.
For example, the U.S. has only 25,000 cotton growers, but they are prosperous (with an average net worth of $800,000) and thus influential. So the U.S. spends $2 billion a year subsidizing them, and American production of cotton has almost doubled over the last 20 years – even though the U.S. is an inefficient, high-cost producer.
And when a poor cotton farmer in West Africa goes bust because of our cotton subsidies, he has no savings to fall back on. Rather, he starves. He cannot afford medicine for his sick baby, and the child dies. He cannot afford a midwife when his wife is pregnant, and so she is crippled in childbirth. He cannot afford worming medication for his children, and so they grow anemic and do poorly in school – and cannot concentrate when Americans lecture them about their poor governance. (Kristof, 2002)

As can be expected, there is a strong link between producer prices of cotton and the economic welfare of people in rural Benin. Minot (2002) estimates that a 40 percent reduction in producer prices of

---

[23] See http://www.fsa.usda.gov/pas/publications/facts/html/dcp03.htm.

cotton causes a reduction in rural per capita income of 7 percent in the short run and 5 to 6 percent in the long run. Rural poverty increases 8 percentage points, or about 334,000 people get pushed below the poverty line.

Several studies have estimated the impact of eliminating export subsidies on the world price of cotton and on African countries. It is difficult to compare results because of differences in estimation methods, assumed elasticities, presentation of the impact (by country, region, or continent), and the amounts of subsidies to be removed. However, all studies confirm that Benin and other African countries would experience net benefits from an elimination of subsidies. Table 4.6 provides a summary of five such studies.

Consider the study by the ICAC (2002) in which they estimate the impact of removing U.S. cotton subsidies. Applying the estimated increases in price on the volume of exports suggests that Benin's export revenue would have been higher in 1999/2000, 2000/2001, and 2001/2002 by about $9 million (5 percent of total merchandise exports), $18 million (9 percent of total merchandise exports), and $30 million (14 percent of total merchandise exports), respectively. In reality, the potential increase in export revenue would have been higher (given the estimated increases in the world price of cotton), because output and exports would have responded positively to the higher prices.

Complete elimination of subsidies in the United States and other countries cannot be expected in the near future. However, with the ruling in 2004 by the WTO against U.S. subsidies in the case brought by Brazil, the cotton industry will start a slow journey toward a level playing field. The dispute settlement panel and the Appellate Body found the product flexibility contracts and direct payments could not be categorized as "decoupled payments" and, thus, are not permissible. Export subsidies by the United States were also determined to be inconsistent with the WTO rules. The spillover benefit of this ruling is that subsidies for other crops will also come under close scrutiny.

TABLE 4.6  Impact of Eliminating Cotton Subsidies

| Study | Policy | Impact |
|---|---|---|
| Gillson et al. (2004) | Removal of subsidies worldwide | Cotton production earnings in Benin increase by 15 to 36 percent |
| Poonyth et al. (2004) | Removal of subsidies worldwide | Cotton export earnings in West Africa (Benin, Burkina Faso, Chad, and Mali) increase by 17 percent |
| Poonyth et al. (2004) | Removal of all subsidies of which the WTO has been officially notified. (This does not include the removal of Chinese cotton subsidies, for example.) | Cotton export earnings in West Africa (Benin, Burkina Faso, Chad, and Mali) increase by 7 percent |
| Fabiosa et al. (2003) | Removal of subsidies worldwide | Cotton export earnings in Africa increase by 17 percent |
| Badiane et al. (2002) | Removal of U.S. subsidies | Cotton revenues in West and Central Africa* increase by $250 million (or by about 12 percent of merchandise exports) |
| ICAC (2002) | Removal of subsidies worldwide | World price of cotton would have been higher in 2000/2001 and 2001/2002 by 17 cents and 31 cents per pound, respectively |
| ICAC (2002) | Removal of U.S. subsidies | World price of cotton would have been higher in 1999/2000, 2000/2001, and 2001/2002 by 3 cents, 6 cents, and 11 cents per pound, respectively. [Nominal annual world price of cotton in 2000, 2001, and 2002 was 59 cents, 48 cents, and 46 cents per pound, respectively (Baffes, 2004).] |

*The West and Central African countries included are Benin, Burkina Faso, Cameroon, Central African Republic, Chad, Côte d'Ivoire, Mali, Senegal, and Togo.

Benin and Chad are the two African countries that joined Brazil's complaint as third parties. However, their voice was heard more forcefully through the "cotton initiative," launched jointly by Benin, Burkina Faso, Chad, and Mali in 2003. These countries sent their complaint directly to the WTO General Council. This was a strategic move because the issue became not only about the U.S. cotton subsidies, but also about cotton subsidies by all countries, including China. The "cotton initiative" made a strong appeal for the reduction and elimination of cotton subsidies. This was done not simply by reminding the alleged culprits of their legal obligations, but also by calling for a sense of fairness and justice for poor countries, especially given the pro-development pronouncements of the Doha Round. The African Group and other developing countries rallied around this initiative, broadening the coalition and making more contentious the issues between developed and developing countries. The 2003 WTO Ministerial Meeting in Cancun, Mexico, failed in part because of an inability to reach a compromise on agricultural subsidies. At the subsequent meeting in Hong Kong in 2005, an agreement was reached to eliminate farm export subsidies by the end of 2013.

Implementation, of course, will depend on the good will of the major subsidizing countries – the United States, China, and those in the EU. It will also depend on whether African countries can remain focused on their demands.

Interestingly, while the United States and other developed countries found it difficult to remove cotton subsidies, they agreed to support development and production of cotton in Benin and other African countries, as discussed in Chapter 2. Benin assumed an important leadership role in negotiating for such assistance. The assistance provided by developed countries and multilateral agencies can have a far-reaching, positive impact on Benin and other African countries. However, African countries must resist the temptation to accept financial aid in lieu of the elimination of subsidies. Unlike financial aid, which may not even get to the capital city let alone to the rural areas, any increase in income through high prices is widely dispersed to millions of farmers.

Likewise, for a reduction in cotton subsidies to have an impact in reducing rural poverty, Benin must continue to reform its agricultural sector to minimize inefficiencies and increase the percentage of the world price that is channeled to farmers.

Subsidies in large cotton-producing countries have negatively affected the African farmer in two major ways. One is the reduction in the world price of cotton. Second, and just as important, is the reduced legitimacy for the United States and the EU to press African governments toward more liberalization initiatives that are friendly to farmers. Auspiciously, after the West African countries' strong appeal to developed countries through the "cotton initiative," the United States and other developed countries now have some leverage, thanks to the provision and promises of assistance, to push West African countries to make some reforms of their own.

# 5 TRANSPARENCY IN GOVERNMENT PROCUREMENT

G OVERNMENTS BUY MANY GOODS AND SERVICES. Government procurement policies can be significant in fostering infant industries, especially in developing countries. However, such policies can also serve as trade barriers. The WTO has a plurilateral Agreement on Government Procurement to prevent governments from having procurement policies that constitute trade barriers. To extend this discipline to all WTO members, developed countries would like to see a multilateral agreement, at least on *transparency* in government procurement. African countries are concerned, though, that such an agreement would hinder them in developing certain industries.

The magnitude of government procurement that is contestable (that is, potentially open to foreign competition) is sizable, ranging from 5 to 15 percent of GDP for various countries (OECD, 2002), as explained below. Government (or public) procurement is a subset of total government expenditure. It is the expenditure by the central government, states, provinces, local government, and government-owned enterprises for the purchase of works, services, and goods. It does not include, for example, wages and salaries, subsidies, transfer payments, and debt redemption. For the purpose of this study and to be consistent with the current WTO language and parameters, government procurement does not include defense spending either.

Interest in and international deliberations about government procurement are neither accidental nor new. The principle of non-discrimination for government purchases was included in the U.S. draft of the International Trade Organization (ITO) charter prepared soon after the establishment of the United Nations and the Bretton Woods institutions. However, it proved difficult to reach an agreement on government procurement. Government procurement was finally exempted from the non-discrimination rules. As discussed in Chapter 1, the ITO itself never came into existence because it was not ratified by the U.S. Congress. Instead, GATT was established as a temporary institution.

Article III of GATT states the national treatment principle, that is, that foreign goods and domestic goods should be treated the same. However, government procurement was excluded from this requirement under Article III:8 (a):

The provisions of this Article shall not apply to laws, regulations or requirements governing the procurement by governmental agencies of products purchased for governmental purposes and not with a view to commercial resale or with a view to use in the production of goods for commercial sale.

Article XVII of GATT describes the non-discriminatory principle for imports or exports by state trading enterprises, but that does not apply to:

imports of products for immediate or ultimate consumption in governmental use and not otherwise for resale or use in the production of goods for sale. With respect to such imports, each contracting party shall accord to the trade of the other contracting parties fair and equitable treatment. (Article XVII:2)

Not surprisingly, these exemptions did not keep government procurement completely out of GATT discussions.

### THE SIZE OF GOVERNMENT PROCUREMENT

Whether due to a lack of transparency, the segmentation of government procurement, or the overall typical shortage of reliable data for African countries, data on government procurement for central governments in Africa, let alone local governments, are rarely available. In 2002, the OECD published an extensive study estimating the size of contestable government procurement for 134 countries, including twenty-nine African countries (OECD, 2002). Among the African countries, Kenya was the only one for which there was sufficient information to determine the size of contestable government procurement.

According to the study, based on expenditures for the period 1990–1997, the weighted average ratio of contestable government procurement to GDP for twenty-eight OECD countries was estimated to be about 8 percent. Based on expenditures for the period 1990–1994, a similar ratio for the 106 non-OECD countries in the study was *extrapolated* to be about 5 percent.[1]

Trionfetti (1999) estimated the ratio of government procurement to GDP for African countries to range from 9 to 13 percent.[2] A relatively thorough study on public procurement in African countries, although limited in terms of the number of countries covered, is one by Odhiambo and Kamau (2003). They estimate the size of the central government procurement in 2000/2001 as a percent of GDP to be (rounded) 11, 9, and, 35, respectively, for Kenya, Tanzania, and Uganda. They explain the apparent outlier level for Uganda as follows:

That Uganda's procurement is higher than in the other countries is not hard to explain. Uganda is a country that is recovering from many years of civil war and destruction. The government is currently spending massively to replace infrastructure and other public amenities, such as schools

---

[1]   The estimated ratio for non-OECD countries was derived based on ten countries whose information was complete. The GDP of those ten countries accounted for about 11 percent of the GDP for the 106 non-OECD countries in the study.

[2]   Five African countries were included in the study: Botswana, Morocco, South Africa, and Tunisia under Africa, and Egypt under the Middle East. See the study by Wittig (1999), which uses Trionfetti's results to estimate dollar values of the range of public procurement for individual Sub-Saharan African countries for 1997.

and hospitals. And on account of its compliance to economic reforms, the country has been receiving huge donor support. (Odhiambo and Kamau, 2003: 13)

Estimating the size of government procurement for African countries will remain a daunting task for years to come. Applying Trionfetti's estimated range of 9 to 13 percent to the general picture, in 2004 the nominal value of government procurement for Africa was in the range of $65 billion to $94 billion. [According to the World Bank (2007), the nominal GDP for the whole continent of Africa in 2004 was $726 billion.]

It is hard to predict the future trend of government procurement in Africa. Reforms are continuing (although at a slower pace than in the 1980s and 1990s) that may further reduce the direct role the government plays in the economy, thus reducing the relative magnitude of government procurement. However, that may be countered by a growing awareness of the need to develop physical infrastructure to expand production capacity and attract private investment. That is, while the relative size of total government spending may decrease, the proportion of development spending within the budget may grow.

## THE AGREEMENT ON GOVERNMENT PROCUREMENT (GPA): A PLURILATERAL AGREEMENT

Although GATT was technically only a provisional treaty, over time it actually amounted to a number of complex agreements, administered and enforced by its operating body. The first six rounds of negotiations under GATT focused on tariff reduction. The seventh round, the Tokyo Round (1973–1979), was relatively far reaching in scope because it additionally reduced non-tariff barriers. This achievement was important because as average tariff rates were decreasing, the propensity to increase non-tariff barriers increased, or at least non-tariff barriers became more conspicuous.

The Tokyo Round also sought an agreement that would extend the national treatment principle to government procurement, given the relative size of government purchases and the inclination for governments to discriminate in favor of domestic producers. Developing countries resisted such an agreement for fear of losing important policy space, especially for their industrial policies. They also resisted because areas that were most relevant to them, such as agriculture and textiles and apparel, were still being kept out of the purview of GATT by developed countries.

This resistance did not derail negotiations on government procurement altogether, however. A plurilateral Agreement on Government Procurement (GPA) was reached in 1979 and took effect in 1981. Twenty-one countries opted to accede to the GPA: Austria, Canada, the ten members of the European Community (EC) at the time,[3] Finland, Hong Kong, Israel, Japan, Norway, Singapore, Sweden, Switzerland, and the United States. The GPA was limited to purchases of goods only (not services), by the central government, and with a value of at least Special Drawing Rights (SDR) 150,000 (equivalent to about $216,000 in March 2006).[4]

Over time, the GPA expanded in scope and coverage. A subsequent round of negotiations on the GPA in the mid-1980s led to a reduction in the threshold for central government purchases of goods to SDR 130,000 (equivalent to about $187,000 in March 2006), effective in 1988. However, the number of parties to the agreement remained constant and government purchases of services remained outside of the agreement.

The major achievement of the Uruguay Round was to establish the WTO, which brought rules and agreements reached under

---

[3] Members of the EC in 1981 were Belgium, Denmark, France, Greece, Ireland, Italy, Luxembourg, the Netherlands, West Germany, and the United Kingdom. Note that the WTO refers to the European Community as the "European Communities."

[4] SDR was created in 1969 by the IMF as an international reserve asset. However, it has been used mainly as a unit of account.

GATT into a single body of operation. This was a departure from the old system under which members could pick and choose the agreements to which they wanted to subscribe. However, some remnants of the *à la carte* approach remained. The GPA was one of only four plurilateral agreements to remain as such when the WTO came into existence.[5]

In 1995 when the WTO was established, one of the new multilateral agreements that came into force was the General Agreement on Trade in Services (GATS). In line with exemptions made for government procurement of goods, Article XIII of GATS exempts government procurement of services from the national treatment principle.

Nonetheless, while the Uruguay Round of GATT was underway, the signatories to the plurilateral GPA successfully negotiated broader coverage for the GPA, taking effect on January 1, 1996. Non-discrimination in government procurement was extended to the purchase of services. Likewise, the definition of "government" was extended to encompass procurement of goods and services not only by the central government, but also by sub-central governments (state and local governments), and government-owned enterprises, such as utility companies.

The number of individual governments that are parties to the GPA has also grown, from twenty-one in 1981 to thirty-nine in 2007, primarily due to the expansion of the EC.[6] The membership of the EC increased from ten in 1981 to twenty-seven in 2007, including Austria, Finland, and Sweden, which were parties to the GPA even before they joined the EC. As of 2007, the only

---

5 The three others were the Agreement on Trade in Civil Aircraft, the International Dairy Agreement, and the International Bovine Meat Agreement. The last two were terminated in 1997 because matters relating to those areas could be dealt with by the Agreements on Agriculture and on Sanitary and Phytosanitary.

6 As of 2007, members of the EC were: Austria, Belgium, Bulgaria, Cyprus, Czech Republic, Denmark, Estonia, Finland, France, Germany, Greece, Hungary, Ireland, Italy, Latvia, Lithuania, Luxembourg, Malta, the Netherlands, Poland, Portugal, Romania, Slovak Republic, Slovenia, Spain, Sweden, and the United Kingdom.

additional non-EC members to the GPA since 1981 were Iceland, Korea, Liechtenstein, and the Netherlands with respect to Aruba.

Table 5.1 shows the thresholds for government procurement covered under the GPA. While there is noticeable uniformity in the thresholds, each contracting government has the prerogative to determine its list of entities and goods and services for the purpose of the agreement. Contracting governments also have the leeway to treat each other differently. They can and do make exceptions for some goods and services on their lists. The general objective is to achieve reciprocity.[7]

The Agreement on Government Procurement is subject to Dispute Settlement Understanding (DSU) enforcement, with some qualifications. Due to the nature of government procurement – the pace and the likely inability to correct a national bias once it happens – panels are required to accelerate the proceedings. In addition, the GPA does not allow cross-retaliation. That means any potential retaliation by a successful complainant cannot be in any other areas, covered by other agreements. (See Chapter 2 for details about the operation of the DSU system.)

According to the WTO website, for the period from 1996 to 2005, five disputes were brought alleging practices that were not consistent with the GPA agreement, as shown below (see also WTO, 2005):

DS163     In 1999, the United States brought a case against South Korea with respect to some practices of certain entities in procurement of airport construction in Korea. A year later, a panel ruled that the entities in question were not included

---

[7]   Two different examples of this are shown by Korea and the United States. (The source is the same website source from which data for Table 5.1 was compiled.) Korea specified that for goods and services (including construction services) of Canada and suppliers of such goods and services, the agreement does not apply to procurement by the entities listed in Annexes 2 and 3 of the agreement. Korea indicated that it is prepared to amend this note at such time as coverage with respect to these Annexes can be resolved with Canada. Separately, the United States noted that "[a] service listed in Annex 4 is covered with respect to a particular Party only to the extent that such Party has included that service in its Annex 4."

TABLE 5.1 Government Procurement Thresholds in Thousands of SDRs

| Country | Central Government | | | Sub-Central Government | | | Government Enterprises | | |
|---|---|---|---|---|---|---|---|---|---|
| | Goods | Services | Construction | Goods | Services | Construction | Goods | Services | Construction |
| Canada | 130 | 130 | 5,000 | 355 | 355 | 5,000 | 355 | 355 | 5,000 |
| European Communities | 130 | 130 | 5,000 | 200 | 200 | 5,000 | 400 | 400 | 5,000 |
| Hong Kong China | 130 | 130 | 5,000 | n.a. | n.a. | n.a | 400 | 400 | 5,000 |
| Iceland | 130 | 130 | 5,000 | 200 | 200 | 5,000 | 400 | 400 | 5,000 |
| Israel | 130 | 130 | 8,500* | 250 | 250 | 8,500* | 355 | 355 | 8,500* |
| Japan | 130 | 130 | 4,500 | 200 | 200 | 15,000 | 130 | 130 | 15,000** |
| Korea | 130 | 130 | 5,000 | 200 | 200 | 15,000 | 450 | none | 15,000 |
| Liechtenstein | 130 | 130 | 5,000 | 200 | 200 | 5,000 | 400 | 400 | 5,000 |
| Netherlands with respect to Aruba | 130 | 130 | 5,000 | n.a. | n.a. | n.a | 400 | 400 | 5,000 |
| Norway | 130 | 130 | 5,000 | 200 | 200 | 5,000 | 400 | 400 | 5,000 |
| Singapore | 130 | 130 | 5,000 | n.a. | n.a. | n.a | 400 | 400 | 5,000 |
| Switzerland | 130 | 130 | 5,000 | 200 | 200 | 5,000 | 400 | 400 | 5,000 |
| United States | 130 | 130 | 5,000 | 355 | 355 | 5,000 | 400*** | 400*** | 5,000 |

One SDR ≈ $1.44 in March 2006; n.a., not applicable.

*Threshold will be reduced to SDR 5,000,000, effective 1/1/2009.

**For some construction services, the threshold is SDR 450,000.

***For some procurement of goods and services, the threshold is SDR 250,000.

Source: WTO website: http://www.wto.org/English/tratop_e/gproc_e/apend_e.htm#cane (March 3, 2006).

in Korea's list of entities subject to GPA reciprocity with the U.S. and, thus, Korea had not violated its obligations.

DS95 and DS88   In 1997, Japan and the EC brought cases against the U.S. with respect to a Massachusetts law enacted in 1996 that barred public authorities in the Commonwealth of Massachusetts from procuring goods or services from any persons who conducted business with Burma. The contention was that the Massachusetts law was in violation of the GPA since Massachusetts entities were included in the U.S. list of sub-central government entities. A panel was established in 1998. However, a resolution was reached between the complainants and the U.S. At the request of Japan and the EC, panel proceedings were halted in 1999.

DS73   In 1997, the EC brought a case against Japan alleging that Japan's tender specifications to purchase a multifunctional satellite for Air Traffic Management referred explicitly to US specifications. The EC contended that due to biased specification, EC's bidders were in effect excluded from the tender. The EC and Japan reached a resolution, eliminating the need to form a panel.

DS40   In 1996, the EC brought a case against Korea alleging that the Korean telecommunications sector discriminated against some foreign suppliers, favoring U.S. suppliers under bilateral agreements between Korea and the United States. The EC and Korea reached a resolution in 1997, eliminating the need to form a panel.

Government procurement is, by its very nature, quite political. This was highlighted by the bold decision of the United States to bar nations that had not supported the U.S.-led war in Iraq from bidding on major U.S.-financed contracts for the reconstruction of Iraq (Branigin and Spinner, 2003). Countries such as Canada, France, and Germany (not to mention China and Russia, which are not parties to the GPA) were left in the cold salivating for the lucrative projects for which they were not allowed to compete, even though they were parties to the GPA. Ironically, the United

States was the formidable force behind the creation of the GPA. Iritani (2003) describes the irony as follows:

Incensed that foreign countries were playing favorites in doling out billions of dollars to build airports, roads and dams, the U.S. became a prime cheerleader for a global agreement on government procurement. Now, the U.S. stands accused of violating the very pact it worked so hard to create.

The decision by the United States incited harsh criticism from the excluded countries and also created a rift within the EC. Some EC countries threatened to lodge a formal complaint with the WTO. Great Britain, an avid supporter of the Iraq war, seemingly forgetting the spirit with which the GPA was established, contended that it was the United States' prerogative to spend its taxpayers' money as it wished (Iritani, 2003).

The U.S. arguments in response to countries contemplating a formal complaint were all over the spectrum. Some U.S. officials claimed that their decision did not violate the GPA because the entity that oversaw reconstruction in Iraq, the Coalition Provisional Authority, was based in Iraq and was not among the entities listed by the United States for the purpose of the GPA. Other officials defended the decision with the national security argument (Neikirk, 2003; Palmeter and Meagher, 2003; Pauwelyn, 2003). In keeping with Article 21 of GATT, Article XXIII of the GPA permits exceptions made on legitimate national security grounds. No country ever ended up filing a formal complaint against the United States for its decision to exclude some countries from reconstruction contracts in Iraq. Nonetheless, dissatisfaction has remained regarding the U.S. position.

### ECONOMIC THEORY AND PREFERENTIAL GOVERNMENT PROCUREMENT

A prevailing argument for free trade is that it brings about an allocation of resources according to comparative advantage, thus increasing total world production and income. Free trade promotes efficiency and innovation and allows firms to take advantage of economies of scale. Free trade brings its own short-term challenges for displaced resources, however, because resources are not perfectly mobile between industries or regions. Countries will often use trade barriers to protect those resources that might be displaced by imports. In addition, trade barriers are often used to protect infant industries, to enable them to lower average production costs and acquire comparative advantage. The infant industry argument (often used by developing countries) is borne of the compelling fact that comparative advantage is dynamic.

Tariffs are the most common form of trade barriers. Supplementing or substituting for tariffs is a wide range of non-tariff barriers that can be as straightforward as a quota or as subtle as a discriminatory government procurement policy. Whether there has been an increase in non-tariff barriers following the reduction in tariffs over the years or the tariff reduction has simply exposed them, non-tariff barriers have received greater attention over time.

A government's procurement policy can constitute a trade barrier by discriminating against foreign firms. The impact of such a policy on domestic production and imports depends on the size of government procurement relative to domestic supply, the preference policy itself and its margins, market conditions (competitive or not), substitutability of domestic goods for foreign goods, and returns to scale (decreasing, constant, or increasing).

Baldwin and Richardson (1972) and Baldwin (1984) show that preferential government procurement has no real impact under the following three conditions: perfect competition, perfect substitutability of an import product for a domestic product, and when the quantity demanded by the government at the free trade price is smaller than the quantity supplied domestically at that price. Under these conditions, an increase in government demand for a domestic product will tend to increase the domestic price of that product. However, the increase in price will be offset by a corresponding switch to imports by private consumers. In this situation, even if the government decided to procure the product entirely from domestic suppliers, the domestic price will be pulled back to the level of the original world price and, therefore, world production will not be affected. Likewise, domestic production will remain constant.

In a situation where government demand at the free trade price exceeds the domestic supply, an increase in government demand for a domestic product would increase the domestic price (paid by the government) and domestic production of the product, and decrease the world price (paid by private consumers). This outcome, in terms of changes in prices, is similar to the impact of a tariff imposed by a large country. Production distortion at home is mitigated by an improvement in the terms of trade. However, government expenditure increases. For African countries that typically face perfectly elastic supply conditions, their government procurement policy would have no effect on the world price.

A study by Miyagiwa (1991) demonstrates that the Baldwin–Richardson ineffectiveness proposition holds even under imperfect competition, as long as the assumption of perfect substitutability is maintained. Miyagiwa extends the Baldwin–Richardson studies by considering discriminatory government procurement where the government pays the domestic supplier a premium beyond the import price. (The import price is the price charged by a foreign supplier for a product.) The model has two firms: Firm 1 is a domestic firm and Firm 2 is a foreign firm. The domestic firm produces purely for domestic consumption. The foreign firm produces purely for export to Firm 1's country. The study concludes that if the two firms' products are perfect substitutes, a price premium given as a fixed mark-up (a specific amount) would have no impact on the volume of imports. This is because a specific price premium is, in effect, a lump-sum subsidy that should not have any impact on the profit-maximizing output. However, if the price premium is a percentage of the import price, the discriminatory government procurement policy would increase the volume of imports.

In Miyagiwa's model, when the price premium is a percentage of the import price, the premium serves as an incentive for Firm 1 to raise (indirectly) the import price. It accomplishes this by reducing its supply to private consumers, thus pushing those consumers to depend more on Firm 2's product (imports). An increase in demand for imports causes the price of imports to increase, which, in turn, causes the preferential price from the government to Firm 1 to increase as well. The loss to Firm 1 of reduced sales to private consumers is offset by the increase in the profit margin from selling to the government.

In the case of differentiated products, Miyagiwa's model shows that the impact of preferential government procurement on the prices of the two firms' products is ambiguous. However, Firm 1 will charge a higher price than Firm 2, or more generally, the domestic price will be higher than the import price, a typical result with trade barriers.

Trionfetti (1999) applies the model developed by Baldwin and Richardson to a small country, that is, a price taker. (In the context of Miyagiwa's model, it would imply that Firm 1 could not influence the price of Firm 2.) Trionfetti (1999) and Brülhart and Trionfetti (2004) also affirm the proposition made by Baldwin and Richardson (1972) and Baldwin (1984) that under perfect competition and product homogeneity, preferential government procurement is inconsequential.

Baldwin and Richardson (1972) showed that the U.S. government's import share was much lower than that of the private sector, meaning a bias was shown by the U.S. government in favor of domestic producers. (An import share is the percentage of total domestic consumption that was supplied by imports.) A more comprehensive study by Trionfetti (2000) also revealed that government purchases are biased in favor of domestic producers. Government import shares were compared with those of the private economy with a focus on thirteen tradable manufactured products in seven industrialized countries.[8] Of the ninety-one ratios (thirteen manufactured products times seven countries) of government import shares to import shares of the private economy, seventy cases had a ratio of less than one, and forty-six of those had a ratio of less than two-thirds.[9]

In another study, Brülhart and Trionfetti (2004) concluded that, in monopolistically competitive industries, home-biased government procurement has a positive impact on international specialization. They found that the impact of government demand on international specialization is larger than that of private demand. It is important to note that Brülhart and Trionfetti (2004) treat home bias as an exogenous variable and, therefore, a question remains over cause and effect in the relationship between home bias and specialization. Nonetheless, the study gives credence to countries that defend discriminatory procurement policies as a way to enhance their competitiveness or to diversify their exports.

Notwithstanding obvious limitations of constrained theoretical models and empirical studies limited by data, what emerges is an important warning not to make categorical assumptions about the impact of discriminatory government procurement policies. Mattoo (1996), who provides an excellent review of the literature and a careful argument for the GPA, agrees that "a zero preference should not be used as a benchmark with which to evaluate the welfare effects of procurement policies in the same way that a zero tariff is used to evaluate the welfare effects of trade policies" (Mattoo, 1996: 12).

---

[8]    The seven countries are Denmark, France, Germany, Ireland, Italy, Spain, and the United Kingdom.
[9]    The study was done using data from 1985.

## AFRICAN COUNTRIES AND THE AGREEMENT
## ON GOVERNMENT PROCUREMENT

Article V of the GPA has provisions for special treatment for developing countries. These provisions would apply to all African countries that become signatories to the agreement. As is the case with other GATT/WTO agreements, the language conveys an understanding of the unique challenges developing countries face, and a commitment to support those countries in their initiatives to develop. The objectives of special treatment include: (a) promoting the development of domestic industry; (b) facilitating increased imports from those countries; and (c) providing technical assistance. The first objective would potentially be achieved by letting developing countries set the parameters of their commitments according to their development goals and strategies. That is, developing countries would be allowed to make their own decisions regarding what is included in their lists of entities, goods, and services to be covered by the agreement. Likewise, they would be able to modify their coverage lists after entering into the agreement. The two other objectives require affirmative action from developed countries. Technical assistance includes translating bidding documentation from suppliers of developing countries and establishing information centers to assist developing countries with reasonable requests about laws, regulations, procedures, notices, future tenders, etc. Least-developed countries are to receive even more extensive special treatment.

Obviously the promise of special treatment has not been convincing enough to attract African countries (and other developing countries) to join the GPA. African countries have kept their distance from the agreement, even from observer status; Cameroon is the only African country with observer status in the GPA.[10]

---

[10] Other countries with observer status (in 2007) are Albania, Argentina, Armenia, Australia, Chile, China, Colombia, Croatia, Jordan, Kyrgyz Republic, Moldova, Mongolia, Oman, Panama, Sri Lanka, Chinese Taipei, and Turkey.

African countries have been resistant even to a weaker version of the GPA that developed countries have been trying to offer all WTO members.

During the Uruguay Round of negotiations, it became evident that a multilateral agreement on government procurement of the scope and coverage of the plurilateral arrangement was highly improbable. However, the United States and other GPA members saw that a scaled-down agreement on government procurement, applied to all WTO members, would be an important starting point. Thus, the bar was lowered to the pursuit of an agreement on transparency in government procurement (TGP).

### THE SINGAPORE ISSUES

The first WTO Ministerial Conference took place in December 1996 in Singapore. Among the Ministerial Declarations of that conference was the establishment of working groups to study issues related to investment policies, competition policies, TGP practices, and trade facilitation (WTO, 1996: paragraphs 20–22). These four areas of exploration came to be known as the "Singapore Issues." At the Doha Ministerial Conference in November 2001, it was declared that, following the preparatory work by the working groups, negotiations on these issues would "take place after the Fifth Session of the Ministerial Conference on the basis of a decision to be taken, by explicit consensus, at that session on modalities of negotiations" (WTO, 2001a: paragraphs 20–27). The discussion that follows focuses on TGP. However, some materials to which reference is made address all the Singapore issues collectively.

The assignment of the working group for TGP was never an easy task. It involved many meetings with various stakeholders and other intergovernmental organizations that have expertise in TGP, such as the United Nations Commission for International

Trade Law (UNCITRAL) and the World Bank. The working group identified twelve important issues:[11]

1. definition and scope of government procurement;
2. procurement methods;
3. publication of information on national legislation and procedures;
4. information on procurement opportunities, tendering and qualification procedures;
5. time-periods;
6. transparency of decisions on qualification;
7. transparency of decisions on contract awards;
8. domestic review procedures;
9. other matters related to transparency;
10. information to be provided to other governments;
11. WTO dispute settlement procedures; and
12. technical cooperation and special and differential treatment for developing countries.

Communications from the working group, comprehensive and painstaking as they may have been, only produced a plethora of incompatible proposals from WTO members. In fact, the introduction of the Singapore issues led to an impasse in the preparation period before the September 2003, Fifth Ministerial Conference (in Cancún, Mexico). On one side were developed countries led by the EC who staged a campaign for the Singapore issues to be incorporated into the Doha Round of negotiations after the Cancún conference. On the other side were African and other developing countries who called for further clarification.

In February 2003, the EC had submitted a proposal which assumed that negotiations of the Singapore issues would commence after the Cancún Ministerial Conference and that the Singapore issues could be discussed as a single undertaking (WTO, 2003c). The

---

[11] Submissions by WTO members and other documents that pertain to the work of the Working Group for Transparency in Government Procurement can be found at http://docsonline.wto.org/ under WT/WGTGP/*.

EC proposal included "elements of modalities" that could guide negotiations. The question of modalities was important because, according to the Doha Ministerial Conference Declaration on TGP, negotiations would take place only after an explicit consensus on modalities of negotiations. In a follow-up communication, the EC declared that members were "on the verge of a decision on modalities for these negotiations" (WTO, 2003e).

The EC presentation of "elements of modalities" came under attack by twelve developing countries, including five African countries (WTO, 2003f)[12]:

Since explicit consensus on modalities is a precondition for commencing negotiations, it is very important to clarify the meaning and issue of modalities. The Doha Declaration itself does not define the term "modalities." It would thus be logical to define it from current WTO practice. It is clear that the "modalities" on negotiations on an issue contains the aspects of the issue that are agreed on and the nature and direction of obligations to be undertaken. Consensus on modalities would therefore require agreement by all Members on the specific issues to be covered, and the substantive treatment of these issues, including the nature and direction of obligations and commitments arising from them.

... Under the section on "elements of modalities", the EC paper simply provides three subject matters, namely procedural issues (number of meetings, etc.), scope and coverage of negotiating agenda, and special and differential treatment. This short and superficial listing of "elements of modalities" fails to capture the breadth and the substance of the discussions on the Singapore issues. Implicit in the EC paper is that explicit consensus on the modalities themselves is not required, only a listing of 'elements of modalities.'

The term "modalities" is elusive. While the challenge from developing countries is technically and procedurally valid, it is also a red herring. There was resistance from the outset as to why an

---

[12] The communication came from Bangladesh, Cuba, Egypt, India, Indonesia, Kenya, Malaysia, Nigeria, Pakistan, Venezuela, Zambia, and Zimbabwe.

agreement on government procurement, even if limited to transparency, should be required of all WTO members. By 2003, developing countries' resistance to negotiating the Singapore issues had gained so much momentum that no amount of work on defining the modalities would have enabled them to pass the "explicit consensus" test. It is likely that a more comprehensive set of "elements of modalities" by the EC would have simply supplied more targets at which developing countries could take aim.

The reluctance and apprehension of African countries concerning the negotiations of the Singapore issues persisted. They communicated their strong opposition, albeit in diplomatic language, through various overlapping groupings, including subsets of developing countries, regional economic blocs such as the Southern African Development Community (SADC), ACP countries, the AU, least-developed countries, and the Group of 77.[13]

The stance of African countries regarding TGP cannot be well understood by simply reading the Singapore Ministerial Declarations. The one on TGP seems rather supportive of African and other developing countries.

These negotiations will build on the progress made in the Working Group on Transparency in Government Procurement by that time and take into account participants' development priorities, especially those of least-developed country participants. Negotiations shall be limited to the transparency aspects and therefore will not restrict the scope for countries to give preferences to domestic supplies and suppliers. We commit ourselves to ensuring adequate technical assistance and support for

---

[13] For example, see these documents at the WTO website: WT/L/409 (a declaration by LDCs, August 2001); WT/L/430 (a declaration by ACP countries, November 2001); WT/MIN(01)/ST/138 (a statement by SADC, November 2001); and WT/GC/W/510 (communication from Benin, Kenya, Mauritius, Nigeria, Senegal, Sierra Leone, Tanzania, Uganda, Zambia, and Zimbabwe, August 2003). See also, the Mauritius Declaration by African Union Trade Ministers (Economic Commission for Africa, 2003); the Maputo Declaration by the African Union Heads of State (African Union, 2003); and the Declaration by the Group of 77 and China on the Fourth WTO Ministerial Conference at Doha, Qatar, October 2001 (http://www.g77.org/Docs/Doha.htm).

capacity building both during the negotiations and after their conclusion. (WTO, 2001a: paragraph 26)

Why would African countries be hesitant, given these promises which appear to reflect awareness of and sensitivity to their needs? There is a Swahili saying, "aliyeumwa na nyoka huogopa gambale!" (One who has been bitten by a snake fears dead snake skin.) Presumably African countries feel they have been "bitten" (or deceived) by previous agreements, despite the fact that WTO agreements routinely include exceptions, extensions, and promises of assistance to developing countries. Pressure, political maneuvering, and paternalism on the part of developed countries toward African countries are also routinely seen in the WTO. There is evidence of hypocrisy on the part of developed countries as well, especially as it relates to their agricultural policies. All of this results in extreme caution, skepticism, or outright defiance on the part of African countries. In short, it is not possible to understand the African countries' position in isolation from other issues in the WTO.

### REASONS FOR AFRICAN COUNTRIES' RESISTANCE TO TGP

Several factors help explain why African countries have specifically resisted negotiations that could lead to a multilateral agreement on TGP. They include: complexity of the issues; scarce resources; limitations in pursuing industrial policy; strategy; and sovereignty.

## Complexity of the Issues

One may ask what is so complex about making government procurement transparent. Moreover, it seems everyone these days is preaching about good governance; it would seem credibility can only begin with transparency. However, the twelve issues identified by the working group give an indication of how complicated the discussion on transparency can get. It does not help that literature on the benefits of procurement reforms is scant (Evenett and Hoekman, 2005). Even if there were a common understanding of the definition and scope of government procurement, questions would remain about procedures and enforcement. There are issues related to monitoring procedures and how to respond to queries and complaints that might arise. Nonetheless, African opposition to proceeding to the negotiations phase has not been categorical. Their one common call has been to continue the process of further clarification.

While African countries have criticized the EC for treating the Singapore issues as a single undertaking, they have used the same "bundling" approach when raising the complexity challenge. The complexity appears overwhelming when the Singapore issues are packaged together.

## Scarce Resources

Negotiations for any agreement are costly, especially if the issues are complex. African countries question whether the expected benefits would justify the opportunity cost of allocating their meager technical and diplomatic resources to these issues; they do not consider these issues to be a priority at this point in their development. Nonetheless, African countries have made use of this opportunity to reiterate their call for effective technical assistance and capacity building. Scarcity of resources for meaningful negotiations is a ubiquitous concern for African countries.

## Limitations in Pursuing Industrial Policy

It is fair to assume that an agreement on TGP is sought with the final goal of reaching a broader agreement on government procurement. Such an agreement would allow for increased competition through greater market access, where developed countries would have a comparative advantage. Nonetheless, while competition is a pre-requisite for an efficient allocation of resources, efficiency is not the only goal. Moreover, comparative advantage is dynamic. Preferential government procurement can be used in the context of a pragmatic industrial policy to support geographical areas, minority groups that have been marginalized in the past, or industries that have the potential to be competitive in the future. African countries are, therefore, apprehensive about any negotiations if the path of those negotiations may lead to an agreement that would undermine their ability to pursue industrial policy.

## Strategy

WTO negotiations are a quid pro quo (something for something) "game." For example, one of the achievements of the Uruguay Round of GATT was to reach an agreement on agriculture that set the agricultural sector en route to trade liberalization. Developed countries, led by the United States and the EC, had protected the agricultural sector from the jurisdiction of GATT. Incorporating this sector (and textiles and apparel) into the WTO was, therefore, a sacrifice (not in an economic sense) by developed countries. In return, African and other developing countries went along with agreements in areas of great interest to developed countries, including intellectual property (TRIPS) and trade in services (GATS). Developed countries have been the demandeurs for the Singapore issues. In return, developed countries have promised to liberalize their agricultural sectors, a promise that is elusive, at best, given that developed countries themselves are not even on common ground.

Such a history raises important questions. Why are developed countries using farm subsidies once again as their major offer, when they agreed to reduce farm subsidies in 1994 as part of the Agreement on Agriculture? How many new agreements to their advantage do they intend to extract out of their promises to reduce farm subsidies?

Resistance by African countries to negotiate the Singapore issues has centered on concerns of potentially excessive burdens in return for uncertain benefits. It has also been a strategic position, to enable them to push their own issues to the forefront. Of course, a reduction in farm subsidies, particularly cotton subsidies, is an important demand, though they wish they did not have to "give up" any more for developed countries to make good on their old promises. Yet in addition to pushing for a reduction in farm subsidies, African countries have used this opportunity to press for increased food aid. Call it a contradiction or simply pragmatism, African countries have argued for implementation of provisions for differential treatment in their favor. In particular, they have called for food aid for least-developed countries and net food-importing countries that would be negatively affected by the reduction in farm subsidies in OECD countries (Economic Commission for Africa, 2003).

It is important to emphasize that the lingering debate is not only about agricultural subsidies and availability of food aid, but also about the form food aid should take. Developed countries, the United States in particular, use their food aid program as a form of farm subsidies, creating the potential for a vicious circle of farm subsidies. U.S. law (and, apparently, political reality) requires food given by the U.S. government as foreign aid to have been produced in the United States, regardless of food prices elsewhere. In 2004, the EU's Agricultural Commissioner characterized the U.S. food aid program as "export dumping under the guise of 'food aid'" (Fischler, 2004: A12). In line with that assessment, African countries have wanted a reduction in farm subsidies to be complemented with food aid in the form of cash-aid.

African countries have also mounted their own offensive by calling for greater transparency within the WTO itself. This is represented by this quote drawn from a proposal by eleven African countries, addressing the Singapore issues:

We reiterate the crucial importance of creating a transparent, democratic, all inclusive and consultative decision-making process in the WTO, as this is vital to enhancing the credibility of the WTO and the multilateral trading system. (WTO, 2003g)

African countries would have missed an important opportunity, had they not pushed for more transparency within the WTO. Of course, this was not the first time such an appeal was made. Yet this was a prime opportunity because developed countries were pushing for negotiations on transparency in government procurement.

Another reflection of strategy is that a display of resistance might win them more concessions in the future in terms of transitional periods, thresholds, and technical assistance, if and when an agreement on government procurement is reached. Should that time come, African countries would like to take a minimalist approach in terms of obligations, while at the same time maximizing potential fringe benefits.

Here is another consideration. Even if the real reason for pushing for TGP is eventually to have market access, it is unlikely that developed countries are craving African markets. The markets are too small and most African countries would have to be treated with special preferences that would exempt them from many obligations anyway. Moreover, a good proportion of government procurement funds for major African projects comes from external sources, accompanied by procurement procedures from those sources. For example, there are elaborate guidelines for procurement for projects funded by the World Bank (World Bank, 2004a).

The World Bank and the International Monetary Fund (IMF) use their expertise and lending leverage to assess and encourage the reform of government procurement procedures for many African countries.[14] Loans issued through the Poverty Reduction Strategy Papers (PRSP) channel have become an important means for pressing for transparency in government procurement. Tanzania was praised in 2003 as one of the first countries to have enacted a government procurement law modeled after the one by the United Nations Commission on International Trade Law (UNCITRAL) (World Bank, 2003).

The point here is that, given their small markets and their dependence on foreign donors, most African countries have hardly any additional market to lose, even if a government procurement agreement increasing market access were to be reached. African countries' opposition to negotiating on TGP must be understood in part as a strategy to be in coalition with the developing countries bloc, which includes large economies like Brazil and India. If African countries had responded positively to the developed countries' prodding, with the position that an agreement on TGP did not make much difference to them, it would have weakened the position of Brazil and India. Brazil, India, and other large developing countries would not have looked very kindly at African countries. African countries must always walk a fine line because "giants" and partners are on either side of them.

## Sovereignty

At the same time, a measure of political independence is important. No one needs to be reminded that less than fifty years ago, African countries were under the colonial oppression of European countries. Colonialism not only created what Ake described as incoherent or disarticulated economies (Ake, 1991). It also left a sense of "who are you to tell me what to do?" The author has had the occasion to speak with many African scholars and policy makers over

---

[14] Country Procurement Assessment Reports (CPAR) prepared by the World Bank can be accessed at www.worldbank.org.

the years. It is not unusual to see Africans resent and reject, as a first reaction, a corrective measure sponsored by developed countries, even though the Africans might already have been speaking of a need for that change. Successful rejection can be a symbol, even if misguided at times, of independence and sovereignty, not necessarily a measure of being on the right side of the issue. Although this phenomenon may be true of all countries, the historical experience of African countries probably makes them more sensitive than others to suggestions and pressure from developed countries.

## THE WTO CONFERENCE IN CANCÚN

When an agreement on TGP might be reached is anyone's guess. The WTO conference in Cancún in September 2003 collapsed primarily over the Singapore issues and farm subsidies. WTO members failed to reach "explicit consensus" on the modalities of negotiations on the Singapore issues. As expected, wrangling and finger pointing ensued, but in the end reality set in. On August 1, 2004, three of the four Singapore issues – investment, competition, and TGP – were dropped from the Doha Agenda, although not from the WTO agenda altogether. The fourth issue, trade facilitation, remained in the Doha agenda.

The collapse of the Cancun Ministerial Conference was greeted with jubilation by anti-globalization groups who seem to take every setback in the WTO as a victory and vindication of their viewpoint. However, a reflection by Supachai Panitchpakdi, Director General of the WTO, suggests there are no winners:

While some non-governmental organizations – and even some delegations – briefly celebrated the collapse in Cancún, I can assure you that no one is celebrating now. There is a sharp realization that failure to restart talks means that the US$1 billion a day spent on farm subsidies in OECD countries will continue unabated. (Panitchpakdi, 2003)

Panitchpakdi might be right. Nonetheless, it is high time OECD countries stopped using the Singapore issues as a smokescreen for the farm subsidies that have been preserved for decades. OECD farm subsidies continue unabated because of a lack of political fortitude to remove them. Some African diplomats in Geneva describe what happened in Cancún as unfortunate, but also as an important wake-up call to developed countries that African and other developing countries cannot simply be manipulated and intimidated.

Notwithstanding these observations, African countries do need to take some time to consider for themselves the role of their government procurement policies in the long run, regardless of how the issue might eventually play out in the WTO. (One can expect that sooner or later, the WTO will have an agreement on transparency in government procurement to which all members will be subject.) African countries may have had valid reasons to stall the discussions on government procurement in the Doha Round. However, transparency is still paramount, if government procurement policies are to have their potentially positive effect on social and economic development. If not for any other reason, transparency would, over time, provide information that could be used to evaluate the role of government procurement policies in development. Moreover, the sheer size of government procurement, and the potential for corruption associated with it, call for transparency.

### CORRUPTION IN AFRICAN COUNTRIES

TGP is not only important in areas where international cooperation or sponsorship is involved; it can also be valuable in reducing corruption in areas where there is no international cooperation. Although some countries have witnessed improvement in governance since the political and economic reforms of the 1980s, they still have a long way to go. A lack of transparency in government services is still common in most African countries. This would likely be encountered whether one is applying for a business license, a driver's license, a birth certificate, a passport, a plot in an urban area, a deed, electricity, landline phone service (less important today given the cellular phone revolution), or public college education. Given the large size of government procurement relative to GDP and its occurrence at all levels of government, TGP can reinforce or be a catalyst for reforms in many other areas of government, as well.

TGP is not an end in itself. Its economic and social values are derived from its potential to increase competition (even just within the country) and reduce corruption. Some people get very defensive when the subject of corruption in African countries is raised and are quick to point to accomplices from developed countries, as well as corruption in developed countries themselves. While these points cannot be dismissed categorically, corruption in many African countries is systemic. More importantly, it is wise to take the advice of Julius Nyerere, a philosopher and the first President of Tanzania, that one should not compare his or her health with that of a sick person, but rather with the appropriate measures of good health. In this case, the appropriate point of reference would be zero corruption.

The best measure of corruption that is available at present is the one produced annually by Transparency International (an NGO), called the Corruption Perception Index (CPI).

The index defines corruption as the abuse of public office for private gain, and measures the degree to which corruption is perceived to exist among a country's public officials and politicians. It is a composite index, drawing on 16 surveys from 10 independent institutions, which gathered the opinions of businesspeople and country analysts. (Transparency International, 2006)

The CPI ranges from 0 to 10, from highly corrupt to highly clean, respectively. Transparency International considers a CPI of 5 as the borderline number that separates countries that do and do not have serious problems with corruption.

Perceptions on corruption vary depending on culture, its transparency, the magnitude of the corrupt acts, the mode of corruption, political campaign regulations, the economic situation of the corrupt individual, the distribution of corruption "benefits," expectations, and other factors.[15] However, this index is not derived out of thin air. Even if it were merely based on perceptions, perceptions do matter, particularly to foreign investors whose perceptions would be influenced in a positive way by a country's adherence to a multilateral agreement. African countries can therefore benefit from an agreement on TGP.

Out of 159 countries in the 2005 survey by Transparency International, forty-three countries had a CPI of 5 or above, with Botswana being the only African country in that class, as shown in Table 5.2. Chad and Bangladesh tied for the lowest CPI in 2005. The African Union estimates that corruption costs Africa $148 billion a year, a value equal to one-quarter of the continent's GDP.[16]

Empirical studies, when and where possible, might help show the magnitude of corruption attributable to the lack of transparency in government procurement. However, considering the costs of corruption, it would be unwise to put TGP on hold until such studies are conducted. The costs of corruption include increased transaction costs, increased rent-seeking activities, increased uncertainty, and reduced productivity. In his study of the impact of corruption on economic growth and income distribution in Africa, Gyimah-Brempong (2002) estimates that a one unit increase in corruption, as measured by corruption perception indices, reduces the growth rate of GDP by between 0.75 and 0.9 percentage points. A unit increase in corruption is associated with between 0.04 and 0.07 units increase in the gini coefficient of income inequality.[17] In other

---

[15] For more on the definition of corruption and caution on the CPI, see Gyimah-Brempong (2002).

[16] See http://www.irinnews.org/report.asp?ReportID=29918. For comments on corruption in Africa, see http://news.bbc.co.uk/1/hi/world/africa/3819027.stm.

[17] The gini coefficient is a measure of inequality in income distribution. Its value ranges from 0 to 1 (or 0 to 100, in percentage terms) representing, respectively, a perfectly even distribution of income and a situation where one person has all the income (with everyone else receiving no income at all).

TABLE 5.2 Corruption Perception Index for African Countries: 1998–2005

| | 1998 | 1999 | 2000 | 2001 | 2002 | 2003 | 2004 | 2005 |
|---|---|---|---|---|---|---|---|---|
| Botswana | 6.1 | 6.1 | 6.0 | 6.0 | 6.4 | 5.7 | 6.0 | 5.9 |
| Tunisia | 5.0 | 5.0 | 5.2 | 5.3 | 4.8 | 4.9 | 5.0 | 4.9 |
| South Africa | 5.2 | 5.0 | 5.0 | 4.8 | 4.8 | 4.4 | 4.6 | 4.5 |
| Namibia | 5.3 | 5.3 | 5.4 | 5.4 | 5.7 | 4.7 | 4.4 | 4.3 |
| Mauritius | 5.0 | 4.9 | 4.7 | 4.5 | 4.5 | 4.4 | 4.1 | 4.2 |
| Seychelles | | | | | | | 4.1 | 4.0 |
| Ghana | 3.3 | 3.3 | 3.5 | 3.4 | 3.9 | 3.3 | 3.6 | 3.5 |
| Burkina Faso | | | 3 | | | | | 3.4 |
| Egypt | 2.9 | 3.3 | 3.1 | 3.6 | 3.4 | 3.3 | 3.2 | 3.4 |
| Lesotho | | | | | | | | 3.4 |
| Morocco | 3.7 | 4.1 | 4.7 | | 3.7 | 3.3 | 3.2 | 3.2 |
| Senegal | 3.3 | 3.4 | 3.5 | 2.9 | 3.1 | 3.2 | 3.0 | 3.2 |
| Rwanda | | | | | | | | 3.1 |
| Benin | | | | | | | 3.2 | 2.9 |
| Gabon | | | | | | | 3.3 | 2.9 |
| Mali | | | | | | 3.0 | 3.2 | 2.9 |
| Tanzania | 1.9 | 1.9 | 2.5 | 2.2 | 2.7 | 2.5 | 2.8 | 2.9 |
| Algeria | | | | | | 2.6 | 2.7 | 2.8 |
| Madagascar | | | | | 1.7 | 2.6 | 3.1 | 2.8 |
| Malawi | 4.1 | 4.1 | 4.1 | 3.2 | 2.9 | 2.8 | 2.8 | 2.8 |
| Mozambique | | 3.5 | 2.2 | | | 2.7 | 2.8 | 2.8 |
| Gambia | | | | | | 2.5 | 2.8 | 2.7 |
| Swaziland | | | | | | | | 2.7 |
| Eritrea | | | | | | | 2.6 | 2.6 |
| Zambia | 3.5 | 3.5 | 3.4 | 2.6 | 2.6 | 2.5 | 2.6 | 2.6 |
| Zimbabwe | 4.2 | 4.1 | 3.0 | 2.9 | 2.7 | 2.3 | 2.3 | 2.6 |
| Libya | | | | | | 2.1 | 2.5 | 2.5 |
| Uganda | 2.6 | 2.2 | 2.3 | 1.9 | 2.1 | 2.2 | 2.6 | 2.5 |
| Niger | | | | | | | 2.2 | 2.4 |
| Sierra Leone | | | | | | 2.2 | 2.3 | 2.4 |
| Burundi | | | | | | | 2.3 | 2.3 |

(*continued*)

TABLE 5.2 *(continued)*

|  | 1998 | 1999 | 2000 | 2001 | 2002 | 2003 | 2004 | 2005 |
|---|---|---|---|---|---|---|---|---|
| Congo, Republic of |  |  |  |  |  | 2.2 | 2.3 | 2.3 |
| Cameroon | 1.4 | 1.5 | 2.0 | 2.2 | 2.2 | 1.8 | 2.1 | 2.2 |
| Ethiopia |  |  | 3.2 |  | 3.5 | 2.5 | 2.3 | 2.2 |
| Liberia |  |  |  |  |  |  |  | 2.2 |
| Congo, Democratic Republic of |  |  |  |  |  |  | 2.0 | 2.1 |
| Kenya | 2.5 | 2.0 | 2.1 | 2.0 | 1.9 | 1.9 | 2.1 | 2.1 |
| Somalia |  |  |  |  |  |  |  | 2.1 |
| Sudan |  |  |  |  |  | 2.3 | 2.2 | 2.1 |
| Angola |  |  | 1.7 |  | 1.7 | 1.8 | 2 | 2 |
| Côte I'voire | 3.1 | 2.6 | 2.7 | 2.4 | 2.7 | 2.1 | 2.0 | 1.9 |
| Equatorial Guinea |  |  |  |  |  |  |  | 1.9 |
| Nigeria | 1.9 | 1.6 | 1.2 | 1.0 | 1.6 | 1.4 | 1.6 | 1.9 |
| Chad |  |  |  |  |  |  | 1.7 | 1.7 |

*Source*: *Transparency International* <http://www.transparency.org/>

words, corruption hurts the poor disproportionately more than it hurts the rich. According to the study, corruption decreases the GDP growth rate directly by reducing productivity and indirectly by reducing investment.

Asiedu (2006) estimates that decreasing corruption in Nigeria to the level of South Africa's would have the same positive impact on foreign direct investment (FDI) as increasing the share of fuels and minerals in total exports by 35 percent. Thus, while natural resources have been the main attraction for FDI in Africa, improving government institutions and reducing corruption are important to enhance the inflow of FDI, whether or not a country is endowed with natural resources.

Causes of corruption include a lack of transparency and competition combined with a lack of accountability in activities that enjoy high monopoly rents, such as government procurement. In such areas, establishing anti-corruption units usually has no real impact. To illustrate this, in the 1960s and 1970s when central banks were the only legal suppliers of foreign currency in many African countries, corruption in foreign exchange was the norm in those countries. This was mainly due to overvaluation of domestic currencies, which created a shortage of foreign currencies. No amount of condemnation and anti-corruption campaigns put a dent in the corruption and parallel markets in foreign exchange. When the foreign exchange market was liberalized, though, mainly due to external pressure, such corruption ended instantaneously. Although corruption in government procurement may never be eliminated completely, the way to deal with it must include transparency and increased competition; this can be encouraged by an agreement on TGP.

One may speculate that an agreement on TGP could have prevented some of the corrupt deeds that have taken place in many countries involving the award of large government contracts to non-existent companies. For example, it might have prevented corrupt individuals in the government of Tanzania from awarding a multi-million dollar contract in 2006 to a bogus company, Richmond Development Company, to supply electricity to Tanzania. A report by a parliamentary committee that investigated the awarding of the contract implicated some cabinet members and the Prime Minister, which led to his resignation and the naming of a new cabinet by President Jakaya Kikwete.

## FORMULATING AN IDEAL GOVERNMENT PROCUREMENT POLICY

With all the discussion about the importance of transparency in government procurement policies, one may well ask just what exactly an ideal government procurement policy would look like. Although a single satisfactory answer to this question may not be found, this question must guide any consideration of government procurement policies. The following (not necessarily in order of importance) should be used as criteria to help determine the best government procurement policy for any given country: the end goals of procurement; integration of procurement goals with broader social-economic goals; competitiveness; clarity and transparency of the selection process; flexibility; and administration of the process and enforceability.

## *The End Goals of Procurement*

It is imperative to be clear about what is being procured. Otherwise, the government will be at the mercy of the potential bidders. Construction services for a new road that would involve building a sophisticated bridge are different from construction services for resurfacing an existing road. Although this point seems very basic, projects are often left uncompleted or abandoned because the goals were not clear and/or realistic, given the funding. To be fair, this is a question to be addressed by people who propose and plan for the project for which they procure goods and services. Nonetheless, careful consideration of the end goals of the procurement can provide a reality check. Although projects fail for many reasons, not necessarily all related to procurement, sometimes projects are not completed because flaws in the procurement system make donors stop funding them.

## *Integration of Procurement Goals with Broader Social-Economic Goals*

External (spillover) benefits can be associated with government procurement. Government procurement can be used in the context of "affirmative action" programs to promote the inclusion of women, minorities, and other historically marginalized people in employment and business opportunities. For example, since 1996, the South African government has had a system of preference points for contracts worth less than 2 million rands (equivalent to about US$324,000 in March 2006) for "previously disadvantaged individuals" (PDIs) and women. PDIs are "individuals who, being South African citizens, are socially and economically disadvantaged by the South African political dispensation prior to April 28, 1994" (Republic of South Africa, 2001: appendix A).

Given South Africa's history of apartheid and its exemplary coordinated approach to increasing opportunities for PDIs, its formula for calculating adjudication points for tenders (i.e., bids) deserves some consideration here. Adjudication points, used to determine who will be most favored in government bidding, are calculated as follows:

$NP = 88[1 - (P\text{-}Pm)/Pm] + 0.1^*$ percentage of equity owned by PDI $+ 0.02^*$ percentage of equity owned by women
where NP is the number of points;
Pm is the price of the lowest acceptable tender on a comparable basis; and
P is the tender price.

The tender is awarded to the bidder with the highest points. In case of a draw, the bidder with the lowest tender price is given priority. Table 5.3 gives a numerical example with three bidders, A, B, and C. Note that the lowest and highest number of points a bidder can get are 88 and 100, respectively. In this hypothetical, simplified example, B would be awarded the tender. For an elaborate manual on how South Africa uses government procurement to enhance opportunities for PDIs, see Republic of South Africa (2001).

Government procurement can also be used in the context of a coherent industrial policy to support domestic industries. Here are a few examples of how government procurement procedures give

TABLE 5.3 Tender Adjudication Points for Previously
Disadvantaged Individuals and Women in South Africa
(A Numerical Example)

| Bidder | Tender Price | Percentage of Equity Ownership | | Number of Points |
|---|---|---|---|---|
| | | PDI | Women | |
| A | 100 | 100 | 100 | 90.22 |
| B | 95 | 80 | 40 | 91.91 |
| C | 90 | 90 | 30 | 91.2 |

preferential treatment to local suppliers and products, according to
the latest reviews by the WTO.[18]

Benin:    Small and medium-size national enterprises may be the
exclusive recipients of certain contracts.

Botswana:    The price advantage for local firms is 40 percent of the local
content ratio. For example, a local firm imports 3 million
pula worth of bicycle parts and uses them to produce 4
million pula worth of finished bicycles. The local content
ratio would be 25 percent (value added divided by total
value of finished bicycles) and the price advantage would
be 10 percent (40 percent of 25 percent).

Burkina Faso:    A price advantage of 10 percent is given to domestic firms.

Côte d'Ivoire:    No apparent restrictions exist regarding the nationality of bidders, except in the case of professional services,
such as those of architects, pharmacists, lawyers, physicians, surveyors, and jurists. Such services are reserved
for Ivorians.

Egypt:    A price advantage of 15 percent is given to domestic
firms. In addition, the government has the discretion to
limit procurement to certain enterprises.

---

[18] WTO reviews of national legislation, regulations, and procedures on government procurement can be found at: http://www.wto.org/english/tratop_e/gproc_e/natleg_e.htm.

Mauritius:     No preferential treatment for domestic firms exist, except where authorized by foreign agencies. For example, for projects financed by the European Development Fund, Article 303 of the Lomé IV Convention provides bidders from ACP countries a price preference of 10 percent for work contracts worth less than €5 million (ACP, 1995).[19] For supply contracts, the price preference is 15 percent for bidders from ACP countries, for all contracts regardless of their value.[20]

Namibia:     A price advantage of up to 20 percent is given for domestic products and up to 10 percent for goods assembled in the country.

Togo:     When a contract is divided into lots, at least one-fourth of the lots must be reserved for local businesses. In calculating adjudication points, national enterprises are given bonus points of up to 7.5 percent. Foreign enterprises that win tenders must subcontract at least 30 percent of the work to local businesses.

Uganda:     Local suppliers receive a 15 to 20 percent preferential margin.

Zambia:     No de jure preferences are given for local suppliers. However, in practice, tender committees have a certain amount of discretion to favor local enterprises in the case of limited orders.

The examples above are not unique to African countries. Typically, developed countries single out small and medium-size businesses for special attention and preference. In the United States, the Small Business Act (Public Law 644 §15(g)) includes statutory goals (as

---

[19]   The threshold was set in 1995 at that amount in terms of the European Currency Unit (ECU). However, when the euro was introduced in 1999, it replaced the ECU at par, that is, at a one-to-one ratio. To qualify for the price preference for works contracts, one-quarter of the capital stock and management staff must originate from one or more of the ACP countries.

[20]   To qualify, at least 50 percent of the suppliers must originate from one or more of the ACP countries.

TABLE 5.4  U.S. Statutory Federal Procurement Goals for Small Business*

| Program | Prime Contracting | Subcontracting |
|---|---|---|
| Small Business | 23 | – |
| Small Disadvantaged Business | 5 | 5 |
| Women-Owned Small Business | 5 | 5 |
| HUBZone Business** | 3 | – |
| Service-Disabled Veteran Owned Business | 3 | 3 |

\* The numbers in this table represent the percentage of overall federal procurement dollars to be spent on contracts with those respective businesses.
\*\* HUBZone, Historically Underutilized Business Zone.
*Source: U.S. Office of Government Contracting (2003)*

of 2006) for small businesses, as shown in Table 5.4. These goals are based on the aggregate of all federal procurement.

The United States uses several laws to authorize the federal government to give preferential treatment to domestic suppliers (WTO, 1999). The two most sweeping of these are the "Buy American Act of 1933" and the "Balance of Payments Program." The Buy American Act provides a price margin of 6 and 12 percent for large and small domestic firms, respectively. (Purchases by the Defense Department are allowed a 50 percent preferential price margin.) The Balance of Payments Program includes a provision on federal procurement of goods for use outside the United States, under which domestic suppliers are allowed a 50 percent price margin. The cost of a domestic product is considered unreasonable if, after including any import duty and the respective price preferential margin, it is above the cost of a similar foreign product. The Buy American Act and the Balance of Payments Program exempt supplies from designated countries, which include GPA members, countries with which the United States has free trade area agreements, the Caribbean Basin countries, and least-developed countries.

Considering social goals and external benefits such as the transfer of knowledge, subsidizing domestic businesses through government procurement (a form of production subsidies) can be
justified. However, to reach their objectives, whether it is industrialization or some social goal, government procurement policies
must be coherent. Government procurement intended to support
women-owned businesses in Africa, for example, must be used
in conjunction with other programs directed toward promoting
women's participation in the economy. These would include education and literacy programs, business training and capacity building programs, special financing programs, and property laws that
allow and enable women to own property (instead of having them
treated as property, as is still the case in many parts of rural Africa).
Unless it is used as part of a coherent set of programs, government
procurement could serve simply as a political tool or bandage for
an intractable challenge that requires a deliberate combination of
solutions.

A government procurement program that gives preferential
treatment to a certain group should ideally aim to make that group
less dependent on the special treatment in the long run. Of course,
for some groups, such as women in African countries, the long run
is many decades to come. At this point in their cultural, political,
and economic history, no African countries can claim to have come
close to reaching the point of optimal support for women, let alone
the point where such support can begin to be reduced.

## Competitiveness

Even the pursuit of industrialization or important social goals such
as empowerment of women must be balanced with an eye to competition and market-induced outcomes – efficiency and the flexibility to change. At best, a well-devised government procurement
program intended to support women's businesses (in conjunction
with other initiatives) would be an incentive for the number of

women-owned businesses to grow and, thus, increase competition and efficiency. At worst, government procurement can be a safe haven for a few businesses owned by women in the capital who are well-connected to government officials. Such a government procurement program could serve as a deterrent to entry into the industry by other women. An effective program would devise ways to incorporate women in all parts of the country, to have more competition and an impact that was farther reaching. A government procurement program (or any other program), even when used in pursuit of key social goals, can be excessively costly and even debilitating to the groups they are supposed to help, if it ignores or assumes away market forces.

Domestic competition is enhanced by competition from other countries. Regional economic blocs provide African countries a logical stepping stone for competitive government procurement. For example, in the East African Community, special treatment by each government could be extended to women-owned businesses in the economic bloc rather than confining it to particular countries. Likewise, a preferential government procurement policy by a least-developed country in Africa could be extended to local enterprises in all least-developed countries in Africa. Thus, regional economic blocs as well as least-developed countries could work at harmonizing their government procurement rules.

The EC's government procurement provision for projects financed by the European Development Fund in ACP countries is a model that can be emulated regarding preferential treatment and competition. It makes local businesses in all ACP countries, and not just in the country in which the project will be implemented, eligible for preferential treatment. Government procurement programs that are cognizant of the merits of competition will avoid the economic losses many African countries suffered during the 1970s with their import substitution policies that insulated inefficient legal monopolies.

## *Clarity and Transparency of the Selection Process*

Government procurement procedures can involve many intricate steps. At times it seems even the most precise procedures may require a lawyer to interpret them. Yet procedures should be clear and easy to understand, especially in terms of the publication of announcements, criteria for different tendering procedures, deadlines, criteria for making decisions on bids, and enforcement. Procedures should also be transparent, that is, announcements about the awarding of contracts should be made publicly, and the records involved in the selection process should be accessible to the public. Procedures must be formulated with social goals, efficiency, and competition in mind.

## *Flexibility*

Changing government procurement rules too often (and without ample notice) creates confusion, unnecessary transaction costs, and loopholes for corruption. Nonetheless, the rules must evolve from experience and technological changes. To be able to learn from experience requires good recordkeeping and a process that can be evaluated against its stated objectives.

New rules may be necessary for more transparency and effective enforcement. For example, Kenya announced new rigorous rules in 2006, following a report that revealed widespread misuse and mismanagement in government procurement (such as buying goods and services at up to three times the market price and paying for goods and services that were never delivered). The new rules make it unlawful for the government to procure goods and services from civil servants (Kathuri, 2006).

Reforms may be needed to allow the use of electronic government procurement as technology gradually improves and becomes more widespread. In March 2006, Morocco agreed to partner with Gateway Development, Italy, and the World Bank to deploy an electronic government procurement system that is expected to streamline procurement processes and reduce government costs.[21]

## Administration of the Process and Enforceability

These criteria go beyond transparency. A transparently corrupt process does not help much. While the transparency of the procurement process helps to reveal violations when they occur, the rules must be enforced. There must be legal and career ramifications (such as losing one's job) of violating the rules, if a transparent procurement process is to be effective. Thus, the process should be administered by an autonomous, independent body that is at the same time accountable to a democratic political system of checks and balances. Unfortunately, for some African countries, this is simply wishful thinking. Malfunction in government procurement processes is often times only a symptom of a broader political malfunction or oppression by the ruling party or personality. For example, the new procurement rules in Kenya aimed at curbing corruption (mentioned above) were not expected to have a significant impact, given the apparent meddling in the procurement enforcement process by the government (Kathuri, 2006a).

### HOW THE WTO CAN HELP AFRICAN COUNTRIES ENHANCE THEIR GOVERNMENT PROCUREMENT POLICIES

No African government is publicly against transparency. In fact, some African countries are establishing reforms in the direction of greater transparency in government policies and services in general. According to various reviews by the WTO, the IMF, the World Bank, and the U.S. State Department, countries such as

---

[21]  The press release can be found at http://home.developmentgateway.org/aboutus/news/ showMoreNewsDetails.do~activeNewsItem=22629.

Botswana, Ghana, Mauritius, South Africa, Tanzania, and Tunisia have made important strides toward transparency and reducing corruption. Other countries have not done so well. Some, such as Angola, Cameroon, Chad, Congo (Republic), Equatorial Guinea, Kenya, Nigeria, and Zimbabwe, have even regressed.

For those governments that are already making concerted efforts toward greater transparency, it is not clear what the additional cost would be of a WTO agreement on TGP. What is also not obvious is how an agreement on TGP would restrain African countries in their development endeavors. Each country would still have the right to determine its own government procurement procedures and objectives. No organization or country, for example, can ask South Africa not to use government procurement as a tool to enhance economic opportunities for PDIs. Moreover, the lack of a WTO agreement on TGP has not spared African countries from external pressure to conform to transparency obligations. The World Bank, the IMF, and developed countries (as donors, lenders, and preference-giving countries) incorporate TGP as a condition.

Given all of this, one may question the relevance of a TGP agreement. Still, an important difference between the current avenues of negotiating transparency, mentioned above, and an agreement on TGP is that the latter would be a multilateral agreement, with minimum standard requirements. The WTO multilateral system can be a useful vehicle for countries to assist each other in achieving greater discipline in the areas of transparency and enforcement of procurement rules. The broad nature of a TGP agreement could also be associated with economies of scale in negotiation costs. That is, instead of negotiating many details with each individual international donor and lender on TGP, the WTO minimum standards on transparency would establish the benchmark. African countries could also benefit from the technical assistance and capacity building that would be associated with such an agreement.

CONCLUSION

It is important that African countries have the ability to use government procurement as a policy tool to achieve their industrial and development goals. Using preferential government procurement as a means to promote industrialization seems logical. Theoretical and empirical studies reviewed above justify preferential government procurement under the right conditions. For example, a case can be made for supporting industries exhibiting increasing returns to scale. Likewise, government procurement policies can be used to support certain industries and businesses owned by minority groups.

Nonetheless, there are economic costs and political ramifications associated with preferential treatment and protection, regardless of the motivation. Notwithstanding its potential as a viable policy tool, discriminatory government procurement can be held hostage by politicians and domestic businesses benefiting from the practice, thereby reducing competition. Moreover, implementing discriminatory policies is not as straightforward as it sounds. In practice, government procurement programs are not fine-tuned to reflect salient features of cost differences between industries (Mattoo, 1996). Preferential government procurement is usually applied uniformly across sectors. At the same time, procedures for preferential treatment are not always transparent and are not easily accessible by all potential suppliers. Trionfetti (1999) warns that in the presence of asymmetrical and incomplete information, preferential government procurement may help sustain inefficient domestic firms at the expense of efficient domestic firms.

Preferential government procurement must be practiced with caution and clear objectives. The potential benefits of preferential treatment must be weighed against the increase in government spending and the increase in costs for private firms buying products similar to those being procured by the government. In addition, discriminatory procurement must be temporary in nature and operate under competitive conditions.

The Singapore issues helped African countries join forces and speak in unison. African countries have shown that when they "stick together," they are no longer "pushovers" in the WTO. Their resolve regarding the Singapore issues shows that they can organize an effective resistance. Of course, not knowing how government procurement might have been affected, removing the discussion on transparency in government procurement from the Doha Round of negotiations in itself does not reveal whether African countries are winners or losers.

Nevertheless, African countries now have the time they felt they needed to think over TGP. Next time it is revived, they can be more specific about the boundaries of an agreement on TGP, rather than simply asking for more clarification. They can prepare to be proactive in terms of the minimum standards of such an agreement, transitional periods for developing and least-developed countries, effective technical assistance, and enforcement. They can do this while taking into account their own capacity, constraints, and development objectives. This preparation should continue in the context of regional economic blocs and the African Union.

In its vow to tackle corruption, the African Union wants to foster transparency and accountability. However, African leaders do not have the culture of disciplining each other. This is true not only in the case of economic corruption, but even in the case of human rights violations and other violations of democratic processes.[22] In the real world, where discriminatory government procurement policies have a high propensity to be driven by politics and rent-seeking incentives, a multilateral agreement on TGP could inject some discipline into the procurement process.

---

[22] For a thoughtful discussion on why African leaders are unable to create a credible peer process to advance good governance, see Taylor (2005).

Competition and real transparency supported by an effective agreement on TGP would "kick away the ladder" with which corrupt leaders (and those who are inefficient and perpetually dependent on subsidies) have been climbing to wealth (and complacency).[23] The likely outcome that the corrupt politician's "ladder" would be "kicked away" by an agreement on TGP should be a reason in itself to support the agreement. This could lead to greater economic development for a nation as a whole. The economic and social values of an agreement on TGP would be derived from its potential both to increase competition (even just within the country) and reduce corruption.

For their part, developed countries need to increase technical assistance to African countries to help them in their efforts to reform government procurement procedures. That is partly what African countries need before discussions on TGP can resume in earnest. Developed countries must also implement past agreements, especially those that have a direct and broad impact on African countries, such as the Agreement on Agriculture. As noted above, discussions on TGP cannot be disentangled from those on agricultural subsidies.

An agreement on TGP must be effective and not simply a diplomatic gesture. When discussions resume and the likelihood of achieving an agreement on TGP increases, some countries will produce endless lists of exemptions. Those must be examined and accommodated responsibly. Trying to incorporate each and every exemption would make the agreement too broad and inconsequential. Considering that was what might have happened had negotiations on TGP been kept in the Doha Round, perhaps removing them was not a bad outcome, for the time being.

---

[23] The concluding chapter provides a commentary on Chang's thesis (Chang, 2002) that developing countries are being asked to "kick away the ladder" that developed countries used to achieve their economic success.

# 6 AID FOR TRADE

G IVEN THE DECLARATION THAT THE DOHA ROUND WAS TO
be a *development* round, it was only a matter of time before
aid became a central issue in the WTO negotiations. However,
from the standpoint of the WTO, aid had to be linked to trade. An
"aid for trade" initiative was formally launched in December 2005
at the WTO Ministerial Conference in Hong Kong. An appeal for
"aid for trade" was carefully crafted in the Hong Kong Ministerial
Declaration to emphasize the role of aid without losing sight of the
importance of removing trade barriers (WTO, 2005b: 11):

Aid for Trade should aim to help developing countries, particularly LDCs
[least-developed countries], to build the supply-side capacity and trade-
related infrastructure that they need to assist them to implement and
benefit from WTO Agreements and more broadly to expand their trade.
Aid for Trade cannot be a substitute for the development benefits that
will result from a successful conclusion to the DDA [Doha Development
Agenda], particularly on market access. However, it can be a valuable
complement to the DDA. We invite the Director-General to create a task
force that shall provide recommendations on how to operationalize Aid
for Trade. The Task Force will provide recommendations to the General
Council by July 2006 on how Aid for Trade might contribute most effectively to the development dimension of the DDA.

The emphasis on more aid comes from African and other developing countries. A recurring theme when one speaks with African
trade officials is that African countries need assistance to increase

[ 245 ]

their capacity: (a) to participate effectively in the WTO negotiations; (b) to take advantage of the WTO agreements and preferential treatment accorded to them by reducing supply constraints; and (c) to mitigate the short-run costs of increased trade liberalization. Regarding the second point, they wonder, for example, how useful the Generalized System of Preferences (GSP), the African Growth and Opportunity Act (AGOA), and Everything But Arms (EBA) are, if they cannot increase their capacity to produce and export more.

Regarding the mitigation of short-run costs of increased trade liberalization, African countries identify three types of such costs. First, an increase in trade liberalization causes a reduction in tariff revenues and a displacement of resources (lost jobs) in the short run. Second, a reduction in agricultural subsidies in developed countries increases the food import bill. Most African countries are currently net food importers, as discussed in Chapter 4. Third, a reduction in the most favored nation (MFN) tariffs erodes the margin of preference. The idea of the MFN principle in the WTO is to have each member country treat all other members equally with respect to trade barriers with exceptions for preferential treatment that benefits developing countries. The margin of preference is the difference between the MFN tariff and the GSP, AGOA, or EBA tariff, for example. The margin of preference erodes whenever MFN tariffs are lowered for goods covered by preferential programs.

Therefore, the objectives of the "Aid for Trade" initiative include reducing supply-side constraints in developing countries and helping those countries adjust to changes. This is an important initiative given its potential to increase the export capacity of African countries, help African countries with adjustment assistance, and improve relations between African and developed countries in the WTO. Nonetheless, discussions about aid – through the WTO no less – can be overwhelming, considering many perennial questions about need, effectiveness, delivery and amounts delivered, purpose, motives of donors, dependency of recipients, accountability,

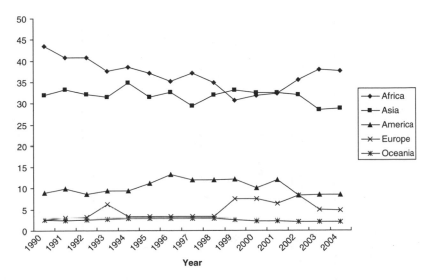

FIGURE 6.1 Regional Shares of Total Net ODA as a Percentage of the World Total ODA

utilization capacity, corruption, competition among potential recipients, duplication, ownership, transaction costs, etc. As such, it should not come as a surprise that a discussion or debate over aid is often marked by contradictions and uncertainties, as illustrated in this chapter.

### MAGNITUDE OF GOVERNMENT AID TO AFRICA[1]

To put the discussion in context, some basic information on the magnitude of aid to Africa is helpful. On average, Africa received 35 percent of the world total net Official Development Assistance (ODA) between 2000 and 2004. The trend of ODA to Africa and other developing regions of the world as a percent of world total ODA is shown in Figure 6.1 and Table 6.1. The actual amounts of disbursement of aid to African countries from 1970 to 2004 are shown in Table 6.2.

---

[1]   The source for all data in this section is OECD (2007), unless indicated otherwise.

TABLE 6.1 Total ODA to the World by Recipient Region: U.S. Dollars (Million), 2003 Prices, Net Disbursements

| | Share (Percent) 2000–2004 | Average Annual Amounts | | | | Annual Amounts | | | | | |
|---|---|---|---|---|---|---|---|---|---|---|---|
| | | 1970–1979 | 1980–1989 | 1990–1999 | 2000–2004 | 2000 | 2001 | 2002 | 2003 | 2004 |
| Africa total | 35.3 | 14,344 | 22,265 | 23,572 | 23,414 | 18,580 | 20,318 | 24,866 | 26,781 | 26,522 |
| America total | 9.4 | 3,971 | 5,646 | 6,467 | 6,215 | 5,639 | 7,123 | 5,865 | 6,132 | 6,318 |
| Asia total | 30 | 19,791 | 22,810 | 19,278 | 19,907 | 17,241 | 19,446 | 21,436 | 20,246 | 21,167 |
| Europe total | 6.5 | 946 | 1,130 | 2,595 | 4,283 | 4,573 | 4,215 | 5,824 | 3,496 | 3,308 |
| Oceania total | 1.3 | 1,479 | 1,827 | 1,710 | 865 | 933 | 935 | 816 | 813 | 828 |
| Unspecified regions | 17.5 | 4,863 | 7,573 | 7,910 | 11,567 | 10,411 | 10,012 | 10,416 | 13,141 | 13,858 |
| World total | 100 | 45,395 | 61,250 | 61,533 | 66,252 | 57,378 | 62,049 | 69,223 | 70,608 | 72,002 |

*Source: OECD (2007).*

TABLE 6.2 ODA from the DAC* to Africa by Recipient Country: U.S. Dollars (Million), 2003 Prices, Net
Disbursements

| | Share (Percent) 2000–2004 | Average Annual Amounts | | | | Annual Amounts | | | | |
| | | 1970–1979 | 1980–1989 | 1990–1999 | 2000–2004 | 2000 | 2001 | 2002 | 2003 | 2004 |
|---|---|---|---|---|---|---|---|---|---|---|
| Algeria | 1.2 | 436 | 285 | 277 | 287 | 250 | 287 | 387 | 235 | 279 |
| Angola | 2.3 | 38 | 176 | 399 | 547 | 366 | 357 | 480 | 497 | 1,036 |
| Benin | 1.3 | 127 | 205 | 277 | 304 | 292 | 338 | 254 | 293 | 343 |
| Botswana | 0.2 | 134 | 201 | 118 | 35 | 36 | 35 | 41 | 28 | 37 |
| Burkina Faso | 2.2 | 252 | 403 | 455 | 503 | 414 | 487 | 556 | 507 | 553 |
| Burundi | 0.9 | 130 | 278 | 215 | 207 | 112 | 176 | 201 | 225 | 320 |
| Cameroon | 2.9 | 338 | 395 | 571 | 686 | 463 | 609 | 773 | 900 | 688 |
| Cape Verde | 0.5 | 31 | 130 | 132 | 118 | 115 | 97 | 108 | 143 | 126 |
| Central African Rep. | 0.3 | 118 | 231 | 173 | 76 | 85 | 82 | 69 | 50 | 95 |
| Chad | 1.0 | 193 | 245 | 259 | 240 | 159 | 234 | 268 | 247 | 292 |
| Comoros | 0.1 | 52 | 80 | 45 | 28 | 24 | 34 | 38 | 24 | 22 |
| Congo, Dem. Rep. of | 7.7 | 587 | 773 | 318 | 1,797 | 225 | 327 | 1,368 | 5,421 | 1,645 |

(continued)

[ 249 ]

TABLE 6.2 *(continued)*

| | 2000–2004 | 1970–1979 | 1980–1989 | 1990–1999 | 2000–2004 | 2000 | 2001 | 2002 | 2003 | 2004 |
|---|---|---|---|---|---|---|---|---|---|---|
| | Share (Percent) | Average Annual Amounts | | | | Annual Amounts | | | | |
| Congo, Rep. of | 0.3 | 137 | 174 | 214 | 75 | 41 | 90 | 68 | 70 | 105 |
| Côte d'Ivoire | 2.0 | 273 | 356 | 910 | 463 | 429 | 229 | 1,266 | 252 | 138 |
| Djibouti | 0.3 | 91 | 147 | 121 | 76 | 82 | 72 | 90 | 79 | 59 |
| Egypt | 5.7 | 3,584 | 2,567 | 3,283 | 1,329 | 1,515 | 1,443 | 1,330 | 988 | 1,368 |
| Equatorial Guinea | 0.1 | 7 | 42 | 45 | 24 | 28 | 17 | 25 | 21 | 26 |
| Eritrea | 1.2 | – | – | 107 | 276 | 210 | 347 | 263 | 316 | 242 |
| Ethiopia | 5.9 | 308 | 856 | 999 | 1,374 | 812 | 1,335 | 1,490 | 1,553 | 1,682 |
| Gabon | 0.1 | 112 | 132 | 111 | 27 | 15 | 10 | 86 | 11 | 34 |
| Gambia | 0.3 | 40 | 123 | 74 | 62 | 57 | 64 | 69 | 63 | 58 |
| Ghana | 3.7 | 244 | 493 | 686 | 878 | 676 | 779 | 746 | 954 | 1,234 |
| Guinea | 1.1 | 65 | 268 | 387 | 258 | 176 | 334 | 284 | 240 | 256 |
| Guinea-Bissau | 0.4 | 45 | 133 | 133 | 93 | 103 | 77 | 71 | 145 | 69 |
| Kenya | 2.3 | 445 | 925 | 772 | 538 | 582 | 561 | 445 | 514 | 586 |
| Lesotho | 0.3 | 89 | 180 | 121 | 75 | 46 | 69 | 88 | 78 | 93 |
| Liberia | 0.4 | 74 | 165 | 123 | 98 | 79 | 46 | 59 | 107 | 197 |

| | | | | | | | | | | |
|---|---|---|---|---|---|---|---|---|---|---|
| Libya | 0.0 | 32 | 17 | 10 | — | — | — | — | — | — |
| Madagascar | 2.5 | 229 | 437 | 458 | 582 | 372 | 450 | 427 | 539 | 1,119 |
| Malawi | 2.0 | 203 | 350 | 525 | 477 | 514 | 489 | 430 | 518 | 432 |
| Mali | 2.1 | 284 | 564 | 473 | 493 | 431 | 434 | 541 | 543 | 516 |
| Mauritania | 1.2 | 272 | 351 | 255 | 279 | 252 | 332 | 410 | 239 | 163 |
| Mauritius | 0.1 | 64 | 82 | 46 | 20 | 25 | 26 | 29 | 15 | 34 |
| Mayotte | 0.7 | 8 | 42 | 102 | 159 | 134 | 158 | 152 | 166 | 186 |
| Morocco | 2.5 | 676 | 1,070 | 815 | 579 | 497 | 649 | 578 | 538 | 636 |
| Mozambique | 6.0 | 98 | 671 | 1,189 | 1,396 | 1,066 | 1,152 | 2,607 | 1,039 | 1,117 |
| Namibia | 0.7 | 0 | 17 | 180 | 160 | 189 | 138 | 159 | 147 | 164 |
| Niger | 1.6 | 303 | 447 | 350 | 371 | 250 | 317 | 345 | 457 | 485 |
| Nigeria | 1.4 | 260 | 127 | 247 | 325 | 210 | 220 | 351 | 318 | 525 |
| Rwanda | 1.6 | 197 | 329 | 461 | 384 | 388 | 365 | 408 | 333 | 426 |
| São Tomé & Principe | 0.2 | 6 | 26 | 54 | 38 | 44 | 49 | 31 | 38 | 30 |
| Senegal | 2.5 | 366 | 751 | 648 | 585 | 507 | 505 | 516 | 446 | 953 |
| Seychelles | 0.1 | 40 | 36 | 22 | 13 | 22 | 16 | 9 | 9 | 9 |
| Sierra Leone | 1.4 | 58 | 140 | 161 | 334 | 217 | 422 | 402 | 303 | 326 |
| Somalia | 0.8 | 311 | 757 | 384 | 177 | 128 | 187 | 222 | 175 | 174 |
| South Africa | 2.5 | — | — | 320 | 578 | 588 | 528 | 591 | 625 | 560 |
| St. Helena | 0.1 | 13 | 31 | 20 | 19 | 22 | 18 | 16 | 18 | 23 |
| Sudan | 2.0 | 547 | 1,446 | 472 | 466 | 269 | 229 | 392 | 617 | 821 |

(continued)

TABLE 6.2  (*continued*)

| | 2000–2004 Share (Percent) | Average Annual Amounts | | | | Annual Amounts | | | | |
|---|---|---|---|---|---|---|---|---|---|---|
| | | 1970–1979 | 1980–1989 | 1990–1999 | 2000–2004 | 2000 | 2001 | 2002 | 2003 | 2004 |
| Swaziland | 0.2 | 61 | 61 | 51 | 42 | 14 | 36 | 26 | 28 | 105 |
| Tanzania | 6.3 | 620 | 1,252 | 1,122 | 1,486 | 1,175 | 1,521 | 1,445 | 1,704 | 1,583 |
| Togo | 0.3 | 137 | 215 | 171 | 60 | 84 | 54 | 60 | 47 | 55 |
| Tunisia | 1.4 | 531 | 408 | 251 | 329 | 262 | 475 | 313 | 298 | 295 |
| Uganda | 4.1 | 111 | 368 | 773 | 961 | 984 | 966 | 818 | 977 | 1,062 |
| Zambia | 3.1 | 248 | 580 | 885 | 733 | 946 | 425 | 741 | 581 | 974 |
| Zimbabwe | 0.8 | 14 | 421 | 471 | 196 | 199 | 199 | 226 | 186 | 169 |
| North of Sahara Unallocated | 0.3 | 15 | 24 | 39 | 76 | 47 | 25 | 36 | 112 | 162 |
| South of Sahara Unallocated | 4.3 | 452 | 638 | 633 | 1,000 | 425 | 806 | 1,082 | 1,362 | 1,327 |
| Africa Unspecified | 2.6 | 235 | 643 | 658 | 620 | 930 | 587 | 581 | 493 | 507 |
| Africa total | 100 | 14,344 | 22,265 | 23,572 | 23,414 | 18,580 | 20,318 | 24,866 | 26,781 | 26,522 |

* DAC, Development Assistance Committee. DAC is the official forum through which OECD countries assist developing countries.

*Source: OECD (2007).*

In the 2000–2004 period, the top ten aid recipients in Africa, listed in descending order (with the country receiving the most aid listed first), were the Democratic Republic of Congo, Tanzania, Ethiopia, Mozambique, Egypt, Ghana, Uganda, Cameroon, Zambia, and Madagascar. Together, they received 48 percent of the total ODA to Africa in that period. ODA varies significantly from country to country, whether measured in terms of dollar amounts, ODA per capita, or ODA as a ratio of gross national income (GNI), as shown in Tables 6.2 and 6.3.[2] Aid is also quite volatile. Bulir and Hamann (2006) find that aid was highly volatile relative to domestic fiscal revenues, in spite of the PRSPs and other initiatives to coordinate and harmonize aid.

ODA to Africa by sector shows an upward trend for the social sector and a downward trend for the economic and production sectors.[3] Comparing the shares of ODA by sector between those in the 1990–1993 period and those in the 2000–2003 period, the share of ODA to the social sector increased from an annual average of 18 percent to an annual average of 34 percent. The share of ODA to the economic and production sectors fell from a combined annual average of 32 percent to 22 percent. Other developing regions experienced similar trends. The downward trend in the share of ODA for the economic and production sectors may explain, in part, the resurgence of efforts to obtain more aid for trade.

Collectively, bilateral aid from individual member countries of the Development Assistance Committee (DAC) constitutes the greatest amount of ODA to Africa.[4] In the three-year period from

---

[2] There are multiple ways of presenting the magnitude of aid. For a careful study on the intensity of aid flows to African countries, see O'Connell and Soludo (2001).

[3] The social sector includes education, health, population programs, water supply and sanitation, and government and civil society. The economic sector includes transport, communications, energy, banking, and business services. The production sector includes agriculture, forestry, fishing, industry, mining, construction, trade, and tourism (OECD, 2007).

[4] Members of the DAC are Australia, Austria, Belgium, Canada, Denmark, Finland, France, Germany, Greece, Ireland, Italy, Japan, Luxembourg, the Netherlands, New Zealand, Norway, Portugal, Spain, Sweden, Switzerland, the United Kingdom, and the United States.

TABLE 6.3  ODA per Capita and ODA as a Ratio of GNI
to African Countries: 2005

| Country | ODA per Capita (US$) | ODA/GNI (Percent) |
|---|---|---|
| Algeria | 11 | 0.38 |
| Angola | 28 | 1.73 |
| Benin | 41 | 8.20 |
| Botswana | 40 | 0.80 |
| Burkina Faso | 50 | 12.78 |
| Burundi | 48 | 46.79 |
| Cameroon | 25 | 2.50 |
| Cape Verde | 315 | 17.05 |
| Central African Republic | 24 | 6.97 |
| Chad | 39 | 8.55 |
| Comoros | 42 | 6.64 |
| Congo, Democratic Rep. of | 32 | 27.54 |
| Congo, Republic of | 362 | 36.82 |
| Côte d'Ivoire | 7 | 0.78 |
| Djibouti | 99 | 10.09 |
| Egypt | 13 | 1.04 |
| Equatorial Guinea | 78 | n.a. |
| Eritrea | 81 | 36.32 |
| Ethiopia | 27 | 17.39 |
| Gabon | 39 | 0.74 |
| Gambia | 38 | 13.06 |
| Ghana | 51 | 10.63 |
| Guinea | 19 | 6.89 |
| Guinea-Bissau | 50 | 27.33 |
| Kenya | 22 | 4.27 |
| Lesotho | 38 | 3.84 |
| Liberia | 72 | 54.12 |
| Libya | 4 | 0.06 |
| Madagascar | 50 | 18.75 |
| Malawi | 45 | 28.37 |
| Mali | 51 | 14.08 |
| Mauritania | 62 | 10.43 |
| Mauritius | 26 | 0.50 |

TABLE 6.3 *(continued)*

| Country | ODA per Capita (US$) | ODA/GNI (Percent) |
|---|---|---|
| Morocco | 22 | 1.28 |
| Mozambique | 65 | 20.78 |
| Namibia | 61 | 1.99 |
| Niger | 37 | 15.17 |
| Nigeria | 49 | 7.41 |
| Rwanda | 64 | 27.39 |
| São Tomé & Principe | 199 | 58.56 |
| Senegal | 59 | 8.44 |
| Seychelles | 235 | 2.83 |
| Sierra Leone | 62 | 29.58 |
| Somalia | 29 | n.a. |
| South Africa | 15 | 0.3 |
| St. Helena | 2,255 | n.a. |
| Sudan | 50 | 7.10 |
| Swaziland | 41 | 1.67 |
| Tanzania | 39 | 12.48 |
| Togo | 14 | 4.00 |
| Tunisia | 38 | 1.38 |
| Uganda | 42 | 14.02 |
| Zambia | 81 | 14.21 |
| Zimbabwe | 28 | 11.55 |
| North of Sahara | 16 | 0.82 |
| South of Sahara | 43 | 5.52 |
| Africa | 39 | 3.33 |
| America | 11 | 0.29 |
| Asia | 13 | 0.49 |
| Europe | 26 | 0.72 |
| Oceania | 142 | 13.04 |
| Developing countries | 21 | 1.26 |

GNI, gross national income; n.a., not available.
*Source:* OECD (2007).

2002 to 2004, bilateral disbursements of ODA from the DAC to Africa accounted for 67 percent of the total ODA to Africa. The rest of the ODA to Africa came almost entirely from multilateral donors, who contributed 32 percent of the total ODA to Africa. Among the multilateral donors, the top two are the International Development Association (IDA) and the European Commission; together they contributed 75 percent of the total multilateral ODA to Africa.[5] The African Development Fund (ADF) is the third top multilateral donor, contributing about 8 percent of the total multilateral ODA to Africa.

The United States is the largest bilateral donor of ODA to Africa, as shown in Table 6.4. With the announcement by President Bush and the U.S. Congress in 2008 that the United States will increase its commitment to fight HIV/AIDS from $15 billion for 2004–2008 to $48 billion for 2009–2013, the United States will remain the most important bilateral donor to Africa.[6] As Table 6.5 shows, overall, medium and smaller donors in the DAC have a higher percentage of their aid going to Africa.[7] Developed countries have set a goal of increasing their aid to the level of at least 0.7 percent of their GNI. Five of the twenty-two members of DAC reached and surpassed that goal in 2005, as shown in Table 6.6. If the remaining seventeen DAC countries had reached an ODA/GNI ratio of 0.7, the total ODA from the DAC in 2005 would have been higher than it was by 133 percent, that is, it would have been more than twice what it was.

It is important to emphasize that this chapter and the negotiations on aid in the WTO are focused on government aid. However,

---

[5] The International Development Association (IDA) is part of the World Bank. It was established in 1960 to assist developing countries by offering them interest-free loans and grants. The major contributors to the IDA are the DAC countries.

[6] Most of the U.S. funds to fight HIV/AIDS go to African countries. Over 60 percent of the people in the world living with HIV/AIDS are in Sub-Saharan Africa.

[7] On average, in the three-year period from 2002 to 2004, 30 percent of the U.S. bilateral ODA went to Africa.

TABLE 6.4  Top Ten Bilateral Donors to Africa: U.S. Dollars
(Million), Current Prices, Net ODA Disbursements

| | 2002 | 2003 | 2004 | Three-year Average | Country's ODA as a Percent of Total DAC's ODA |
|---|---|---|---|---|---|
| United States | 3,189 | 5,063 | 4,186 | 4,146 | 24 |
| France | 2,602 | 3,585 | 3,728 | 3,305 | 19 |
| United Kingdom | 1,048 | 1,508 | 2,432 | 1,663 | 10 |
| Germany | 1,007 | 2,059 | 1,400 | 1,489 | 9 |
| Netherlands | 955 | 1,027 | 1,225 | 1,069 | 6 |
| Japan | 700 | 704 | 838 | 747 | 4 |
| Belgium | 363 | 1,053 | 549 | 655 | 4 |
| Italy | 810 | 744 | 393 | 649 | 4 |
| Sweden | 409 | 683 | 676 | 589 | 3 |
| Norway | 452 | 581 | 627 | 553 | 3 |
| Other DAC countries | 1,826 | 2,151 | 3,245 | 2,407 | 14 |
| Total DAC countries | 13,362 | 19,158 | 19,301 | 17,273 | 100 |

*Source: OECD (2007).*

government aid is not the only aid that developing countries
receive, nor is it necessarily the most effective. In the United States,
government foreign aid amounts to much less than private foreign
aid. The amount of U.S. private assistance to developing countries
is, at least, three times larger than U.S. government foreign aid
(Hudson Institute, 2006). The Hudson Institute (2006) notes that
private giving in Europe is significantly less because Europeans
traditionally rely on government aid to assist their own poor, as
well as developing countries.

TABLE 6.5 Top Ten Donors by Share of Aid to Africa: U.S. Dollars (Million), Current Prices, Net ODA Disbursements

| | 2002 | 2003 | 2004 | Three-Year Average | Aid to Africa as a Percent of Each Donor's Total ODA |
|---|---|---|---|---|---|
| Ireland | 191 | 247 | 290 | 243 | 85 |
| Portugal | 97 | 113 | 804 | 338 | 84 |
| Belgium | 363 | 1,053 | 549 | 655 | 83 |
| Italy | 810 | 744 | 393 | 649 | 82 |
| France | 2,602 | 3,585 | 3,728 | 3,305 | 76 |
| Denmark | 408 | 469 | 529 | 469 | 59 |
| Netherlands | 955 | 1,027 | 1,225 | 1,069 | 56 |
| Luxembourg | 54 | 66 | 84 | 68 | 52 |
| Canada | 388 | 516 | 632 | 512 | 52 |
| Sweden | 409 | 683 | 676 | 589 | 51 |
| Other DAC countries | 7,085 | 10,654 | 10,390 | 9,376 | 35 |
| Total DAC countries | 13,362 | 19,158 | 19,301 | 17,273 | 45 |

*Source: OECD (2007).*

### FROM AID FOR DEVELOPMENT TO AID FOR TRADE

Aid and discussions about aid are not new. In the 1960s and 1970s, the discussion with respect to Africa was framed in the context of aid for development. The term development carried a lot of weight as Africans were experimenting with different strategies to undo the ills of colonialism and put their countries on a positive development trajectory. European countries gave various forms of aid in recognition of legitimate efforts by some African countries to accelerate economic growth and equitable development. Countries like France and Great Britain were willing to give aid in part to maintain their strong influence in Africa. Aid from former colonial masters also served as a gesture of recognition of the economic,

TABLE 6.6 DAC Members' Net Official Development Assistance: 2005, Current Prices

| Country | ODA U.S. Dollars (Million) | ODA/GNI (Percent) |
|---|---|---|
| Norway | 2,786 | 0.94 |
| Sweden | 3,362 | 0.94 |
| Luxembourg | 256 | 0.82 |
| Netherlands | 5,115 | 0.82 |
| Denmark | 2,109 | 0.81 |
| Belgium | 1,963 | 0.53 |
| Austria | 1,573 | 0.52 |
| France | 10,026 | 0.47 |
| United Kingdom | 10,767 | 0.47 |
| Finland | 902 | 0.46 |
| Switzerland | 1,767 | 0.44 |
| Ireland | 719 | 0.42 |
| Germany | 10,082 | 0.36 |
| Canada | 3,756 | 0.34 |
| Italy | 5,091 | 0.29 |
| Japan | 13,147 | 0.28 |
| New Zealand | 274 | 0.27 |
| Spain | 3,018 | 0.27 |
| Australia | 1,680 | 0.25 |
| United States | 27,622 | 0.22 |
| Portugal | 377 | 0.21 |
| Greece | 384 | 0.17 |
| Total DAC | 106,777 | 0.33 |

*GNI, gross national income*
*Source: OECD (2007).*

social, and cultural damage they inflicted on Africans (reflecting some sense of guilt). During the Cold War era, aid from the United States and the former Soviet Union was primarily based on the side with which a recipient country was affiliated.

When development failed to materialize in the vast majority of African countries, questions were raised about the relevance of financial aid to Africa. Researchers started to pay closer attention to the domestic policies of African countries and those of the developed countries. From the 1960s to the 1980s, most African countries maintained inward-looking policies (import substitution policies and high export taxes) and overwhelming government monopolies and monopsonies. In developed countries, with which African countries trade the most, agricultural subsidies were mounting and so were direct trade barriers, such as quotas and tariffs, in agriculture and textiles and apparel. Given these problems, the prescription for African development started to emphasize a shift from aid to trade. The slogan was "trade not aid."

African countries were asked to reform their economies – to be more open to trade and to allow the private sector to play a larger role. The instructions for reform were packaged in the structural adjustment programs designed by the International Monetary Fund (IMF) and the World Bank. Aid became conditioned on reform. Starting in the late 1980s, African countries started to reduce or remove the monopoly and monopsony powers of the government over agricultural exports. In addition, price controls and trade barriers were reduced and financial markets were liberalized, thus reducing or eliminating the overvaluation of domestic currencies. These reforms have been ongoing by most African countries, to various degrees.

Regarding subsidies and trade barriers in developed countries, the international community did not have much leverage to push those countries to open their markets and stop flooding the world market with subsidized agricultural commodities. Seven rounds of negotiations and repeated appeals from developing countries had failed even to integrate agriculture and textiles and apparel into the General Agreement on Tariffs and Trade (GATT). The decision to include these areas in GATT was not to come until the conclusion of the Uruguay Round of GATT in 1993.[8] The Agreement on

---

[8]  Unlike the previous rounds of negotiations, developing countries had some leverage in the Uruguay Round, thanks to the demand by developed countries to extend GATT

Agriculture and the Agreement on Textiles and Apparel became effective in 1995, when the WTO replaced GATT.

Associated with the structural adjustment programs in African countries was a decline in social services – particularly in education and health-related services – as governments were required to reduce their budget deficits and bring about macroeconomic stability through contractionary fiscal and monetary policies. The downturn in services became apparent in the 1990s. This was compounded by the HIV/AIDS epidemic in Sub-Saharan Africa and the debt burden, all of which generated criticism against the structural adjustment programs and their prime architects, the IMF and the World Bank. In an effort to repair their image and to achieve sustainable poverty reduction, in 1999 the IMF and the World Bank came up with a different mechanism for issuing loans – Poverty Reduction Strategy Papers (PRSPs). Under this framework, countries are to take the initiative to prepare nationally owned PRSPs (IMF and the World Bank, 2000). According to the IMF, five principles underlie the PRSP approach. Poverty reduction strategies should be: country-driven, results-oriented, comprehensive, partnership-oriented (involving coordinated participation of development partners), and based on a long-term perspective (IMF, 2005).

Poverty Reduction Strategy Papers have continued to provide the context within which to approach various challenges, set goals and policies, mobilize resources, and integrate programs for developing countries. The PRSP framework and its link to the Heavily Indebted Poor Countries (HIPC) initiative have provided least-developed countries with debt relief savings that have been allocated to education, health, and other social services.

Meanwhile, trade is linked to poverty reduction in an indirect way through its potential to create economic growth. There is evidence

discipline to the areas of intellectual property rights and services. It is unlikely that the agreements on intellectual property rights and trade in services could have been achieved without an agreement that promised the integration of the agriculture and textile sectors into GATT.

that trade played an important role in bringing economic success to countries like Brazil, China, India, and Mauritius. African countries have acknowledged the potential benefits of trade. However, they have also maintained that to take advantage of trade, they need aid directed toward trade-enhancing projects. They have argued that without additional aid, adhering to the WTO rules would lead them to suffer the costs of trade liberalization, without gaining the benefits of trade. Thus, in 2005, four years into a troubled Doha Round, the "Aid for Trade" initiative became an agenda item that warranted a task force.

As discussed in Chapter 1, trade is an important mechanism through which countries can allocate their scarce resources efficiently. However, in the years following independence, many African countries viewed trade with skepticism. Colonialism had left them with the limited role of producing raw materials without any internal backward and forward linkages in production. With the objective to industrialize and diversify their economies, they embarked on an import substitution strategy, applying various trade and exchange rate controls that ended up taxing both exports and imports. This strategy produced a number of undesirable outcomes. Domestic currencies were overvalued, factories built in the name of import substitution were severely underutilized due to a lack of imported inputs, and there was a general shortage of goods. This bleak economic reality, combined with external pressure, pushed African countries to start embracing (grudgingly, for some) export-oriented policies.

Developed countries had their own share of protection and agricultural subsidies that were harmful to African countries. At the same time, developed countries gave and continue to give foreign aid to African countries. As African countries were reducing their trade restrictions, developed countries were urged to remove their own trade distorting policies because that might benefit developing countries even more than giving them direct aid. Adam and O'Connell (2004) show that where the export sector is an important source of productivity spillovers in a recipient country, the economic benefits of preferential tariffs can be significantly higher than those of equivalent grants. A trade preference equivalent to a grant is one that increases the export revenue of a beneficiary country by the same level as the grant.

The Aid for Trade initiative, which primarily represents the perspectives of developing countries, takes into account the catalytic role of the export sector. However, while African countries recognize the benefits of trade and preferential treatment, it is unlikely that they would consider preferential treatment better than direct aid. Given a choice of preferential treatment or aid, Adam and O'Connell (2004) suggest that governments would prefer aid, especially in those countries where the government is not fully committed to private sector development. The government controls the disbursement of aid funds, whereas the benefits of preferential trade are distributed to the recipient country's exporters through market channels. African countries want both preferential treatment and aid – and more of each is better than less. The argument for more aid has gained even more momentum as developing countries face an anticipated erosion of the margin of preference.

### THE SCOPE OF THE AID FOR TRADE INITIATIVE

The task force on Aid for Trade specified five categories to be covered by the initiative (WTO, 2006b):[9]

(a) *Trade policy and regulation*: Training and technical assistance for effective participation in negotiations and dispute settlements, implementation of trade agreements, and adaptation of and compliance with rules and standards.

(b) *Trade development*: Assistance for market analysis and trade promotion, business support services and institutions, public-private sector networking, and e-commerce.

---

[9]  See also ECA (2007) and Smaller (2006).

(c) *Trade-related infrastructure*: Assistance in building roads and ports.

(d) *Building productive capacity*: Assistance to reduce supply constraints to improve national capacity to produce goods and services and help countries to diversify and add value to their exports.

(e) *Trade-related adjustment*: Assistance to meet adjustment costs associated with trade policy reform, including balance-of-payments problems resulting from loss of tariff revenue or erosion of the margin of preference.

In addition to these five categories, the task force deliberately included a general (and ambiguous) category titled "other trade-related needs." The task force wanted the scope of Aid for Trade to be broad enough to reflect the diverse trade needs of developing countries. The task force also made many other recommendations that are conventional in aid initiatives, as discussed further below.

### RATIONALE FOR AID FOR TRADE

Regardless of what happens to the Aid for Trade initiative, the call for aid within the WTO is here to stay. Therefore, it is important to analyze the rationale for Aid for Trade. The five categories of Aid for Trade listed above can be grouped into four main areas: participation, implementation costs, supply constraints, and adjustment costs.

*1. Participation.* Effective participation in the WTO negotiations frequently requires specialized technical expertise in various trade issues and trade-related areas. In addition, it requires a technical and structural capacity for effective communication and collaboration between a country's representatives in Geneva and the capital. Foreign aid has already helped to improve communications between African representatives in Geneva and their associates in Africa. Likewise, various donor agencies and governments support economic policy studies by institutions like the African Economic Research Consortium (AERC), the Economic Commission for Africa (ECA), and African regional blocs. These studies have helped African countries to prepare for WTO ministerial conferences.

The AERC is particularly notable for its collaborative research and training programs. It is a classic model for research capacity-building in Africa. It produces high-quality policy papers and organizes forums for policy dialogue. In addition, in collaboration with African universities, it offers M.A. and Ph.D. programs in economics. Effective participation in the WTO is based on the capacity to introduce and analyze proposals. For Africa, any serious Aid for Trade initiative must include an explicit plan to enhance the endeavors of the AERC.

The reasons for the low participation of African countries in the dispute settlement mechanism are discussed in Chapter 2. Some have to do with cost and technical capacity. To help address the high cost of bringing cases to the Dispute Settlement Understanding (DSU), the Advisory Center on WTO Law (ACWL) provides legal training and highly subsidized services to developing countries. With additional aid, the ACWL's services can be expanded and possibly provided at the regional level in Africa. (See the case on ACWL at the end of Chapter 2.)

*2. Implementation costs.* Implementation of WTO agreements requires an allocation of technological and human resources to amend existing legislation and enact new laws. Some agreements may even require the establishment of new institutions (in addition to revamping old ones). For example, the Agreement on Trade-Related Aspects of Intellectual Property Rights (TRIPS) and the Agreement on the Application of Sanitary and Phytosanitary Measures require effective regulatory bodies that may not exist in African countries. For most African countries, establishing such national regulatory bodies would take years and would require external technical expertise and financial support. Some individual WTO agreements have provisions for implementation or technical assistance for developing countries. Ideally, the Aid for Trade initiative would put those provisions under one umbrella, with the objective of creating coherence in providing technical assistance for the implementation of agreements.

*3. Supply constraints*. The reality about supply constraints in Africa is arguably the most important challenge to be addressed by the Aid for Trade initiative. Supply constraints have left African countries with a narrow range of exports and a limited capacity to respond to favorable price and market opportunities. These constraints run through the whole supply chain – production, product sorting and grading, storage, packaging, and transportation. Other supply constraints include health standards requirements, labeling requirements, complex procedures for exports, and corruption. In addition, inadequacies in macroeconomic policies, research and development, educational systems, protection of private property, infrastructure, and the judicial system further constrain the supply of goods and services (Lyakurwa, 2007).

Some of the supply constraints, in particular transaction costs associated with customs procedures, are the focus of the negotiations on trade facilitation in the Doha Round. Trade facilitation is the only one of the four Singapore issues that remains in the Doha Round. The other three – investment, competition, and transparency in government procurement – were dropped from the Doha Round in 2004. The future and outcome of these negotiations are unpredictable. However, what is certain is that negotiations on trade facilitation and on aid for trade are intrinsically linked. Noteworthy improvements in customs procedures in developing countries would require substantial financial aid and technical support for those countries (Sutherland, 2005).

The wide range and interconnectedness of supply constraints raise doubt about the potential effectiveness of Aid for Trade, as discussed in the following section. Despite the broad nature of the Aid for Trade initiative, aid given to advance trade, in practice, would tend to be limited to supply constraints most closely linked to trade. This would be a problem to the extent that weaknesses in additional links in the supply chain are not addressed.

*4. Adjustment costs*. When a country implements freer trade policies, inevitably a reallocation of resources occurs that produces winners and losers. Although the economy as a whole benefits, tariff revenue may decrease and workers who are displaced by more efficient producers in other countries may not find new jobs immediately.

For developed countries, tariff revenue reductions are not an important problem. Taxes on international trade activities are an insignificant source of government revenue in developed countries – they contribute less than 1 percent of the total government revenue. Regarding displaced workers, developed countries have various labor-market policies that provide assistance to workers displaced by freer trade. For example, even the few workers in the United States who are displaced by production shifts due to the African Growth and Opportunity Act (AGOA) are eligible for trade-adjustment assistance. Trade-adjustment assistance in developed countries includes unemployment compensation, retraining, small business start-up assistance, job-search support, relocation allowances, tax credits on health insurance premium costs, and subsidies to employers (OECD, 2005a).

African countries face a different situation. Some of them depend heavily on import and export duties as a source of government revenue. In 2005, international trade taxes contributed at least 20 percent of the government revenue in at least twelve African countries (World Bank, 2007). Furthermore, African countries do not have trade-adjustment assistance programs. Individuals displaced by reductions of trade barriers have to bear the cost on their own.

Still, the reduction of trade barriers required of most African countries by the WTO agreements is typically spread out over many years of transitional periods. Moreover, a reduction in tariff rates does not necessarily cause a decrease in tariff revenues. What happens to tariff revenues when tariff rates are lowered depends on the elasticity of demand for imports, that is, how responsive imports are to changes in the tariff rates. If demand for imports is sufficiently elastic, the increase in the volume of imports can overcompensate for the decrease in the tariff rate and actually cause tariff revenue to increase. Improvements in tariff administration, often prompted by tariff rate reductions, could also cause tariff revenue to increase.

In addition to adjustment costs borne by African countries as a result of their domestic policy changes, other adjustment costs emanate from the erosion of the margin of preference. The objective of preferential market access for African products in developed countries is to help African countries stimulate their economies through growth and diversification of exports. However, successful reductions in the most favored nation (MFN) tariff rates (and the accession of China to the WTO in 2001) erode the preferential margin. The Aid for Trade initiative has been justified, in part, as a way to help developing countries adjust to this erosion.

Yet only a few African countries have really utilized the preferential market access granted by developed countries (Brenton and Ikezuki, 2006; Hoekman et al., 2006). Table 6.7 shows the percentage of exports (of various African countries) that take advantage of preferences offered by the EU, Japan, and the United States. As the table indicates, in 2002, only five of forty-eight Sub-Saharan African countries had more than 10 percent of their total non-oil exports taking advantage of preferences in the EU, Japan, and the United States combined. Even when utilized, only a portion of the preference premium is captured by African exporters. Take, for example, the textile and apparel sector in Africa, considered to have benefited the most from AGOA. Olarreaga and Özden (2005) estimate that Africa's apparel exporters and their intermediaries outside Africa capture only about one-third of the difference between the preferential (AGOA) and non-preferential export price. Their analysis suggests that a large portion of the price difference is captured by importing companies, presumably due to their market and bargaining power. This phenomenon, in itself, may be an important explanation for the low utilization of the preferential treatment given to African products.

TABLE 6.7 Classification of Sub-Saharan African Countries
by Magnitude of the Value of Combined (Non-Oil) Preferences
in the European Union, Japan, and United States Relative to Total
(Non-Oil) Exports: 2002

| | |
|---|---|
| < 1 percent | Angola, Burundi, Central African Republic, Chad, Congo, Democratic Republic of Congo, Djibouti, Equatorial Guinea, Gabon, Guinea, Liberia, Mali, Niger, Nigeria, Rwanda, São Tomé & Principe, Somalia, South Africa |
| Between 1 percent and 5 percent | Benin, Botswana, Burkina Faso, Cameroon, Cape Verde, Comoros, Eritrea, Ethiopia, Ghana, Ivory Coast, Mauritania, Sierra Leone, Sudan, Tanzania, Togo, Uganda, Zambia |
| > 5 percent but < 10 percent | Gambia, Guinea-Bissau, Kenya, Madagascar, Mozambique, Namibia, Senegal, Zimbabwe |
| > 10 percent | Lesotho, Malawi, Mauritius, Seychelles, Swaziland |

*Source: Table 2 in Brenton and Ikezuki (2006). Reprinted by permission.*

It is interesting that countries that have utilized preferential
treatment *and* countries that have failed to take advantage of preferential treatment are asking for additional aid to help them adjust
to reduced preferential margins. The Economic Commission for
Africa (ECA, 2007) reports that in 2006, Mauritius, a country that
has benefited considerably from preferential treatment, estimated
it would need $4.5 billion over a period of ten years to deal with
reduced preferences. The ECA further states that "Mauritius is a
more developed economy than most African countries. This means
the Aid for Trade financial needs of other African countries are
likely to be substantial" (ECA, 2007: 3).

For those African countries that have not been able to take advantage of preferential treatment, it would be purely opportunistic to suggest that they need this specific adjustment support. On the other end of the spectrum, it could be argued that those countries that have been able to take the fullest advantage of preferential treatment should be assisted the most in adjusting to the erosion of the margin of preference. However, a counter-argument is that those countries have already benefited; if their businesses operated strategically with a long-term perspective, they should be in a position to withstand an erosion of the margin of preference. Moreover, the erosion of preferential margin takes place over time. For all these reasons, although an erosion of preferential margin has often been used as a rationale for Aid for Trade, it does not carry much weight when examined objectively.

Providing financial assistance for diminished preference margins also raises a more fundamental question. Is preferential market access a right or a privilege? Financial assistance for adjustment costs is to come from the same countries that have offered preferential treatment to African countries in the first place. In a way, countries that offer preferential treatment are held hostage by their preferential openness. Preferential treatment, which by its very design is meant to be temporary, is portrayed in the Aid for Trade initiative as if it were a perpetual entitlement for developing countries.

Ultimately, the objective of Aid for Trade is to achieve real development in developing countries. This raises the question about the effectiveness of aid, which is determined in part by its coherence with other development initiatives.

### EFFECTIVENESS OF AID

The Millennium Development Goals (MDGs) adopted in 2000 have provided long-term targets for which aid is sought and analyzed.[10] The most cited is MDG number one – *to eradicate extreme poverty and hunger.* One of the targets under this goal is to reduce by half the proportion of people living on less than one dollar a day (purchasing power) by 2015. The base year is 1990. For Africa, it means reducing the proportion of people living on less than one dollar a day from 45 percent of the population in 1990 to 22.5 percent of the population in 2015 (ECA, 2005).

Given the topic of this chapter, it is fitting also to mention MDG number eight – *to develop a global partnership for development.* While this goal is important in its own right, it mainly serves to enable countries to achieve the other goals. Global partnership is a vital pre-requisite for the other MDGs to be realized. MDG number eight recognizes the contribution to development that countries can make through rule-based trade and special and preferential treatment for least-developed countries. Likewise, this goal recognizes the contribution that developed countries can make through development assistance, debt relief, and providing access to essential medicines and new technologies.

Aid can have a direct impact on poverty by improving education and health services and directly providing food, clothing, and shelter to the poor. However, if the provision of these services and basic necessities does not produce economic growth, the impact of aid on poverty is transient, to the extent that aid itself is temporary. Ideally, with this line of attacking poverty, aid initially reduces poverty directly; the reduction of poverty leads to economic growth; and economic growth leads to a further reduction of poverty. Except in dire situations, aid programs are normally designed to address poverty in an indirect way, through economic growth. It is for this reason that most studies assess the effectiveness of aid by focusing

---

[10] There are eight development goals altogether: eradicate extreme poverty and hunger; achieve universal primary education; promote gender equality and empower women; reduce child mortality; improve maternal health; combat HIV and AIDS, malaria, and other diseases; ensure environmental sustainability; and develop a global partnership for development (http://www.unmillenniumproject.org/goals/index.htm).

on its impact on economic growth (World Bank, 1998; Burnside and Dollar, 2000; Dalgaard et al., 2004). A few studies that have focused on the impact of aid on poverty include Collier and Dollar (1999) and Mosley et al. (2004).

One conclusion that has emerged from empirical studies is that aid is effective in countries with good policies (World Bank, 1998; Burnside and Dollar, 2000).[11] This conclusion, expressed in the quote below, can serve to guide aid programs.

Consistent with other authors, we found that aid has had little impact on growth, although a robust finding was that aid has had a positive impact on growth in good policy environments. This effect goes beyond the direct impact that the policies themselves have on growth. (Burnside and Dollar, 2000: 864)

The experience of Botswana tends to support this conclusion when one looks at the simple relationship between aid, policy index, and the growth rate of real GDP per capita. According to Burnside and Dollar (2000), Botswana had the sixth highest (of fifty-six countries) annual average of aid to GDP ratio, the highest policy index, and the highest real GDP per capita growth rate for the period 1970–1993. Studies on Botswana have found that it has consistently focused on economic development and instituted effective measures to achieve it. Botswana has used its inflows of aid effectively by integrating them into national strategies. When specific aid inflow did not fit with national policies and priorities, the government of Botswana was willing to reject it (Commission for Africa, 2005: Annex 8). Wangwe (2006) describes the uniqueness of Botswana as follows[12]:

Botswana provides a unique case study of aid dependence in Africa. It has gone from being one of the poorest, most aid dependent countries to a middle-income country no longer in need of significant amounts of

---

[11] For a critical analysis of the World Bank study, see Lensink and White (2000).
[12] See also Lancaster and Wangwe (2000).

external assistance and where donors have begun to phase out aid. Four lessons are drawn from the success of Botswana. First, the government demonstrated competence, cleanliness, discipline and effectiveness in managing aid as well as prudent management of the economy including mobilization of domestic resources including those from the extractive industry and the collected revenues have been utilized to undertake investments in human and physical infrastructure. Second, success has been associated with ability to plan and implement economic policies and programmes effectively for growth. Third, success has been associated with reasonably good governance and political stability. Fourth, a success factor has been the ability of the government to manage its aid effectively making sure that aid supported projects fit into the national development framework carefully integrating aid into its broader development plans and priorities. (Wangwe, 2006: 3–4)

There still remains the intricate question of causality among aid, economic growth, and good policies. Nonetheless, if most African countries had been able to emulate the experience of Botswana, development agencies would by now have moved beyond persistent appeals for the "Big Push" for aid (UNCTAD, 2006).

Notwithstanding the impressive experience of Botswana, the conclusion that aid is effective in countries with good policies seems to be a tautology. Economic policies are not intrinsically good; they are good because they produce desired outcomes. Moreover, policies, "good" or "bad," are not independent of aid. Econometric studies estimate the impact of aid on growth and poverty, with the policy index treated as an exogenous (independent) variable. However, economic policies are endogenous, determined by other factors, including aid. In addition, some policy variables used to develop the policy index are only proxies of the real policy variables. For example, the inflation rate is typically used as a proxy for monetary policy. This would not constitute a problem in econometric studies if monetary policy were the only determinant of inflation. However, there are other determinants of inflation, including fiscal policy and trade policy.

The difficulty in measuring the impact of aid on economic growth and poverty, particularly for African countries from the

1960s to the 1980s, goes beyond the definition of variables, reliability of data, and econometric methods. Empirical studies have been conducted with an implicit assumption that aid was provided to African countries for sound economic development. This was not the case for all countries and for all aid. Aid was given to some countries – to some heads of states, to be more precise – to buy their political allegiance and to gain access to minerals. Although economic development was desired, when it happened, it was incidental. The motive for giving "aid" from the 1960s to the 1980s must be understood in the context of the Cold War and the overall geopolitics of the era. In its overview about aid, the World Bank (1998) makes a rather revealing remark about aid to former Zaire.

[F]oreign aid has been, at times, an unmitigated failure. While the former Zaire's Mobutu Sese Seko was reportedly amassing one of the world's largest personal fortunes (invested, naturally, outside his own country), decades of large-scale foreign assistance left not a trace of progress. Zaire (now Democratic Republic of Congo) is just one of several examples where a steady flow of aid ignored, if not encouraged, incompetence, corruption, and misguided policies. (World Bank, 1998)

As the remark implicitly suggests, the flow of aid to Zaire has been exaggerated. Aid was not given to Zaire. The money was flowing to Mobutu and his political aristocracy and their bank accounts in Europe and elsewhere. It was the price the United States and other Western powers were willing to pay to have Mobutu on their side. In that respect, money given to Mobutu achieved its objective; Mobutu stayed loyal to the West. To suggest that money given to dictators like Mobutu Sese Seko of Zaire (1965–1997), Jaafar Nimery of Sudan (1969–1991), Siyad Barre of Somalia (1969–1991), or Jean-Bédel Bokassa of the Central African Republic (1966–1979) was for economic development is naïve at best.[13] To suggest it was due to their misguided policies that development

---

[13] The years in parentheses indicate the period they ruled.

did not take place, is likewise naïve. Certainly, no one would be surprised that the $22 million spent by France in 1977 to fund the coronation of "Emperor" Bokassa (Underhill, 2003), for example, did not reduce poverty in the Central African Republic.

The study by Burnside and Dollar (2000), which has been cited extensively, provides some insights about the role of good policies on the effectiveness of aid. However, the results of this study (and similar studies) must be viewed with caution. The study covers twenty-four years (1970–1993), a period that includes years when a number of developing countries were led by dictators who were given money for their loyalty to donors and for the construction of "white elephants," not necessarily for real economic development.[14]

To summarize the discussion thus far, three basic points can be made. First, although it is difficult to measure the impact of aid on economic growth and poverty, aid seems to be effective in countries with good policies; it has a positive impact that goes beyond the direct impact of the good policies themselves. Second, not all foreign aid was meant for development (directly or indirectly). Therefore, it is misleading to evaluate all foreign aid in terms of its impact on economic growth, especially when many developing countries are lumped together. Third, the policies (and motives) of donor countries determine the type of and conditions for aid and, in turn, have an impact on the effectiveness of aid on economic growth and poverty reduction.

Further complicating the overall effect of aid is the fact that aid is fungible (World Bank, 1998: Chapter 3). That is, aid can simply replace another source of funding for a project, rather than

---

[14] The study by Burnside and Dollar (2000) has fifty-six recipient countries, twenty-five of which are African countries, including former Zaire and Somalia. A "white elephant" project is one that is economically unprofitable, but may be glamorous and may produce political benefits. See Robinson and Torvik (2005) for a theoretical discussion on why politicians may prefer inefficient projects rather than efficient projects. The political benefits of inefficient projects may be larger than those of socially efficient projects.

increase spending by the amount of aid. This makes it difficult to measure what impact the aid has actually had. If foreign aid in the amount of $10 million for export diversification, for example, does not increase spending on export diversification by $10 million, that aid is said to be fungible. In other words, that aid simply reduces the amount of funds the government would have spent on that project in the absence of aid. The maximum reduction is the aid amount. Aid for any given project or for the general budget may not even increase overall government spending by the amount of aid. Aid may simply allow the central government to lower taxes. Fungibility implies:

$$G_{na} \leq G_a < (G_{na} + \beta), \text{ when } G_{na} > \beta \text{ or } \beta \leq G_a < (G_{na} + \beta),$$
$$\text{when } G_{na} < \beta$$

where $G_a$ is the total spending on a project with aid available; $G_{na}$ is the total spending on the project with no aid available; and $\beta$ is the amount of aid. Aid is fully fungible when the amount the government would have spent from its own resources $(G_{na})$ exceeds the amount of aid $(\beta)$.

From a macroeconomic perspective, the effectiveness of aid is also reduced by a real appreciation of the domestic currency as a result of the increase in the supply of foreign currency (aid). In other words, if the supply of foreign currency increases, the amount of domestic currency demanded increases, and the resulting appreciation of the domestic currency reduces the competitiveness of domestic exports. This is a concern that sometimes puts the Ministry of Finance (the guardian of macroeconomic stability) at odds with other ministries. For example, in Uganda in 2002, when the Ministry of Health was asking for more aid for health projects, the Ministry of Finance was warning that too much aid could destabilize Uganda's economy (Phillips, 2002). Of course, the concern about real exchange rate appreciation must be balanced with the purpose of the aid. Moreover, even a surge in aid inflow would not necessarily hurt exports, if it is used to increase domestic capacity utilization and productivity or if it is mainly used to purchase tradable goods (Nkusu, 2004; Gupta et al., 2006). Considering that the Aid for Trade initiative is meant to deal with supply bottlenecks, it is unlikely that increases in aid under that initiative would hurt exports. Moreover, a serious real appreciation of domestic currency caused by capital inflows can be prevented by the central bank selling bonds. Such an action would sterilize (offset) the foreign capital inflows and increase the central bank's holdings of foreign reserves.[15]

### IMPLEMENTING THE TASK FORCE RECOMMENDATIONS FOR AID FOR TRADE

The discussion that follows considers the prospects for implementation of the task force recommendations for the Aid for Trade initiative. These task force recommendations are not unique. They have become standard when planning or analyzing any form of aid initiative for Africa, be it through an international governmental organization such as the World Bank, IMF, or the WTO, or through international aid agencies such as Oxfam or Catholic Relief Services (CRS). Thus, the discussion is important regardless of what happens to the initiative. The core set of recommendations involve: donor coordination and harmonization of procedures; real additional aid; aligning Aid for Trade with MDGs, national development strategies, and PRSPs; and ownership by recipient countries.

---

[15] Although sterilization can prevent real appreciation of the domestic currency, this strategy "is tantamount to using aid to simply increase a country's foreign exchange reserves rather than provide additional purchasing power over real resources." (UNCTAD, 2006: 38) There is concern that some African countries are accumulating foreign reserves to levels that appear too large relative to what would be needed to guard against speculative attacks on foreign currency and capital flight. In the 1990s, at least one-third of capital inflow to Africa was used to boost foreign reserves. This phenomenon of diverting aid from the acquisition of resources to boosting foreign reserves has continued and even increased (UNCTAD, 2006).

*1. Donor coordination and harmonization of procedures.* The task force recommended that the Aid for Trade initiative be guided by the Paris Declaration on Aid Effectiveness and build on existing trade-related assistance initiatives. The Paris Declaration on Aid Effectiveness is a resolution by governments of developed and developing countries and multilateral and bilateral development institutions to take concrete and effective actions to harmonize and align aid recipient countries' priorities, systems, and procedures (WTO, 2006b: Annex I).

The objective of this recommendation is to reduce the administrative costs to be borne by recipient countries that typically must send hundreds of applications to potential donors, host numerous outside monitoring missions, and produce many different reports for various donors who are financing a variety of projects. In the late 1990s, the government of Tanzania produced an average of 1,200 reports a year for donors and received over 500 missions a year (De Renzio and Mulley, 2006).

While donor coordination is usually accomplished by funneling aid through multilateral organizations such as the World Bank, IMF, UNCTAD, or the WTO, direct aid from donor countries is generally difficult to coordinate. Every governmental aid agency, including the Australian Agency for International Development, the Canadian International Development Agency, EuropeAID, Japan's office of Official Development Assistance, and the U.S. Agency for International Development, has its own mission statement and wants to be unambiguously (and even singularly) identified as a donor for a project. Moreover, donor countries are often in competition with each other for positive publicity, influence, and access to investment and trade opportunities in the recipient countries. Collier (2007: 101) describes a case of three donors each wanting to build a hospital in the same place. Their compromise, which came after two years of finding ways to coordinate, was for each to build one floor of the hospital under its own rules.

Even harmonizing procedures is not easy. Government development agencies are accountable to their respective ministries (or departments) and subject to those ministries' accounting procedures. Those procedures, in turn, determine the guidelines for issuing aid and for reporting aid expenditure. A donor country would be reluctant to harmonize aid procedures with other countries if that meant the country had to change other accounting procedures unrelated to foreign aid. Moreover, government institutions are generally slow to change.

Although the Aid for Trade initiative is to be built on existing trade-related assistance programs, that is easier said than done considering the number of overlapping aid programs. Existing trade-related assistance initiatives include the Integrated Framework for Trade-Related Technical Assistance for Least-Developed Countries (IF), the Joint Integrated Technical Assistance Programme (JITAP), and the Program for Building African Capacity for Trade (PACT). The IF was launched in 1997. It is supported by six core international agencies, namely, the International Monetary Fund (IMF), the International Trade Center (ITC), the United Nations Conference on Trade and Development (UNCTAD), the United Nations Development Program (UNDP), the World Bank, and the WTO. The main objective of the IF is to help least-developed countries use trade as an engine for growth and poverty reduction. JITAP was launched in 1996 to provide technical assistance in building the trade capacity of African countries. It is supported by the ITC, UNCTAD, and the WTO. PACT, launched in 2002, is a program similar to JITAP, also for African countries and supported by the same three organizations as JITAP, plus Canada's Trade Facilitation Office. All of these programs cover African countries, but none of them covers all African countries. In addition to these programs, there is the Common Fund for Commodities (CFC), an intergovernmental organization, whose objective is to finance research and development projects that are geared toward improving productivity, competitiveness, diversification, investment, marketing, and the optimal use of natural resources. The CFC is linked to twenty-four intergovernmental commodity bodies.

Considering the number of aid programs already in place, it is clear why donor coordination is needed and, at the same time, why optimal coordination is virtually unattainable. Among other things, the duplication of aid programs benefits people who work for the aid programs (governmental or non-governmental) in donor countries; it also benefits those who have jobs in developing countries directly because of those programs. Interestingly enough, it is usually the same people (in organizations such as the World Bank, the IMF, and UNCTAD) who are asked to propose how to coordinate aid and reduce cost, which literally means to propose ways to eliminate their jobs. The simple fact is that some organizations benefit from a lack of donor coordination. If there is to be a serious effort to coordinate aid, the movement should be toward consolidating some of the existing aid programs, rather than initiating new programs that are similar to the old ones.

Some existing donor organizations are even expanding their roles to cover areas already covered by other organizations. Take the IMF and the PRSPs, for example. While the PRSPs approach adopted by the IMF in 1999 reflected a healthier attitude toward the recipient countries' ownership, an important question must be raised. The mandate of the IMF is (a) to ensure that countries follow some set rules of conduct in international trade and finance; and (b) to provide short-term loans to assist countries with temporary balance of payments difficulties. How can the IMF reconcile these short-term objectives with poverty reduction, which is a long-term goal? Naturally, there is a link between macroeconomic stability and poverty reduction. However, the link is complex and cannot be addressed adequately by an institution that thinks in terms of the short run unless it expands its mandate, as it appears the IMF has implicitly done.

Notwithstanding these constraints, some donor coordination and harmonization of procedures have been achieved where there is a clearly defined target for aid on which donors agree, as is the case for certain diseases. The Global Fund to Fight AIDS, Tuberculosis and Malaria is funded by Canada, the EC, France, Germany, Italy, Japan, the Netherlands, the United Kingdom, the United States, and the Bill and Melinda Gates Foundation. Likewise, in 2005, the G8 countries jointly agreed to write off $40 billion in debt owed by eighteen low-income countries, mostly in Africa, to allow these indebted countries to direct more resources to health services (WHO, 2006a).

Although it is hoped that the Aid for Trade initiative will present "trade" as a clear target, trade is too broad and too dynamic to receive sustained, coordinated donor funding the way HIV/AIDS has. However, there may be a silver lining in this. Coordinated donor funding may not always be advantageous to recipient countries. It is possible for donor coordination to lead to contributions by individual donor countries that are lower than they would be in the absence of coordination. This could happen as publicity focuses on the aggregate amount contributed by the donor countries – an amount that would often seem very large.

Donor coordination can also give donor countries "coordinated" leverage over the recipient (poor) countries. At least it can create the perception of such leverage. Either way, that could be damaging to the WTO, where negotiations between rich and poor countries are often polarized.

The issue of donor coordination should not only rest on donor countries. Recipient governments can reduce administrative costs and increase the effectiveness of aid by taking a sector-wide approach (SWAp) to planning and aid applications. The SWAp can allow recipient countries to draw donors together for a set of coordinated and integrated projects. However, the WHO (2002) notes that some development agencies do not fully embrace the policy of joint planning, budgeting, and accountability and that some prefer planning using a project approach, not the SWAp. Although some development partners are not going to accept the SWAp, this approach can still develop better donor coordination, allow for comprehensive problem analysis, provide a clear basis for setting priorities, and reduce fragmentation in implementation and monitoring. The SWAp can also lead to wider participation by local stakeholders in development initiatives and an equitable distribution of resources (WHO, 2002; Hutton, 2004). A few African countries, including Ghana, Tanzania, and Uganda, have developed successful SWAps for the health sector. However, it is still a relatively new and complex approach that needs time and *aid* to develop.

2. *Real additional aid.* This is an appeal for developed countries actually to increase financial aid instead of simply redistributing current levels to allocate more for trade. This recommendation reveals the real reason for the Aid for Trade initiative – the hope for real additional resources. By disaggregating appeals for aid into various initiatives – aid to deal with HIV/AIDS, aid for clean water, aid for education, aid to combat deforestation, aid to fight terrorism, aid to fight poverty, aid to combat global warming, and aid for trade – the objective is to highlight particular needs and have those needs met by real additional aid. However, the recommendation for real additional aid for trade encounters three fundamental challenges.

The first challenge is that there is no agreed upon "current levels of aid" on which additional aid can be based, regardless of the promises by rich countries to raise aid. For example, it is not clear if additional aid for Africa should be based on current or previous real values of aid; the conditions of a donor country's gross national income (GNI); current or previous aid as a percent of a recipient country's GNI; current or previous aid per capita for African countries; the current or previous percentage of global aid given to Africa; Africa's aid absorption capacity; or Africa's requirements for aid. Note that even if there was an agreement as to which one of these measures additional aid should be based on, the actual quantitative calculation would still be a matter of dispute. Estimates of Africa's requirements for aid vary from $35 to $64 billion per year (UNCTAD, 2006).[16]

---

[16] Net Official Development Assistance (ODA) to Africa averaged $23 billion (2003 prices) for the period 2000–2004 (OECD, 2007).

The second challenge is that, in practice, various initiatives for aid cannot be neatly separated from each other. In other words, the Aid for Trade initiative cannot be isolated from other initiatives, as suggested by the discussion above regarding the sector-wide approach. Trade is so intertwined with other activities that a donor country does not even need to redistribute aid to allocate more aid for trade projects; it can simply reclassify or broaden the official declared use of aid. For example, aid that was for irrigation could be reclassified as aid for export production, or it could be described as aid for irrigation *and* export promotion. Aid for health services, education, and peace initiatives could be classified as aid for trade. Note that proposals to increase cotton production and exports of African countries include improvement of the judicial system (WTO, 2005a).

The third challenge regarding real additional aid is that influential constituencies in donor countries may oppose the Aid for Trade initiative. Unlike aid initiatives for HIV/AIDS or poverty reduction which resonate easily with the general public, the Aid for Trade initiative is not likely to receive the active support of NGOs and movie and rock stars usually associated with aid efforts. In fact, many groups that work hard and successfully to raise awareness of the HIV/AIDS epidemic and overall poverty in Africa are often the same groups that are skeptical of trade (if not outright averse to trade). They view the international trading system (embodied by the WTO rules and conditionalities of the IMF and the World Bank) as unfair and harmful to developing countries, despite the fact that trade can be an effective engine for growth that, in turn, can reduce poverty.

Activists in donor countries may object to the very rationale for the Aid for Trade initiative, which states:

Aid for Trade is about assisting developing countries to increase exports of goods and services, to integrate into the multilateral trading system and to benefit from liberalized trade and increased market access. Effective Aid for Trade will enhance growth prospects and reduce poverty in developing countries, as well as complement multilateral trade reforms and distribute the global benefits more equitably and within developing countries. (WTO, 2006b)

This rationale is not going to appeal to groups that already think the root cause of inequality and poverty in the world is globalization. Therefore, it should not come as a surprise to the WTO if the very constituencies in the donor countries who are activists for more aid are indifferent or even opposed to the Aid for Trade initiative. Moreover, taxpayers in donor countries may also think that their money is being misallocated to "nonessentials" like Aid for Trade instead of funding crises management. Some in donor countries may disapprove of Aid for Trade for fear of competition that may come from recipient countries as a result of such aid.

Donor countries have promised that by 2010, they will have increased official development assistance (ODA) to Africa by $25 billion a year. They have also promised to increase overall ODA to 0.7 percent of GNI. In 2005, the unweighted average of ODA from the DAC was 0.47 percent of GNI; the income-weighted average was 0.33 percent (OECD, 2007). Because donor countries typically fail to reach their promised targets, promised levels are mainly suggestive, leaving aid disbursement uncertain and volatile. This reality is a source of frustration for African diplomats in the WTO and, in part, is why they have been pushing the aid agenda hard through the WTO.

The WTO is based on trade, rules, capacity, and predictability. African representatives in the WTO stress that aid for capacity building must not only increase – it must also be predictable, just as the rules of trade are predictable. Although that would be ideal, it is unlikely to be the case. Aid is not reciprocated the way trade rules are. Foreign aid is not an economic entitlement (even if one can make a moral argument for it) and cannot be indexed to some inflation rate or to some need index. Whether it is aid for trade or aid for some emergency, the amount of aid disbursed will always ultimately depend on the will of the donor countries and not necessarily on the requests they receive or even the promises they make.

African countries are asking that the Aid for Trade initiative deliver new financial resources and not simply reallocate funds already pledged. Another issue related to this appeal for real additional aid has to do with the fungibility of aid. Can African countries also promise that funds available through Aid for Trade will not be fungible? In other words, can they promise to increase spending on trade-related projects by the full amount of the increase in aid? They cannot and should not. It is important to note that fungibility of aid does not imply corruption or inconsistency in the classification of spending. It reflects rational behavior of individuals, firms, or governments in allocating additional funds.

As discussed above, still another issue is that a surge of aid could cause a real appreciation of domestic currency and hurt domestic exports. This would be ironic, given the objectives of the Aid for Trade initiative. While it is important not to exaggerate the potential impact of aid flow on the exchange rate, it is important to keep it in mind, nonetheless. This is especially true considering that appeals are not only for additional aid, but also for the additional aid to be frontloaded. In other words, appeals are for aid to be disbursed in a concentrated way in the initial stages of the project.

*3. Aligning Aid for Trade with MDGs, national development strategies, and PRSPs.* The Millennium Development Goals (MDGs) adopted in 2000 have become widely used as targets for which aid is sought. In fact, one often gets the impression that these goals are optimal and that the amount of aid needed to achieve them can be determined with precision. Of course, in reality, it is difficult, if not impossible, to determine an optimal set of goals for any country. Likewise, it is not possible to know precisely how much aid is needed, aid being just one of many diverse ingredients needed to achieve the goals (Easterly, 2005). Nonetheless, the MDGs can be useful as targets and benchmarks by which individual countries and the world community as a whole can evaluate their progress and be held accountable.

If the Aid for Trade initiative is to be aligned with the MDGs, national development strategies, and Poverty Reduction Strategy Papers (PRSPs), it must take a very broad approach. While each African country has a ministry of trade (or a ministry of trade and industry), trade cuts across *all* ministries – agriculture, communication and transportation, defense, education and technology, environment, finance, health, labor, law and justice, natural resources, regional cooperation, tourism, etc. Although the Aid for Trade initiative is, in essence, an effort to adopt a sector-wide approach to trade, trade is not confined to one sector.

On the one hand, the broad range of trade issues suggests there is a need for an integrated approach to coordinate both aid for trade and the implementation of various programs. A program to diversify agricultural exports, for example, that concentrates solely on obtaining aid to increase production, would not be successful until there is reliable infrastructure, property rights, and macroeconomic stability. Consider the case of cut flowers in Tanzania. There was always suitable land for the production of cut flowers in Tanzania and a profitable foreign market for them. Nonetheless, actual production and exports did not take place until the early 1990s, after the following conditions were in place: producers had access to Nairobi International Airport in Kenya, an ordinance prohibiting the uprooting of coffee trees (in areas where cut flowers could be grown) was removed,[17] export taxes were reduced, the foreign currency market was liberalized, and investment rules began to encourage direct foreign investment. These were changes

---

[17] Some regulations, like this one which had essentially asked farmers to produce a particular crop, are supposedly meant to help farmers make good decisions – on production, on how to spend their incomes, or on other matters. However, often times those regulations become disincentives for increasing output. Amavilah provides an example of how livestock production declined in Angola in the 1980s partly because the government of Angola discouraged lavish slaughtering of livestock for weddings and funerals (Amavilah, 2005).

that involved various government ministries, local governments, and a neighboring country. Some deliberate coordination may have accelerated the diversification of exports.

On the other hand, it is the multitude of elements involved in trade that makes planning for trade difficult. A plan for trade must have as its principal goal an increase in the private sector's opportunities for production and trade.[18] The plan could be a genuine regional economic integration initiative that would involve, among other things, trade liberalization, the building and sharing of roads, ports, and other infrastructure, standardizing business and labor laws, and establishing regional research institutes. The pursuit of these endeavors can benefit from foreign aid and can lead to economic growth, which in turn can reduce poverty. Thus, it is important that Aid for Trade aim to be aligned with MDGs, national development strategies, and PRSPs.

4. *Ownership by recipient countries.* Ownership is a sensitive issue in any relationship between recipient and donor countries. If recipient countries do not have decisive ownership over programs to be implemented, the chance of those programs being completed and sustained is small. However, the level of ownership is a question of degree, determined by the recipient country's leaders, leverage, technical expertise, and overall governance. It is also

---

[18] Easterly (2006: 5–6) describes a dichotomy that he argues exists between what he calls planners and searchers:

In foreign aid, Planners announce good intentions but don't motivate anyone to carry them out; Searchers find things that work and get some reward. Planners raise expectations but take no responsibility for meeting them; Searchers accept responsibility for their actions. Planners determine what to supply; Searchers find out what is in demand. Planners apply global blueprints; Searchers adapt to local conditions. Planners at the top lack knowledge of the bottom; Searchers find out what the reality is at the bottom. Planners never hear whether the planned got what it needed; Searchers find out if the customer is satisfied.

This is an exaggerated and very simplified classification of aid agencies and government institutions (Planners) on one side and the private sector (Searchers) on the other side. Aid agencies and government institutions (whose planning, of course, includes searching) can play a unique role in empowering the private sector (whose searching must include *planning*) and those marginalized by the private sector.

determined by the operative philosophy of the donor agencies and the motives of the donors.

To expect or even suggest complete ownership of aid-financed projects by recipient countries is naïve. Complete ownership by recipient countries may not even be desirable. Often it is the donor organizations that carry out valuable needs assessment in the recipient countries, identify priorities, and prepare project proposals to meet those needs. Ideally, this is done in full consultation and collaboration with domestic experts and domestic stakeholders. In acknowledging the inevitable influence of the donor countries and organizations, the term that is used to describe the relationship between recipient and donor countries is *partnership*. African countries refer to donor countries and organizations as "our partners in development."

Another dimension of the ownership problem occurs within the recipient country. Suppose the IMF agrees with a country-driven PRSP approach, but the Minister of Finance in the country does not involve other stakeholders in the country in preparing the PRSP. Aware of such possibilities, the task force for Aid for Trade recommends to recipient countries that commitment to country ownership must mean an approach that includes local (and regional) private sector actors, women and minority groups, and other stakeholders. Such an approach would enhance transparency, monitoring, and accountability. The extent to which African countries take an inclusive approach regarding aid for trade will depend on the government structure, the existence and know-how of private sector organizations, and the amount of aid at stake.

To improve chances for inclusion and coherence, the task force recommended that recipient countries form national aid-for-trade committees (and possibly regional aid-for-trade committees). Current structures of aid committees and sub-committees in any given country would determine what would be appropriate for that country, although it is difficult to isolate trade from other initiatives, as discussed above. While it may seem to contradict the commitment to recipient country ownership, donor countries and organizations have an obligation to see that recipient countries take an inclusive approach.

## CONCLUSION

Tension always exists between developing countries and rich countries in WTO negotiations, regardless of what the agenda item might be. An African diplomat in Geneva described his perspective to the author as follows: "You must always be alert, even when they (rich countries) agree with you, because the likelihood is that there is something you are not aware of that made them agree with you." Some African representatives were skeptical of the Aid for Trade initiative even before the task force started its assignment. They did not think donor countries would actually deliver on their promises. Nonetheless, they have been encouraged because the Aid for Trade initiative has brought the discussion on aid to the forefront. They have viewed the initiative as an opportunity to determine the extent of the commitment of donor countries to increase aid. The Aid for Trade initiative gives African countries some leverage; they could always delay implementation of agreements or stall negotiations on new areas of trade if the Aid for Trade initiative were to fail. In addition, because it is possible that the initiative could actually produce some additional resources, they have in fact supported Aid for Trade.

Donor countries, for their part, want to use the Aid for Trade initiative to demonstrate their willingness to assist African countries. The initiative also allows donor countries to emphasize to African countries their obligations to WTO rules. With promises to increase aid, donor countries might even persuade African countries to consider new agreements. Whatever the motives of the recipient and donor countries might be, the Aid for Trade initiative is a political asset that neither side would want to see lost.

African countries sometimes approach the WTO negotiations as if they are doing the world a favor by liberalizing trade. Therefore, they feel they should be compensated and rewarded for it. They are often quick to point out the implementation and adjustment costs of trade reforms, but reluctant to acknowledge and estimate the cost of protection. This is a phenomenon that adds to the division between recipient and donor countries. Recipient countries tend to highlight the costs of trade liberalization, and donor countries tend to highlight the cost of protection in the recipient countries.

There are legitimate implementation costs and supply constraints that deserve aid. However, it is important to evaluate the impact of liberalization on its own merit. Short of that, hasty adjustments could be carried out only because aid was made available. Likewise, trade and growth-enhancing adjustments could be put off just because aid was not available. Aid should facilitate trade reforms; it should not be the reason for reforms. Moreover, some impediments to trade have nothing to do with limited technical capacity or inadequate infrastructure. When it is routine for truckers to spend days and sometimes weeks at the border (sometimes even between countries with a free trade area arrangement) to obtain clearance, the key problem is not a lack of computerized systems or the lack of well-trained and experienced personnel. The root cause of the problem is corruption and the lack of strong and effective leadership. In such cases, no amount of aid for trade facilitation will solve the fundamental problem.

The fact that donor countries have the upper hand regarding aid, does not give them the right to tease poor countries with promises they do not intend to fulfill. They must also refrain from using aid as bait to persuade recipient countries to sign new agreements. Moreover, the WTO must allow developing countries ample time to analyze proposals and implement agreements.

In the late 1990s, the Overseas Development Council and the African Economic Research Consortium sponsored a study to:

examine the nature, extent, and impact of aid dependence and address the critical challenge of how to lessen the dependence of most African governments on bilateral and multilateral aid, while accelerating the continent's economic and social progress. (Lancaster and Wangwe, 2000: vi)

The Aid for Trade initiative is an indicator that most African countries have not made progress toward lessening aid dependence. Some still depend on aid to help them identify priority needs and build their capacity to utilize aid.

Yet Africa has noticeably changed from the one-man rule in many countries in the first two and a half decades after independence to democracies in many countries in the twenty-first century. Likewise, the world is no longer divided by the Cold War. Both recipient and donor countries are now in a better position to focus on economic development and poverty reduction and, therefore, to make better use of aid for trade. Aid used effectively to facilitate trade can be an important tool to foster economic growth and, in turn, to reduce poverty.

# 7 CONCLUSION

THE DISCUSSION IN THIS BOOK HAS FOCUSED ON understanding and analyzing some of the WTO agreements and proposals in the context of Africa. It is not possible to describe the relationship between African countries and the WTO precisely, as one might when describing the relationship between two mutually exclusive entities. African countries are an important part of the WTO, constituting 28 percent of the membership (42 of 152 members in 2007).

Many overlapping coalitions exist within the WTO, including the African Group. While at some level each WTO member negotiates on its own behalf, negotiations are typically between one coalition or a set of coalitions and other coalitions, depending on the agenda item. These negotiations are fluid, dynamic, and complex, and can be frustrating, as seen in the Doha Round. The nature of the negotiations (and the relationships among countries) is explained, in part, by the economic and political diversity and history of the WTO members.

The WTO membership includes the richest and the poorest countries in the world. Some of those rich countries were colonizers of the poor countries, whose poor economic conditions can be attributed, in part, to colonialism. Some of the WTO members have mature democratic systems, and some are under a one-party system, a monarchy, or a dictatorship. These differences not only produce diverse economic interests – they also explain diverse capacities to negotiate.

WTO negotiations are complicated further (though also complemented) by the fact that WTO members have other formal multilateral and bilateral forums in which to discuss trade issues. It further complicates matters that demonstrators against the WTO converge on the WTO ministerial meetings and demand that their own diverse voices be heard as well. Demonstrations have certainly brought the WTO into the limelight, although not exactly in the way it would like to be portrayed. Most in the general population know something about the WTO *only* through the demonstrations against it. It should be noted that international organizations such as the WTO, the International Monetary Fund, and the World Bank, are easy and safe targets. Their positions are, relatively speaking, more conspicuous than domestic rules and policies in many developing countries, for example. In addition, these international institutions cannot (and, of course, should not) intimidate demonstrators the way that rulers in some developing countries can. In short, while trying to focus on the overall benefits of freer and more predictable trade, WTO negotiations must also try to accommodate the interests of many different countries, business sectors, and interest groups.

Although the African Group is a viable coalition in the WTO, African countries do not, in fact, have much economic leverage. This is due to their relatively small markets. In addition, the diversity of African countries means they cannot always speak in unison. Moreover, African countries receive financial aid from developed countries and preferential access to OECD markets, making African countries that much more vulnerable and cautious in their approach. The donor–recipient relationship between the OECD countries and African countries explains, in part, the low participation by African countries in the dispute settlement mechanism.

One of the major accomplishments of the Uruguay Round of GATT was reaching the Dispute Settlement Understanding (DSU). This agreement took effect when the WTO replaced GATT in 1995.

The DSU provides a coherent and predictable timetable for consultation and enforcement of WTO obligations. No African country has been involved as a principal complainant in any WTO case thus far. Some African countries have been involved as third parties on the complainants' side, however. The high cost of bringing a case has often been given as the main reason for the limited utilization of the dispute settlement mechanism by African countries. Although cost is undoubtedly a factor, it is unlikely that it is an important one. Moreover, to help address the cost of bringing cases through the DSU, the dedicated and highly skilled Advisory Center for WTO Law (ACWL) provides legal training for developing countries, as well as heavily subsidized services in dispute settlement proceedings.

A more significant reason for the limited participation of African countries in the dispute settlement mechanism is the preferential treatment accorded to them by their major trading partners, that is, the OECD countries. Because the OECD countries could unilaterally remove the preferential treatment, African countries would presumably want to avoid upsetting them. In addition, and more importantly, preferential treatment implies that the preference-giving countries have already opened their markets to African products beyond the minimum requirements of the WTO obligations. Therefore, from an obligatory point of view, as determined by WTO agreements, African countries typically have very little on which to base complaints through the DSU system. Of course, this does not render the DSU irrelevant to African countries. The DSU system has reduced tendencies for a blatant disregard of WTO rules; in so doing, it has elevated the significance of all WTO agreements. Even with its imperfections, the DSU promotes a sense of obligation and discipline and, thus, a more predictable trade environment.

Nonetheless, the WTO's authority to enforce obligations has a downside. On one hand, fear of enforcement may make countries hesitant to negotiate any new agreements, as the resistance by developing countries to negotiate the Singapore issues has demonstrated. On the other hand, some countries may try to push agreements into the WTO that ideally belong in other international organizations, only to gain the legal authority to enforce those agreements. It seems many agreements can be justified as being appropriate for the WTO by categorizing them as "trade related." An example of this is the Agreement on Trade-Related Aspects of Intellectual Property Rights (TRIPS), which brought into the WTO rules and agreements that were under the World Intellectual Property Organization (WIPO).

The TRIPS Agreement is among the new agreements that came into effect with the establishment of the WTO. This agreement has been both a challenge and an opportunity for the African Group. It has been a challenge because it has had the potential to interfere with the availability of generic drugs; these are critical in dealing with the HIV/AIDS epidemic and other diseases in Africa and other developing areas of the world. The TRIPS Agreement has had a waiver that allows the use of compulsory licensing in the case of a public health crisis. However, the waiver was initially temporary and had its own other limitations. In fact, when South Africa applied this waiver to ease access to HIV/AIDS drugs, an association representing thirty-nine pharmaceutical companies filed a court case against the government of South Africa. Three years later the association withdrew its case.

Although African countries would have preferred a friendlier TRIPS Agreement from the very beginning, the inadequacy of the agreement gave the African Group a unique opportunity to work closely together toward a common goal. The group's resolve, ingenuity, and collaboration with other groups paid off. The waiver that allowed the use of compulsory licensing was amended to become broader and more useful. In addition, a decision was reached to make the waiver permanent, pending ratification by at least two-thirds of the WTO members. This is certainly a victory for the African Group. Assuming the waiver becomes a permanent amendment, it will be the first time a core WTO agreement has been amended. The experience that the African countries acquired and the coalitions they forged in the process of negotiating this amendment to the TRIPS Agreement are assets transferable to other endeavors in the WTO.

The experience with the Agreement on Agriculture has been different. The Uruguay Round, the last and longest round of negotiations under GATT (1986–1993), barely managed to incorporate the agricultural sector into the WTO. The Doha Round of the WTO, launched in 2001, was described as a development round that would give priority to the interests and challenges of developing countries. Given that agriculture is the most important economic sector in most developing countries, it was expected that developed countries would reduce their agricultural subsidies. Yet the Doha Round of negotiations has suffered a number of setbacks, mainly due to disagreement between developed and developing countries and between developed countries themselves over these subsidies.

Agricultural subsidies cause increases in production and decreases in world prices, hurting developing countries that depend on agricultural exports. However, some developing countries stand to lose from a reduction of agricultural subsidies in OECD countries. This is due to preferential treatment that OECD countries give to developing countries, such as market access to higher OECD domestic prices for imports from developing countries. The level of benefits from that market access is directly connected to the level of OECD subsidies. In addition, net food-importing countries are concerned about the potential increase in their food-import bills if agricultural subsidies are reduced.[1]

---

[1]   The recent increases in world food prices have certainly highlighted the dilemma of the net-food importing countries regarding OECD agricultural subsidies. If reductions of those subsidies are expected to increase food prices even more, it is unlikely that net-food importing countries would support such reductions.

In negotiating extensions to the Agreement on Agriculture, subsidies may be the most contentious issue, but they are certainly not the only issue. Other issues include market access and the selection of "special products" by developing countries. Still, the dispute over agricultural subsidies will continue to be a dominant issue in the WTO in the years to come. The agricultural sector, in developed and developing countries alike, reflects entrenched domestic policies which contradict the spirit of free trade promoted by the WTO. Agricultural subsidies in developed countries have the support of powerful political constituencies. Even the evidence that cotton subsidies in the United States and other countries hurt poor African countries has not produced meaningful reductions in subsidies. Although the free-trade argument for the removal of subsidies is a very strong argument, it is not necessarily enough to overcome domestic politics.

A more effective case (from a political point of view) for the removal of subsidies and other production-distorting policies may be the cost of those policies to other domestic constituencies. In the 1980s when OECD countries took a critical look at their agricultural policies, they did so because their governments could no longer afford to spend so much money (billions of dollars) on those subsidies. Agricultural subsidies and protection also put the agricultural sector at odds with domestic consumers and manufacturers that use agricultural products as inputs. In addition, within the agricultural sector itself, the inadequate distribution of subsidies causes discontent with agricultural subsidies. There is also concern that agricultural policies in OECD countries fail to achieve some of their goals, such as helping disadvantaged areas, supporting small producers, and promoting environmentally friendly practices. All these costs and failures of subsidies could be used to build a strong case for the reduction or even removal of subsidies.

African countries must continue to negotiate in the WTO for the reduction of OECD subsidies and other commitments that would allow them to grow their agricultural sectors more. However, they must also focus on their own domestic policies. Given the direction that the debate over "special products" has been taking and given the announcement that the Doha Round is a *development* round, it appears developing countries, particularly least-developed countries, will be left with a great deal of flexibility and ample policy space. Nonetheless, even unilateral trade liberalization can benefit African countries. Although adjustment costs and income distribution objectives must be considered, freer domestic trade policies increase the efficiency with which resources are allocated (Anderson et al., 2006). The fact that African countries (least-developed countries, in particular) may not be called upon to open their agricultural markets, must not be interpreted as an affirmation of their current policies. The policy space they have is meant to allow them to liberalize at a pace that they determine to be in harmony with their overall development strategies. Furthermore, over time they will be expected to open their markets more, as their trading partners have done for them.

It should also be expected that the signatories to the plurilateral Agreement on Government Procurement (GPA) will strive to increase the number of countries that are parties to this agreement. In addition, developed countries will make new attempts to pursue an agreement on transparency in government procurement (TGP). It can be expected that African countries will resist such attempts – African countries want complete flexibility to use government procurement policies as part of a broader policy to support infant industries and achieve other development and social goals. Flexibility is important. However, the considerable size of government procurement, and the potential for corruption associated with it, call for transparency. In the real world, discriminatory government procurement policies have a high propensity to be driven by politics and rent-seeking incentives; a multilateral agreement on TGP could inject some discipline into the procurement process. Meanwhile, developed countries would need to increase technical assistance to African countries to help them in their efforts to reform government procurement procedures. That is part of what African countries need before discussions on TGP can resume in earnest.

The Aid for Trade initiative is an acknowledgment of the financial and technical support that African and other developing countries need. These countries need training and technical assistance for effective participation in negotiations and for the implementation of trade agreements. They also need assistance to address supply-side constraints that limit their production and trade capacity. In addition, they need assistance to cover the costs associated with the displacement of workers (such as job re-training) and other adjustments following the implementation of agreements.

Notwithstanding these legitimate needs, one must wonder if the Aid for Trade initiative may further polarize negotiations between developing and developed countries in the WTO, without producing any actual increase in the level of aid provided. Assistance for trade programs is sometimes demanded as if it were an entitlement. At the same time, financial assistance can be used to coerce developing countries into making new commitments. This last point is neither to suggest that developed countries necessarily use aid to pressure developing countries, nor that developing countries are necessarily gullible. It is only to suggest the reality that financial aid is never totally unconditional. Although WTO negotiations will always include discussions about financial and technical assistance, it is important for African countries to evaluate the impact of liberalization on its own merit. That is not to say the availability of assistance is not important, but rather that it should not take precedence over consideration of a given policy's own merits, even in the absence of assistance.

The preceding discussion has highlighted some of the apprehension of African countries in the WTO. The uneasiness comes in part from: their inability to participate fully and effectively in negotiations; concerns about agreements that may constrain them in their development efforts and reduce their policy space; concerns about policies in developed countries that limit their ability to get the most from their exports; and the lack of sufficient resources to implement, take full advantage of, and adjust to agreements. On a more fundamental level, though, reluctance to be "constrained" by WTO agreements (as is often the perception) reflects an underlying sense of being treated unfairly. Specifically, they sense they are being asked to implement policies which developed countries themselves did not have to implement when their economies were in the developing stages.

Chang (2002) captures that sentiment well. African and other developing countries believe they are being asked to "kick away the ladder" that developed countries used to climb to their economic might. The ladder, according to Chang, is a set of institutions and protectionist policies that developed countries used to nurture their once infant industries. The contention is that developed countries are "demanding from developing countries institutional standards that they themselves had never attained at comparable levels of development" (Chang, 2002: 135). This apparent double standard was alluded to in Chapter 3.

While Chang provides a thoughtful analysis overall, certain of his arguments are misleading. For example, he portrays the co-existence of high tariffs and relative high economic growth as a positive causal relationship, implying that high tariffs caused growth in developed countries. No careful examination is provided of the role of increased productivity and resources which, most likely, were the most important catalysts for growth. In fact, it is more plausible that those economies grew in spite of the protection, not because of it. Chang also contends that the policies of the 1960s and 1970s in Sub-Saharan Africa caused faster economic growth. He goes so far as to argue that those "bad policies" of the 1960s and 1970s in Africa and other developing areas were better than the "good policies" of the 1990s. Yet the policies of the 1960s and 1970s resulted in shortages from price and interest rate ceilings, overvaluation of domestic currencies, high taxes on subsistence farmers, prohibitive trade barriers, and uncontrolled increases in the supply of money. How could they have caused faster economic growth? Rather than assuming causality, this question warrants careful examination – both to consider the economic performance of different countries and to consider their causes.

The underlying theme in Chang (2002) is that measures to protect infant industries have been important to the success of developed countries. The infant industry argument for protection is well known and its historical context is presented well by Chang. However, a few caveats regarding the infant industry argument must be kept in mind: (a) it is difficult, for economic and political reasons, to identify viable infant industries (when each one is "infant"); (b) government protection is not the only (or best) method to nurture infant industries; and (c) protection involves costs.

Developed countries are still bearing the costs (current and residual) of tariffs and other support mechanisms they instituted more than a century ago. For example, U.S. tariffs to protect sugar growers date back to the nineteenth century.[2] The U.S. government still protects sugar growers in the twenty-first century, at a high cost to U.S. consumers. According to the estimates of the U.S. General Accounting Office, in 1998 the sugar program cost U.S. consumers $1.9 billion. Even if gains to U.S. sugar producers are taken into account, the net loss to the U.S. economy was $900 million (U.S. General Accounting Office, 2000). The same point about costs can be made regarding protection of the textile and apparel industry in developed countries and agricultural policies of those countries in general.

Trade barriers implemented to protect infant industries are difficult to remove, whether the industry remains an "infant" or it matures – a lesson that developing countries can learn from

---

[2]   U.S. tariffs used primarily to generate government revenue date back to the eighteenth century.

developed countries. In either case, it becomes politically very risky (for politicians) to remove protection. Of course, this does not mean protecting infant industries should be avoided at all costs. The point is to consider carefully the political ramifications and economic costs of protection, regardless of the motivation.

Another problem with the "kicking away the ladder" assertion is its implicit assumption that developed countries do not want the economies of developing countries to grow. Presumably they are afraid of the potential increase in competition from developing countries. The problem with this notion is that trading partners not only compete with each other (which, in fact, has its own benefits); they also serve as markets for each other's products. Developed countries actually have an interest in seeing that the economies of developing countries grow, so consumers in those countries can buy more products from developed countries. Moreover, strong economies can provide more political stability and security.

Collier (2007) does not see the reason for poor countries to be in the WTO. He asks:

What are the countries of the bottom billion doing in the WTO? ... It does not have resources to disburse to countries, nor an objective that its staff must achieve with such resources. It is not a purposive organization but rather a marketplace. The WTO secretariat is there merely to set up the stalls each day, sweep the floors each evening, and regulate the opening hours. What happens is made by the bargaining. ... But the markets of the bottom billion are so tiny that even if their governments were prepared to reduce trade barriers, this would not confer any bargaining power on them. If the U.S. government decides that the political gains from protecting cotton growers outweigh the political cost of making American taxpayers finance a hugely expensive farm bill, the offer of better access to the market in Chad is not going to make much difference. (Collier, 2007: 170–171)

It is no secret or surprise that a country's economic strength is important in determining its leverage in negotiating agreements.

This phenomenon is not unique to the WTO. Collier's comments on the WTO seem to imply that bargaining is an invention of or an imposition by the WTO. However, bargaining between poor countries and rich countries would take place with or without the WTO. Imperfect is it might be, the WTO provides a more predictable trade environment. In addition, the WTO plays an important role in facilitating negotiations between very diverse countries. It is highly unlikely that poor countries would be better off relying on bilateral bargaining, rather than actively engaging in multilateral bargaining and forming coalitions with other WTO members. The unity of developing countries contributed in no small part to developed countries agreeing to bring the agricultural and textile and apparel sectors into the WTO. At least now poor countries can challenge the United States on its cotton subsidies, as Benin and Chad have done through the dispute settlement system as third parties, as well as through the "cotton initiative" that they launched jointly with Burkina Faso and Mali.

Negotiations in the WTO will always be complex and at times contentious. This is due to wide economic and political differences among countries with conflicting interests and goals, as well as a degree of mistrust among some member countries. Furthermore, freer trade is sometimes at odds with objectives such as those concerning the environment and income distribution. In addition, some people are quite vocal in their opposition to freer trade and globalization, and this can also influence negotiations.

What some people fail to understand is that when it comes to trade, differences between rich and poor countries do not always have to be a cause for concern. Differences provide an opportunity for a mutually beneficial exchange of goods and services, as well as ideas. The economic gap between countries does not have to grow. On the contrary, when they take advantage of their differences through trade, all can do better and move in the direction to achieve their potential. Trade can be an effective engine for growth that, in turn, can reduce poverty. At their best, the African Group and other coalitions of African countries in the WTO articulate and advance the interests of African countries, while strengthening the WTO in its mission to facilitate freer trade guided by predictable international rules. At *its* best, the WTO helps all member countries make the most of their strengths and parlay their differences for the benefit of all.

# BIBLIOGRAPHY

Abbott, Frederick (2002), "WTO TRIPS Agreement and Its Implications for Access to Medicines in Developing Countries." Study Paper 2a, Commission on Intellectual Property Rights.

(2005), "The WTO Medicine Decisions: World Pharmaceutical Trade and the Protection of Public Health." *The American Journal of International Law*, **99**, 317–358.

ACP (2005), "ACP Proposal on Market Access in Agriculture." JOB(05)/257/ Rev.1, October 28. http://www.acpsec.org/geneva/ACP_PROPOSAL_ ON_MARKET_ACCESS_IN_AGRICULTURE_en.pdf

ACP Group (1995), *Agreement Amending the Fourth ACP-EC Convention of Lomé Signed in Mauritius on 4 November 1995.* Brussels: ACP Group.

ACWL (2005), "The ACWL after Four Years: A Progress Report by the Management Board." Geneva: Advisory Center on WTO Law.

(2006), "Report on Operations 2005." Geneva: Advisory Center on WTO Law.

Adam, Christopher and Stephen O'Connell (2004), "Aid Versus Trade Revisited: Donor and Recipient Policies in the Presence of Learning-by-Doing." *Economic Journal*, **114** (482), 150–173.

African Union (2001), *The New Partnership for Africa's Development (NEPAD)*. http://www.nepad.org/2005/files/documents/inbrief.pdf

(2003), "Assembly of the African Union, Second Ordinary Session, 10–12 July 2003, Maputo, Mozambique: DECISIONS AND DECLARATIONS." Addis Ababa: African Union.

(2005), "Arusha Declaration and Plan of Action on African Commodities." AU/Min/Com/Decl.Rev.1. Addis Ababa: African Union.

(2005a), "The Cairo Declaration and Road Map on the Doha Work Programme." TI/TMIN/EXP/6-b (III) Rev. 4. Addis Ababa: African Union.

Ake, Claude (1991), *A Political Economy of Africa*. New York: Longman.

(1996), *Democracy and Development*. Washington, D.C.: Brookings Institution.

Amavilah, Voxi (2005), "The National Wealth of Selected Countries – A Descriptive Essay." REEPS Discussion Paper 2005 (4). Phoenix: Resource and Engineering Economics Publication Series.

Anderson, Kym (2002), "Peculiarities of Retaliation in WTO Dispute Settlement." *World Trade Review*, 1(2), 123–134.

Anderson, Kym, et al. (2006), "Would Multilateral Trade Reform Benefit Sub-Saharan Africans?" *Journal of African Economies*, 15 (4), 626–670.

Asiedu, Elizabeth (2006), "Foreign Direct Investment in Africa: The Role of Natural Resources, Market Size, Government Policy, Institutions and Political Instability." *The World Economy*, 29 (1), 63–77.

Badiane, Ousmane, et al. (2002), "Cotton Sector Strategies in West and Central Africa." World Bank Policy Research Working Paper 2867. Washington, D.C.: World Bank.

Bafalikike, Lokongo (2002), "Jammeh: 'NEPAD will never work.'" *New Africa*. Issue 410, p. 18, September.

Baffes, John (2004), "Cotton: Market Setting, Trade Policies, and Issues." World Bank Policy Research Working Paper 3218. Washington, D.C.: World Bank.

(2005), "Cotton: Market Setting, Trade Policies, and Issues." In Atman Aksoy and John Benghin (editors), *Global Agricultural Trade and Developing Countries*, 259–273. Washington, D.C.: World Bank.

Bagwell, Kyle, et al. (2004), "The Case of Tradable Remedies in WTO Dispute Settlement." World Bank Policy Research Working Paper No. 3314. Washington, D.C.: World Bank.

Baldwin, Robert (1984), "Trade Policies in Developed Countries." In Ronald Jones and Peter Kenen (editors), *Handbook of International Economics, Volume I*, 571–619. The Netherlands: Elsevier Science Publishers.

Baldwin, Robert and David Richardson (1972), "Government Purchasing Policies, Other NTBs and the International Monetary Crisis." In H.E. English and Keith Hay (editors), *Obstacles to Trade in the Pacific Area: Proceedings of the Fourth Pacific Trade and Development Conference* (October 7–10, 1971). Ottawa: School of International Affairs, Carleton University.

Barros, A.R. (1992), "Sugar Prices and High-Fructose Corn Syrup Consumption in the United States." *Journal of Agricultural Economics*, 43 (1), 64–73.

Basso, Maristela and Edson Beas (2005), "Cross-retaliation through TRIPS in Cotton Dispute." *Bridges*, 9, 5, May. Geneva: International Center for Trade and Sustainable Development.

Beeching, Jack (1975), *The Chinese Opium Wars*. New York: Harcourt Brace Jovanovich.

Berthélemy, Jean-Claude and Ludvig Söderking (2001), "The Role of Capital Accumulation, Adjustment and Structural Change for Economic Takeoff: Empirical Evidence from African Growth Episodes." *World Development*, **29** (2), 323–343.

Bhagwati, Jagdish (2004), *In Defense of Globalization*. New York: Oxford University Press.

Bhagwati, Jagdish and Arvind Panagariya (2002), "Wanted: Jubilee 2010. Dismantling Protection." *OECD Observer* No. 231/232, May.

Blackhurst, Richard and William Lyakurwa (2005), "Markets and Market Access for African Exports." In Ademola Oyejide and William Lyakurwa (editors), *Africa and the World Trading System*, 55–106. Trenton: Africa World Press.

Blustein, Paul (2005), "U.S. Accused of Flouting Global Trade Rules: Angered Commerce Partners Try to Prod Washington into Compliance." *The Washington Post*, D6, October 26.

Branigin, William and Jackie Spinner (2003), "War Opponents Denounce U.S. Rules on Iraq Contracts: EU Studying If Ban Violates Trade Rules." *The Washington Post*, December 10. http://www.washingtonpost.com/ac2/wp-dyn/A52262-2003Dec10?language=printer

Brenton, Paul and Takako Ikezuki (2005), "The Impact of Agricultural Trade Preferences, with Particular Attention to the Least-developed Countries." In Atman Aksoy and John Benghin (editors), *Global Agricultural Trade and Developing Countries*, 55–73. Washington, D.C.: World Bank.

(2006), "The Value of Trade Preference in Africa." In Richard Newfarmer (editor), *Trade, Doha, and Development: A Window into the Issues*, 223–229. Washington, D.C.: World Bank.

Brewer, Thomas L. and Stephen Young (1999), "WTO Disputes and Developing Countries." *Journal of World Trade*, **33** (5), 69–182.

Brink, Gustav (2005), "The 10 Major Problems With the Anti-Dumping Instrument in South Africa." *Journal of World Trade*, **39** (1), 47–157.

Brülhart, Marius and Federico Trionfetti (2004), "Public Expenditure and International Specialization and Agglomeration." *European Economic Review*, **48** (4), 851–881.

Bulir, Ales and A. Javier Hamann (2006), "Volatility of Development Aid: From the Frying Pan into the Fire?" IMF Working Paper No. 06–65. Washington, D.C.: IMF.

Burnside, Craig and David Dollar (2000), "Aid, Policies, and Growth." *American Economic Review*, **90** (4), 847–868.

Butler, Leah (2006), "Effects and Outcomes of *Amicus Curiae* briefs at the WTO: An Assessment of NGO Experiences." http://socrates.berkeley.edu/~es196/projects/2006final/butler.pdf

# Bibliography

Chang, Ha-Joon (2002), *Kicking Away the Ladder: Development Strategy in Historical Perspective*. London: Anthem Press.

Chang, Pao-Li (2002), "The Evolution and Utilization of the GATT/WTO Dispute Settlement Mechanism." Research Seminar in International Economics, Discussion Paper 475, University of Michigan.

Chomthongdi, Jacques Chai (2005), "The G-groupings in the WTO Agricultural Negotiations." http://www.focusweb.org/content/view/632/36/

Collier, Paul and David Dollar (1999), *"Aid Allocation and Poverty Reduction."* World Bank Policy Research Working Paper No. 2041. Washington, D.C.: World Bank.

Collier, Paul (2007), *The Bottom Billion: Why the Poorest Countries Are Failing and What Can Be Done About It.* New York: Oxford University Press.

Commission for Africa (2005), *Our Common Interest: Report of the Commission for Africa.* London: Department of International Development, Commission for Africa.

Correa, Carlos (2000), *Intellectual Property Rights, the WTO and Developing Countries.* London and New York: Zed Books Ltd.

Crouch, Gregory (2002), "Europeans Investigate Resale of AIDS Drugs." *The New York Times*, New York, W1, October 29.

Dalgaard, Carl-Johan, et al. (2004), "On the Empirics of Foreign Aid and Growth." *Economic Journal*, **114** (496), 191–216.

De Renzio, Paolo and Sarah Mulley (2006), "Donor Coordination and Global Governance: Donor-Led and Recipient-Led Approaches." Oxford: Oxford University Department of Politics and International Relations.

Deen, Thalif (2006), "Zimbabwe: Economy Crumbles in Africa's Former 'Breadbasket.'" *Global Information Network*. June 14, p.1.

Drahos, Peter (2002), "Negotiating Intellectual Property Rights: Between Coercion and Dialogue." In Peter Drahos and Ruth Mayne (editors), *Global Intellectual Property Rights: Knowledge, Access, and Development*, 163–182. New York: Palgrave Macmillan.

Dreier, Thomas (1996), "TRIPS and the Enforcement of Intellectual Property Rights." In Friedrich-Karl Beir and Gerhard Schricker (editors), *From GATT to TRIPS – The Agreement on Trade-Related Aspects of Intellectual Property Rights*, 248–277. Munich: Max Planck Institute for Foreign and International Patent, Copyright and Competition Law.

Drimie, Scott (2003), "HIV/AIDS and Land: Case Studies from Kenya, Lesotho, and South Africa," *Development Southern Africa*, **20** (5), 647–658.

Easterly, William (2005), "How to Assess the Needs for Aid? The Answer: Don't Ask." New York University Development Research Institute, Working Paper No.18.

(2006), *The White Man's Burden: Why the West's Efforts to Aid the Rest Have Done So Much Ill and So Little Good*. New York: Penguin Press.

ECA (2005), "The Millennium Development Goals in Africa: Progress and Challenges." Addis Ababa: Economic Commission for Africa.

(2007), "Aid for Trade: Emerging Issues and Challenges." E/ECA/COE/26/7, March 1. Addis Ababa: Economic Commission for Africa.

Economic Commission for Africa (2003), "Report of the High-Level Brainstorming Meeting of African Trade Negotiators Preparatory to the Fifth WTO Ministerial Conference." Addis Ababa: Economic Commission for Africa.

Evenett, Simon and Bernard Hoekman (2005), "International Cooperation and the Reform of Public Procurement Policies." World Bank Policy Research Working Paper No. 3720. Washington, D.C.: World Bank.

Fabiosa, Jay, et al. (2003), "Agricultural Markets Liberalization and the Doha Round." In *Proceedings of the 25th International Conference of Agricultural Economists*, 867–873. Durban, South Africa.

Fagerberg, Jan, et al. (1997), *Technology and International Trade*. Vermont: Edward Elgar.

Faizel, Ismail (2005), "A Development Perspective on the WTO July 2004 General Council Decision," *Journal of International Economic Law*, 8 (2), 377–404.

FAO (1996), "World Food Summit," 13–17 November. Rome: Food and Agricultural Organization. http://www.fao.org/documents/show_cdr. asp?url_file=/docrep/003/x0736m/rep2/oau.htm

Feinberg, Robert and Kara Reynolds (2006), "The Spread of Antidumping Regimes and the Role of Retaliation in Filings." *Southern Economic Journal*, 72 (4), 877–890.

Fischler, Franz (2004),"Why Can't America Be More Like Us?" *Wall Street Journal*, A12, February 19.

Flam, Harry and Elhanan Helpman (1987), "Vertical Product Differentiation and North-South Trade." *American Economic Review*, 77 (5), 810–822.

Fox, Tom and William Vorley (2004), "Concentration in Food Supply and Retail Chains." UK Department for International Development Working Paper 13. London: DFID.

G-33 (2005), "Special Products – Contribution by the G-33." JOB(05)/230, October 12. http://www.tradeobservatory.org/library.cfm?refid=77130

(2005a), "G33 Proposal on Special Safeguard Measures." JOB(05)/92, June 3. Geneva: Permanent Mission of the Republic of Indonesia in Geneva. http://www.mission-indonesia.org/modules/article.php?lang= en&articleid=284&preview=1

Gardner, Bruce (1990), "Origin and Evolution of U.S. Farm Policies." In Fred H. Sanderson (editor), *Agricultural Protectionism in the Industrialized World*, 9–63. Washington, D.C.: Resources for the Future.

GATT (1985), "Canada – Measures Affecting the Sale of Gold Coins, Report of the Panel." L/5863, http://www.worldtradelaw.net/reports/gattpanels/goldcoins.pdf

Gibb, Richard (2004), "Developing Countries and Market Access: the Bitter-Sweet Taste of the European Union's Sugar Policy in Southern Africa." *Journal of Modern African Studies*, **42** (4), 563–588.

Gillson, Ian, et al. (2004), "Understanding the Impact of Cotton Subsidies on Developing Countries." Overseas Development Institute Working Paper, AG0107. London: Overseas Development Institute.

Glass, Amy Jocelyn (1997), "Product Cycles and Market Penetration." *International Economic Review*, **38** (4), 865–891.

Goreux, Louis and John Macrae (2003), "Reforming the Cotton Sector in Sub-Saharan Africa." World Bank Africa Region Working Paper Series No. 47. Washington, D.C.: World Bank.

Gupta, Sanjeev, et al. (2006), *Macroeconomic Challenges of Scaling Up Aid to Africa: A Checklist for Practitioners.*" Washington, D.C.: IMF.

Gyimah-Brempong, Kwabena (2002), "Corruption, Economic Growth, and Income Inequality in Africa." *Economics of Governance*, **3**, 193–209.

Haley, Stephen, et al. (2006), *Sugar and Sweeteners Outlook/SSS-245.* Washington, D.C.: Economic Research Service, USDA.

Harman, Danna (2006), "Caribbean's Bittersweet New Reality: New EU Subsidy Will Cripple Island Sugar Industries Created Centuries Ago to Serve European Markets." *Christian Science Monitor*, p. 4, March 22.

Herbert, Bob (1996), "Banana Bully." *The New York Times*, **A15**, May 13.

Hoekman, Bernard, et al. (2006), "Preference Erosion: The Terms of the Debate." In *Trade, Doha, and Development: A Window into the Issues*, edited by Richard Newfarmer, 333–343. Washington, D.C.: World Bank.

Holmes, Peter, et al. (2003), "Emerging Trends in WTO Dispute Settlement: Back to the GATT?" World Bank Policy Research Working Paper, 3133. Washington, D.C.: World Bank.

Hudec, Robert (1990), *The GATT Legal System and World Trade Diplomacy.* 2nd Edition (1st edition, New York, Praeger, 1975). Salem, New Hampshire: Butterworth Legal Publishers.

(1993), *Enforcing International Trade Law: The Evolution of the Modern GATT Legal System.* Salem, New Hampshire: Butterworth Legal Publishers.

(2002), "The Adequacy of WTO Dispute Settlement Remedies." In *Development, Trade and the WTO*, 81–91. Washington, D.C.: World Bank.

Hudson Institute (2006), *The Index of Global Philanthropy.* Washington, D.C.: Hudson Institute.

Hutton, Guy (2004), "Case Study of a 'Successful' Sector-wide Approach: the Uganda Health Sector SWAp." Basel: Swiss Tropical Institute.

# Bibliography

ICAC (2001), *Survey of the Cost of Production of Raw Cotton.* Washington, D.C.: International Cotton Advisory Committee.

(2002), *Production and Trade Policies Affecting the Cotton Industry.* Washington, D.C.: International Cotton Advisory Committee.

ICTSD (2001), "EC-ACP Cotonou Waiver Finally Granted." *BRIDGES Weekly Trade News Digest,* 5 (39), November 15. Geneva: International Center for Trade and Sustainable Development.

(2005), "Brazil Suspends Cross-Retaliation Request Against US in Cotton Case." *BRIDGES Weekly Trade News Digest,* 9 (40), November 23. Geneva: International Center for Trade and Sustainable Development.

(2006), "Falconer Paper on Special Products Splits G-33, Farm Exporters." *BRIDGES Weekly Trade News Digest,* 10 (16), May 10. Geneva: International Center for Trade and Sustainable Development.

(2006a), "Ecuador Unpeels New Chapter in Banana Dispute With EU." *BRIDGES Weekly Trade News Digest,* 10 (39), November 22. Geneva: International Center for Trade and Sustainable Development.

(2006b), "Colombia Joins Ecuador in Bananas Dispute Against EU." *BRIDGES Weekly Trade News Digest,* 10 (41), December 6. Geneva: International Center for Trade and Sustainable Development.

(2007), "Rwanda Becomes First Country to Try to Use WTO Procedure to Import Patented HIV/AIDS Drugs." *BRIDGES Weekly Trade News Digest,* 11 (27), July 25. Geneva: International Center for Trade and Sustainable Development.

(2007a), "WTO Panel: US Has Failed to Comply with Cotton Ruling in Dispute with Brazil." *BRIDGES Weekly Trade News Digest,* 11 (35), October 18. Geneva: International Center for Trade and Sustainable Development.

(2007b), "TRIPS Council Extends Public Health Deadline; Discusses Biodiversity, LDC Aid." *BRIDGES Weekly Trade News Digest,* 11 (37), October 31. Geneva: International Center for Trade and Sustainable Development.

(2008), "First Batch of Generic Drugs En Route to Africa under 5-Year Old WTO Deal," *BRIDGES Weekly News Digest,* 12 (31), September 24. Geneva: International Center for Trade and Sustainable Development.

IFPRI (2004), *Assuring Food and Nutrition Security in Africa by 2020: Prioritizing Actions, Strengthening Actors, and Facilitating Partnerships.* Washington, D.C.: International Food Policy Research Institute.

IMF (2005), "Poverty Reduction Strategy Papers (PRSP): A Factsheet." Washington, D.C.: IMF. http://www.imf.org/external/np/exr/facts/prsp.htm

IMF and the World Bank (2000), "Poverty Reduction Strategy Papers – Progress in Implementing." Washington, D.C.: IMF and the World Bank. http://www.imf.org/external/np/prsp/2000/prsp.htm

Ingco, Merlinda (1996), "Tariffication in the Uruguay Round: How Much Liberalization?" *The World Economy,* **19** (4), 425–446.

Iritani, Evelyn (2003), "U.S. Is Accused of Violating Pact in Iraq Bid Policy: Under a procurement accord lobbied for by Washington, American officials must allow open competition, excluded nations say." *Los Angeles Times,* **A11,** December 16.

Jackson, John H. (1998), *The World Trade Organization: Constitution and Jurisprudence.* London: Royal Institute of International Affairs.

Kathuri, Benson (2006), "New Procurement Rules Lock Out Public Servants." *The East African Standard,* Nairobi, February 17. http://www.eastandard.net/archives/cl/hm_news/news.php?articleid=36542&date=17/2/2006

(2006a), "Experts Decry Political Interference In Tenders." *The East African Standard,* Nairobi, March 23. http://www.eastandard.net/archives/cl/hm_news/news.php?articleid=38319&date=23/3/2006

Khor, Martin (2002), "Rethinking Intellectual Rights and TRIPS." In Peter Drahos and Ruth Mayne (editors), *Global Intellectual Property Rights,* 201–213. New York: Palgrave Macmillan.

Kristof, Nicholas (2002), "Farm Subsidies That Kill." *The New York Times,* **A19,** July 5.

Laird, S. and A. Yeats (1990), *Quantitative Methods for Trade-Barrier Analysis.* New York: New York University Press.

Lancaster, Carol and Samuel Wangwe (2000), *Managing a Smooth Transition from Aid Dependence in Africa.* Washington, D.C.: Overseas Development Council and African Economic Research Consortium.

Lee, Karen and Silke von Lewinski (1996), "The Settlement of International Disputes in the Field of Intellectual Property." In Friedrich-Karl Beir and Gerhard Schricker (editors), *From GATT to TRIPS – The Agreement on Trade-Related Aspects of Intellectual Property Rights,* 278–328. Munich: Max Planck Institute for Foreign and International Patent, Copyright and Competition Law.

Lensink, Robert and Howard White (2000), "Aid Allocation, Poverty Reduction and the Assessing Aid Report." *Journal of International Development,* **12** (3), 399–412.

Lyakurwa, William (2007), "The Business of Exporting: Transaction Costs Facing Suppliers in Sub-Saharan Africa." Framework Paper Presented at the African Economic Research Consortium – Collaborative Research Workshop on Export Supply Response Constraints in Sub-Saharan Africa, Dar-es-Salaam, Tanzania, April 23–24, 2007. Nairobi: African Economic Research Consortium.

Mattoo, Aaditya (1996), "The Government Procurement Agreement: Implications of Economic Theory." *The World Economy,* **19** (6), 695–720.

Mattoo, Aaditya and Arvind Subramanian (2004), "The WTO and the Poorest Countries: the Stark Reality." *World Trade Review*, 3 (3), 385–407.

Mazzoleni, Roberto and Richard Nelson (1998), "Economic Theories About the Benefits and Costs of Patents." *Journal of Economic Issues*, 32 (4), 1031–1052.

May, Ernesto (1985), "Exchange Controls and Parallel Markets in Sub-Saharan Africa: Focus on Ghana." World Bank Staff Working Paper, 711. Washington, D.C.: World Bank.

Minot, Nicholas and Lisa Daniels (2002), "Impact of Global Cotton Markets on Rural Poverty in Benin." Washington, D.C.: International Food Policy Research Institute.

Miyagiwa, Kaz (1991), "Oligopoly and Discriminatory Government Procurement." *American Economic Review*, 81 (5), 1320–1328.

Mosley, Paul, et al. (2004), "Aid, Poverty, and the 'New Conditionality.'" *Economic Journal*, 114 (496), 217–243.

Mosoti, Victor (2006), "Africa in the First Decade of WTO Dispute Settlement." *Journal of International Economic Law*, 9 (2), 427–453.

Moss, Charles and Andrew Schmits (2002), "Price Behavior in the US Sweetener Market: A Cointegration Approach." *Applied Economics*, 34 (10), 1273–81.

Mshomba, Richard (1993), "The Magnitude of Coffee Arabica Smuggled From Northern Tanzania into Kenya." *Eastern Africa Economic Review*, 9(1), 165–175.

——— (2000), *Africa in the Global Economy*. Boulder, Colorado: Lynne Rienner Publishers.

Mutume, Gumisai (2006), "New Barriers Hinder African Trade: Health Standards in Rich Countries Limit Continent's Ability to Export." *Africa Renewal*, 19 (4), 18–19.

Naik, Gautam (2002), "Profiteers Divert AIDS Medicines Meant for Africa." *Wall Street Journal*, B4, October 4.

Neikirk, William (2003), "White House Hints at Relaxing Ban on War Opponents on Iraqi Contracts." *Knight Rider Tribune Business News*, p. 1, December 11.

NEPAD (2003), *Comprehensive Africa Agriculture Development Programme*. Midrand, South Africa: NEPAD.

Nkusu, Mwanza (2004), "Aid and the Dutch Disease in Low-Income Countries." IMF Working Paper, WP/04/49. Washington, D.C.: IMF.

O'Connell, Stephen and Charles Soludo (2001), "Aid Intensity in Africa." *World Development*, 29 (9), 1527–1552.

Odhiambo, Walter and Paul Kamau (2003), *Public Procurement: Lessons from Kenya, Tanzania, and Uganda*. OECD Development Center Working Paper No. 208. Paris: OECD.

OECD (1995), *The Uruguay Round: A Preliminary Evaluation of the Impacts of the Agreement on Agriculture in the OECD Countries.* Paris: OECD.

(2002), *The Size of Government Procurement Markets.* Paris: OECD.

(2004), *OECD Agricultural Policies 2004 At a Glance.* Paris: OECD.

(2005), *Agricultural Policies in OECD Countries: Monitoring and Evaluation 2005.* Paris: OECD.

(2005a), "Trade-adjustment costs in OECD labour markets: a mountain or a molehill?" Chapter 1 in *OECD Employment Outlook.* Paris: OECD.

(2007), *International Development Statistics CD-ROM.* Paris: OECD.

Ohiorhenuam, John (2005), "Capacity Building Implications of Enhanced African Participation in Global Trade Rules-Making and Arrangements." In Ademola Oyejide and William Lyakurwa (editors), *Africa and the World Trading System,* 355–387. Trenton: Africa World Press.

Olarreaga, Marcelo and Çaglar Özden (2005), "AGOA and Apparel: Who Captures the Tariff Rent in Presence of Preferential Market Access?" *World Economy,* 28, 1, 63–77.

Otsuki, Tsunehiro et al. (2001), "Saving Two in a Billion: Quantifying the Trade Effect of European Food Safety Standards on African Exports". *Food Policy,* 26 (5), 495–514.

Oxfam International (2002), *Cultivating Poverty: The Impact of US Cotton Subsidies on Africa.* Oxford: Oxfam International.

Pacón, Ana Maria (1996), "What Will TRIPS Do For Developing Countries." In Friedrich-Karl Beier and Gerhard Schricker (editors), *From GATT to TRIPS – The Agreement on Trade-Related Aspects of Intellectual Property Rights,* 329–356. Munich: Max Planck Institute for Foreign and International Patent, Copyright and Competition Law.

Palmeter, David and Niall Meagher (2003), "WTO Issues Relating to U.S. Restrictions on Participation in Iraq Reconstruction Contracts." Washington, D.C.: American Society of International Law. http://www.asil.org/insights/insigh123.htm

Panagariya, Arvind (2005), "Agricultural Liberalization and the Least Developed Countries: Six Fallacies." *The World Economy,* 28 (9), 1277–1299.

Panitchpakdi, Supachai (2003), "Moving Beyond Cancún," *OECD Observer,* No. 240/241, pp. 11–12, December. Paris: OECD.

Pauwelyn, Joost (2003), "Iraqi Reconstruction Contracts and the WTO: 'International Law? I'd Better Call my Lawyer.'" Pittsburgh: University of Pittsburgh School of Law (JURIST). http://jurist.law.pitt.edu/forum/forumnew133.php

Phillips, Michael (2002), "Uganda Fears Help Could Hurt; Officials Split on Currency Effect." *The Wall Street Journal,* A4, May 29.

Piccioto, Sol (2002), "Defending Public Interest in TRIPS and WTO." In Peter Drahos and Ruth Mayne (editors), *Global Intellectual Property Rights*, 224–243. New York: Palgrave Macmillan.

Poonyth, Daneswar, et al. (2004), "The Impact of Domestic and Trade Policies on the World Cotton Market." FAO Commodity and Trade Policy Research Working Paper No. 8. Rome: Food and Agricultural Organization.

Posner, M.V. (1961), "International Trade and Technical Change." *Oxford Economic Papers*, **13** (3), 323–341.

Pretorius, Willem (2002), "TRIPS and Developing Countries: How Level is the Playing Field." In Peter Drahos and Ruth Mayne (editors), *Global Intellectual Property Rights*, 183–197. New York: Palgrave Macmillan.

Raby, Geoff (1994), "Introduction." In *The New World Trading System: Readings*. Paris: OECD.

Raghavan, Chakravarthi (2000), "Tilting the Balance Against the South: The World Trade Organization and Its Dispute Settlement System." *Trade and Development Series*, No. 9. Penang, Malaysia: Third World Network.

Raj, Dev (1990), *Economic Development: Critical Analysis of GSP*. New Delhi: Anmol Publications.

Raspberry, William (1999), "Behind the Baba Dispute." *The Washington Post*, **A17**, March 15.

Read, Robert (2001), "The Anatomy of the EU-US WTO Banana Trade Dispute." *Estey Center Journal of International Law and Trade*, **2** (2), 257–282. Saskatoon, Canada: Estey Center Journal of International Law and Trade.

Republic of South Africa (2001), *The Use of Targeted Procurement to Implement An Affirmative Procurement Policy: Implementation Manual*. Pretoria: Department of Public Works, Republic of South Africa.

Robinson, James and Ragnar Torvik (2005), "White Elephants." *Journal of Public Economics*, **89** (2–3), 197–210.

Rodrik, Dani (2007), *One Economics, Many Recipes: Globalization, Institutions, and Economic Growth*. Princeton: Princeton University Press.

Sanderson, Fred H., et al. (1990), *Agricultural Protectionism in the Industrialized World*. Washington, D.C.: Resources for the Future.

SEATINI – Southern and Eastern African Trade Information and Negotiations Institute (2005), *Compilation of the Formal African Proposals to the WTO*. Harare, Zimbabwe: Southern and Eastern African Trade Information and Negotiations Institute.

Shaffer, Gregory (2006), "What's new in EU trade dispute settlement? Judicialization, public-private networks and the WTO legal order." *Journal of European Public Policy*, **13** (6), 832–850.

Sharma, Devinder (2005), "Bhagwati, Globalization and Hunger." Global Policy Forum. http://www.globalpolicy.org/socecon/trade/subsidies/2005/0329bhagwati.htm

Smaller, Carin (2006), "Can Aid Fix Trade? Assessing the WTO's Aid for Trade Agenda." Minneapolis: The Institute for Agriculture and Trade Policy.

Subramanian, Arvind and Devesh Roy (2003), "Who Can Explain the Mauritian Miracle? Meade, Romer, Sachs, or Rodrik?" In Dani Rodrik (editor), *Search for Prosperity: Analytic Narratives on Economic Growth*. Princeton: Princeton University Press.

Subramanian, K. (2003), "Deception in the Name of TRIPS." *The Hindu Business Line*, March 17. http://www.blonnet.com/2003/03/17/stories/2003031700100900.htm

Sutherland, Peter (2005), "The Doha Development Agenda: Political Challenges to the World Trading System – A Cosmopolitan Perspective." *Journal of International Law*, 8(2), 363–375.

Tangermann, Stefan (1996), "Implementation of the Uruguay Round Agreement on Agriculture: Issues and Prospects." *Journal of Agricultural Economics*, 47(3), 315–337.

Taylor, Ian (2005), *NEPAD: Toward Africa's Development or Another False Start?* Boulder: Lynne Rienner Publishers.

Tomz, Michael, et al. (2005), "Membership Has Its Privileges: The Impact of GATT on International Trade." Working Paper No. 250, Stanford Center for International Development, Stanford University.

Transparency International (2006), "The 2005 Transparency International Corruption Perceptions Index." http://www.infoplease.com/ipa/A0781359.html

Trionfetti, Federico (1999), "Trade and Public Procurement: The Perspective of Small Open Economies." Center for Economic Performance Working Paper No. 1025. London: Center for Economic Performance.

(2000), "Discriminatory Public Procurement and International Trade." *The World Economy*, 23 (1), 57–76.

UNAIDS (2006), *2006 Report on the Global AIDS Epidemic*. Geneva: Joint United Nations Program on HIV/AIDS.

UNCTAD (2005), *2005 Statistical Profiles of the Least Developed Countries*. Geneva: United Nations.

(2006), *Economic Development in Africa – Doubling Aid: Making the "Big Push" Work*. Geneva: UNCTAD.

Underhill, William (2003), "Lives of the Dictators; In a New Series of Riveting Interviews, Exiled Despots Show no Remorse – only Self-absorption and Delusion." *Newsweek*, p.68, March 17.

UNDP (2006), *Human Development Report 2006*. New York: United Nations Development Program.

United Nations (2004), *2003 International Trade Statistics Yearbook Volume I*. New York: United Nations.

(2004a), *2003 International Trade Statistics Yearbook Volume II*. New York: United Nations.

U.S. Congressional Budget Office (2006), *Research and Development in the Pharmaceutical Industry*. Washington, D.C.: U.S. Congressional Budget Office.

U.S. General Accounting Office (2000), *Sugar Program: Supporting Sugar Prices Has Increased Users' Costs While Benefiting Producers*. Washington, D.C.: U.S. General Accounting Office.

U.S. International Trade Commission (1994), *The Year in Trade: Operation of the Trade Agreements Program*. USITC Publication 2769. Washington, D.C.: U.S. International Trade Commission.

U.S. Office of Government Contracting (2003), *Goaling Guidelines for the Small Business Preference Programs for Prime and Subcontract Federal Procurement Goals & Achievements*. Washington, D.C.: U.S. Office of Government Contracting.

Vernon, Raymond (1966), "International Investment and International Trade in the Product Cycle." *Quarterly Journal of Economics*, 80 (2), 190–207.

Wangwe, Samuel (2006), "Managing the Transition from Aid Dependence in Africa." *Research News*, No. 9. Nairobi: African Economic Research Consortium.

WHO (2002), *A Framework to Assist Countries in the Development and Strengthening of National and District Health Plans and Programmes in Reproductive Health*. Geneva: World Health Organization.

(2006), "Progress in Scaling up Access to HIV Treatment in Low and Middle-Income Countries, June 2006." Geneva: World Health Organization.

(2006a), *Progress on Global Access to HIV Antiretroviral Therapy: A Report on "3 by 5" and Beyond*. Geneva: World Health Organization.

Wittig, Wayne (1999), "Building Value Through Public Procurement: A Focus on Africa." Geneva: International Trade Center.

World Bank (1998), *Assessing Aid: What Works, What Doesn't, and Why*. New York: Oxford University Press.

(2003), *Tanzania: Country Assessment Procurement Report (CAPR) – Executive Summary*. Washington, D.C.: World Bank.

(2004), *2004 African Development Indicators*. Washington, D.C.: World Bank.

(2004a), *Guidelines: Procurement Under IBRD Loans and IDA Credits*. Washington, D.C.: World Bank.

(2005), *2006 World Development Report*. Washington, D.C.: World Bank.

(2005a), *2005 World Development Indicators*. Washington, D.C.: World Bank.

(2006), *2006 World Development Indicators*. Washington, D.C.: World Bank.

(2007), *2007 World Development Indicators*. Washington, D.C.: World Bank.

WTO (1996), *Singapore WTO Ministerial 1996: Ministerial Declaration*. WT/MIN(96)/DEC, December 18. Geneva: WTO.

(1998), "United States – Import Prohibition of Certain Shrimp and Shrimp Products." WT/DS58/AB/R, October 12. Geneva: WTO.

(1999), "Trade Policy Review: United States." WT/TPR/S/56, June 1. Geneva: WTO.

(2000), "European Communities – Regime for the Importation, Sale, and Distribution of Bananas: Recourse to Arbitration by the European Communities Under Article 22.6 of the DSU." WT/DS27/ARB/ECU, March. Geneva: WTO.

(2001), "Declaration on the TRIPS Agreement and Public Health." WT/MIN(01)/DEC/2, November 20. Geneva: WTO.

(2001a), *Doha WTO Ministerial 2001: Ministerial Declaration*. WT/MIN(01)/DEC/1, November 20. Geneva: WTO.

(2002), "Contributions of the United States to the Improvement of the Dispute Settlement Understanding of the WTO Related to Transparency." TN/DS/W/13, August 22. Geneva: WTO.

(2002a), "Negotiations on the Dispute Settlement Understanding – Proposal by the African Group." TN/DS/W/15, September 25. Geneva: WTO.

(2002b), "Negotiations on the Dispute Settlement Understanding – Proposals on DSU by Cuba, Honduras, India, Malaysia, Pakistan, Sri Lanka, Tanzania, and Zimbabwe." TN/DS/W/18, October 7. Geneva: WTO.

(2002c), "Negotiations on the Dispute Settlement Understanding – Proposal by the LDC Group." TN/DS/W/17, October 9. Geneva: WTO.

(2002d), "Negotiations on Improvements and Clarifications of the Dispute Settlement Understanding – Proposal by Mexico." TN/DS/W/23, November 4. Geneva: WTO.

(2003), *Dispute Settlement System Training Module*. Geneva: Legal Affairs Division, WTO. http://www.wto.org/English/tratop_e/dispu_e/disp_settlement_cbt_e/intro1_e.htm

(2003a), "Negotiations on Agriculture – First Draft of Modalities for Further Commitments." TN/AG/W/1. Geneva: WTO. http://www.wto.org/English/tratop_e/agric_e/negoti_mod1stdraft_e.htm#thepaper

(2003b), "Text for the African Group Proposals on Dispute Settlement Understanding Negotiations – Communication from Kenya." TN/DS/W/42, January 24. Geneva: WTO.

(2003c), "Singapore Issues – The Question of Modalities, Communication from the European Communities." WT/GC/W/491, February 27. Geneva: WTO.

(2003d), "WTO Negotiations on Agriculture – Poverty Reduction: Sectoral Initiative in Favour of Cotton." TN/AG/GEN/4, May. Geneva: WTO.

(2003e), "Positive Effects of Transparency in Government Procurement and Its Implementation." WT/WGTGP/W/41, June 17. Geneva: WTO.

(2003f), "Comments on the EC Communication on the Modalities for the Singapore Issues." WT/GC/W/491, July 8. Geneva: WTO.

(2003g), "Proposal for Inclusion in the Draft Text for Cancún." WT/GC/W/510, August 14. Geneva: WTO.

(2003h), "Implementation of Paragraph 6 of the Doha Declaration on the TRIPS Agreement and Public Health." WT/L/540, September 2. Geneva: WTO.

(2004), "Text of the 'July Package' – the General Council's post-Cancun Decision." WT/L/579, August 2. Geneva: WTO.

(2004a), "Implementation of the Development Assistance Aspects of the Cotton-Related Decisions in the July Package." WT/GC/83/Add.1, December 3. Geneva: WTO.

(2005), *Update of WTO Dispute Settlement Cases.* WT/DS/OV/24, WTO, June 15. Geneva: WTO.

(2005a), "Implementation of the Development Assistance Aspects of the Cotton-Related Decisions in the July Package." WT/GC/97/Add.1, November 21. Geneva: WTO.

(2005b), "Doha Work Programme: Ministerial Declaration." WT/MIN(05)/DEC, December 22. Geneva: WTO.

(2006), "United States – Subsidies on Upland Cotton – Recourse to Article 21.5 of the DSU by Brazil." WT/DS267/30, August 21. Geneva: WTO.

(2006a), "Joint Communication from the G-33, African Group, ACP, and LDCs on Special Products and the Special Safeguard Mechanism." WT/AG/GEN/17, May 11. Geneva: WTO.

(2006b), "Recommendations of the Task Force on Aid for Trade." WT/AFT/1, July 21. Geneva: WTO.

Yu, Wusheng and Trine Vig Jensen (2005), "Tariff Preferences, WTO Negotiations and the LDCs: The Case of 'Everything But Arms' Initiative." *The World Economy*, **28** (3), 375–405.

Zimmermann, Thomas (2005), "WTO Dispute Settlement at Ten: Evolution, Experiences, and Evaluation." *Aussenwirtschaft*, **60** (1), 27–61.

Zwane, Teetee (2008), "ACP/EU sign interim trade agreements." *The SWAZI Observer*, Mbabane, Swaziland, January 11.

# INDEX

absolute advantage, vs. comparative, for poor countries, 3
Abuja Treaty, 79
accountability, lack, and corruption, 231
accounting procedures, harmonization by donor countries, 279
ACP. *See* African, Caribbean, and Pacific Countries (ACP) Group
acquired immune deficiency syndrome (AIDS). *See* HIV/AIDS
Adam, Christopher, 262, 263
ADF (African Development Fund), 256
adjudication points, in South Africa, 233, 234*t*
adjustment costs, 266–8
administration of government procurement transparency, 240
administrative costs of aid, reducing for recipient countries, 278
ADMS (AIDS Medicines and Diagnostics Service), 137
Advisory Center on WTO Law (ACWL), 47, 89, 90–9, 265, 294
  African Group concerns, 98
  autonomy of, 93–4
  budget, 91
  memberships, 90–1, 92

subsidized legal services from, 94
summary of services rendered, 95–7*t*
United States and, 93
AERC (African Economic Research Consortium), 264, 265
affirmative action, 214
  and government procurement, 232–3
Africa
  estimates of aid requirements, 282
  magnitude of government aid to, 247–57
  map, *xxiif*
  as net importer of food, 148
  ODA per capita and as ratio of GNI, 255*t*
  Official Development Assistance, 252*t*
  top ten bilateral donors, 257*t*
African, Caribbean, and Pacific Countries (ACP) Group, 9
  African countries' membership, 10–1*t*
  percentage of African countries in, 12*t*
African Alternative Framework to Structure Adjustment for Social-Economic Recovery and Transformation, 79

[ 321 ]